KU-607-247

The MAKING *of the* ENGLISH GARDEN

THE SUNDAY TIMES

The MAKING *of the* ENGLISH GARDEN

MACMILLAN
LONDON

Acknowledgements

First published 1988 by
MACMILLAN LONDON LIMITED
4 Little Essex Street London WC2R 3LF
and Basingstoke

Associated companies in Auckland, Delhi, Dublin, Gaborone, Hamburg, Harare, Hong Kong, Johannesburg, Kuala Lumpur, Lagos, Manzini, Melbourne, Mexico City, Nairobi, New York, Singapore and Tokyo

British Library Cataloguing in Publication Data
The Making of the English garden.
1. England. Gardens, to 1988
I. Girling, Richard II. Rose, Graham, *1928-*
712′.6′0942

ISBN 0-333-48230-1

Typeset by Bookworm Typesetting, Manchester

Printed in Italy by IMAGO

Page 1: the garden at Arley Hall in Cheshire has one of the oldest herbaceous borders in the country. The painting by Piers Egerton Warburton is from around 1830

Pages 2–3: poppies, delphiniums and lupins make a minor English classic

Opposite: the value of changing ground-levels is graphically illustrated at Fitz House in Wiltshire

The editors would like to thank the following people for their help in producing this book:
Jane Hutchings, Primrose Minney and Rachel Martin of the *Sunday Times*
Silvia FitzGerald, Kim Meacher and Marilyn Ward of the Library, the Royal Botanic Gardens, Kew
Dr Brent Elliott of the Royal Horticultural Society
John Creasey of the University of Reading, Institute of Agricultural History

Illustrations are by:
Jeane Colville, pp. 60, 163
Lynda Gray, pp. 32/33
Vana Haggerty, pp. 112/113, 114/115
Sue Hitchens, pp. 14/15
David Johnston, pp. 152/153
Gillian Kenny, pp. 94/95
Vivien Monument, p. 159
Jill Frances Ogilvy, p. 149
Roger Payne, pp. 20/21, 22/23, 86/87
Charles Raymond, pp. 48/49
Paul Richardson, p. 67
Anthony Sidwell, pp. 42/43, 76/77, 106/107, 170, 197
Gill Tomblin, pp. 168, 172/173, 177, 181, 185, 188/189, 193
Harry Willock, p. 119
Calligraphy by:
Robin Brockway, pp. 48/49
Diagrams by:
Line & Line, pp. 17, 20, 21, 22, 23, 96, 170

Photographs are reproduced by kind permission of:
The Ashmolean Museum, Oxford, pp. 84, 85
Clive Boursnell, pp. 8/9, 27, 82/83, 166/167, 178/179, 190, 200, 201, 205, 216/217
Alecto Historical Editions, British Museum (Natural History), pp. 98, 99 (Castanospermum australe)
Eric Crichton, pp. 5, 40/41, 47, 92/93, 110/111, 124, 125, 144, 146/147, 151, 157, 161, 203, 204
David Cripps, pp. 36/37
The Hon. Michael Flower, Arley Hall, p. 1
Garden News, pp. 72/73
Andrew Lawson, pp. 2/3, 10/11, 19, 52/53, 62/63, 79, 80, 81, 96, 101, 102/103, 104/105, 107, 121, 122, 126, 127, 133, 158, 164, 165, 170, 174/175, 182/183, 191 (Paths), 194/195, 210, 212, 214, 218
Nick Meers, pp. 207, 213
The William Morris Gallery, London, p. 180
The National Council for Conservation of Plants & Gardens, p. 137
The National Trust, pp. 146/147, 207, 213
Vincent Page, pp. 24, 30, 31, 134/135, 154/155, 191 (Wild flowers)
James Pipkin, pp. 74/75, 140/141, 208
Public Record Office, Crown Copyright, pp. 50, 58, 59
Ransomes, Sims & Jefferies Ltd, pp. 32, 33 (Heath Robinson drawings), top, 34
University of Reading, Institute of Agricultural History, pp. 34, 38/39, 44, 65, 68, 71, 109, 138, 150
Katharina Rieppel, p. 136
The Royal Botanic Gardens, Kew, pp. 54, 55, 56, 57, 77, 86, 88, 89, 90, 98 (Banks), 99 (Pagoda), 117, 129, 130, 131, 142/143, 176
Skyscan Balloon Photography Copyright, p. 198
Sotheby's, London, p. 148
The Yale Center for British Art, Yale University, pp. 28/29

Editor Richard Girling
Gardening Consultant Graham Rose
Designer Gilvrie Misstear
Picture Editor Vincent Page

Principal Contributors

John Brookes, landscape architect
Stefan Buczacki, plant pathologist and member of BBC Radio 4's *Gardeners' Question Time* panel
Dr Ted Collins, Director, Institute of Rural Life, Reading University
Gareth Huw Davies, wildlife and environment writer
Geoff Hamilton, presenter of BBC television's *Gardeners' World*
Arthur Hellyer, gardening correspondent, *Financial Times*
Penelope Hobhouse, garden designer
Brian Jackman, feature writer, *Sunday Times Magazine*
Hugh Johnson, dendrologist and Editorial Director of *The Garden* and *The Plantsman*
Mary Keen, gardening correspondent, *Evening Standard*
Hazel Le Rougetel, rosarian
Charles Lyte, gardening correspondent, *Daily Mirror*
Richard Mabey, author and ecologist
Dr Richard Muir, landscape historian
Peter Seabrook, journalist and television gardening presenter
Professor William Stern, plant taxonomist
Dr Christopher Thacker, garden historian

CONTENTS

Editor's Introduction

This book, like a great garden, has been shaped by many hands. The idea initially was a simple one: to trace the development of the English garden and explain exactly why it looks the way it does. Why are we so incurably addicted to lawns and borders? Why are our favourite flowering plants all foreign introductions and not 'natives'? Why are we so *competitive*?

In designing the *Sunday Times Magazine* series from which the book began, it very quickly became clear that simple questions were not necessarily going to yield simple answers, and that a straightforward chronology of major events could obscure as much as it revealed. This is why we devised the unusual format which we have retained in extended form for the book. Instead of treating gardening as a single subject and slicing up its history into chapter-length segments, we have instead divided the garden itself into its component parts and told the story of each one separately: the uneasy partnership with nature in the struggle to control the

Beauty undimmed by the rain: watercolour freshness at Ham House, Richmond

wilderness; the development of food plants and the techniques of growing them; the determined – and often dangerous – worldwide search for trees and shrubs; the introduction and 'improvement' of flowering plants; the social and aesthetic impetus for changing patterns in garden design. All these are major subjects in their own right – a fact which we hope is reflected in our treatment of them. A new section, specially commissioned for this book, is garden historian Christopher Thacker's description of a hundred outstanding historic gardens to visit, based on his authoritative listing for English Heritage.

We were guided throughout by an editorial board of lofty credentials, and a cast of contributing writers and experts whose names read like a Who's Who of the garden. With their help, we believe we have achieved a unique chronicle of colour, adventure and discovery, tracing each significant step from the first budding of the first cultivated plant to the age of plant genetics and the geodesic dome.

I

Taming the Wilderness

By Richard Muir

Britain has one of the poorest native floras in Europe. It also has many of the most beautiful gardens. How has this happened? If they are not indigenous, then where did our trees, shrubs, vegetables and flowers actually come from? What exactly *is* the English garden? The story begins with the bare elements of the earth and climate, their limitations and the gardener's determination to overcome them.

The "ordinary" English garden, admired and emulated throughout the world, is a miracle of imagination, determination and adventure. As the following chapters will show, it draws its influences – and its material – from every corner of the globe.

Gardening is a game of unnatural selection. We provide artificial environments to cosset the plants we have chosen, and we ruthlessly eliminate their competitors. Only the wildest of nature gardens are self-sustaining. To see what would happen to a garden after just a few years of neglect one need only explore the embankments and cuttings of an abandoned railway line, where the stage-by-stage progression – or regression – towards deciduous woodland will be in progress. Before the arrival of man the farmer, around 5000 BC, most of what are today's gardens were covered by broadleafed wildwood or marshland. Most parts of the country subsequently became ploughland, pasture or meadow, so that the gardener has inherited the efforts of countless generations of peasant farmers.

Gardening, like politics, is the art of the possible. But the bounds of possibility can be stretched, depending on the extent to which the gardener is prepared to refine and modify his natural resources – soil, climate, water and plants. The range of possible improvements extend all the way from digging a few barrowloads of farmyard muck into the vegetable plot to installing a climatically- and humidity-controlled orchid house.

The gardener always has a view of how an attractive garden ought to look, but his notion of perfection has changed enormously through time. Today we regard the Cotswolds as the summit of English rural beauty. Other generations saw things differently. In the early 19th century, Sidney South wrote of the Cotswolds: "After travelling . . . over this region of stone and sorrow, life begins to be a burden and you wish to perish."

Whatever your conception of beauty, one thing remains the same. Real success is given only to those who understand the soil. What actually *is* it? What is it made of? How can it be improved? Soil basically consists of finely-worn detritus eroded from rocks, the mineral grains being set, one hopes, in a dark matrix of sticky humus, produced from the decomposition of organic matter. In a geological sense, soil might be regarded as an intermediate stage between rock and rock. For example: crystals eroded from a granite outcrop might be washed out to sea, where they are first deposited as sand grains on the sea bed, then compressed into sandstone. The subsequent uplifting and eventual erosion of the sandstone then sets off a whole new sequence of soil formation.

From the gardener's point of view, it is not the complexities of geological history that matter but rather the structure and composition of the soil. If the mineral particles are large, as in sand, then the soil will be light and free-draining. It may also be "hungry", with humus and fertilisers easily flushed out by water. Clays, on the other hand, have very fine mineral particles and present very different problems. Though they are potentially fertile, it is difficult for excess water to percolate through them. Such heavy soils tend, if they are left unimproved, to be cold and waterlogged in winter and spring, then to bake into large clods in the summer sun. Loams, bridging the gap between the sands and the clays, are generally the easiest types of soil to work.

Chalk and limestone soils have their own peculiarities. Both are composed of calcareous debris from sea creatures which accumulated millions of years ago on the beds of warm oceans. Both rocks are associated with dry gardening conditions and, with their high concentrations of calcium carbonate, both weather to produce alkaline soils. Limestone tends to be highly fractured and jointed. As acidic soil water widens the fissures, so rainwater and fine topsoil can be swiftly flushed away. Chalk is porous, and chalk soils which are sticky and grey after a downpour soon become light and workable as the bedrock absorbs the moisture.

Some soils, which are said to be "immature", closely mirror their bedrock. Only after a long period of stability does a "mature" profile evolve as organisms go to work on dead vegetable matter and produce a deep, humus-rich topsoil. During the warm interlude between the last two Ice Ages, mature soils will have evolved in many parts of Britain. The most recent glaciation, however, will have undone all the good and left the countryside looking like the aftermath of an explosion in a builder's yard. Soil accumulations were either buried beneath great swathes of glacial debris or washed away in the torrents of meltwater. The long process of soil creation had to begin anew.

The result of all this is that a great many of our gardens are on boulder clay or "drift" – layers of finely-ground rock debris smeared on the landscape by glaciers; or they may stand on plains or fans of sand and silt flushed out of the glacial debris by rivers of meltwater. Over the years many of them will have changed beyond recognition. Suburban gardeners now frequently work on topsoil which the building contractors have imported from somewhere else. When a friend moved into a new house at Waterbeach in Cambridgeshire, I was impressed to see chunks of Roman pottery jutting through the topsoil. Evidently it had come from near the Roman kilns at Horningsea a couple of miles away. At my own village in Nidderdale, Yorkshire, other forces have been at work. The rich black earth in the gardens of the older cottages is a legacy from the earth-closet lavatories of former times. Of such things are gardens made. Different histories produce different soils favouring different plants and requiring different treatments. To reach a clear understanding of this is the first essential step in achieving success as a gardener.

It would be hard to find any other area the size of Britain which has such a diversity of climates. The climate varies not only from region to region and from one corner of the garden to another, but also from year to year. In the first half of January

The Climatic Landscape

Local climatic variation and differing soil-types impose severe restrictions on the wild flora of the "natural" landscape above. Exactly the same restrictions apply to cultivated plants in the "developed" version on the right

By Kevan Chambers

If the wind is moist from the sea, those areas on the right of each illustration would be drier and affected by chill east winds. Areas 1, 2, 3, 4, 5, 13, 14, 15, 16 are the most exposed. Areas 6 and 7 would be the coldest. Areas 25 and 26 are protected by the hill from the worst winds, but would be prone to heavy frost.

Many plants which would benefit from the shelter of the tors, 23, would not tolerate greater exposure on the open hillside, 22.

The townspeople in area 30, who would have to cope with heavy soils and heavy frosts, would have to strive hard to make good gardens. Along the valley, 31, warm sea air moving up the valley would reduce the incidence of frost.

The most fortunate gardeners would be those living in the seaside town, 9 and 10; their soils would be light, sandy, well-drained; their plots frost free; but they might suffer from wind-blown sea spray.

1 **Exposed peak of usually acid rock:** lichens, moss, Least willow; on lime-rich rocks, rare alpines such as drooping saxifrage. In gardens: saxifrages, stonecrops, edelweiss, woolly willow.
2 **Exposed ridges:** mountain azalea, moss campion. In gardens: prostrate alpine willows, alpine lady's mantle.
3 **Crags of lime-rich or acid rocks:** blue rock speedwell, rose root, parsley fern, alpine forget-me-not. In gardens: all these do well.
4 **Mountain streams:** yellow saxifrage, starry saxifrage, birdseye primrose. In gardens: these grow well alongside water.
5 **Mild and humid western slopes:** butterworts, bog pimpernel. In gardens: these will grow in permanently moist soil.
6 **Scots pine forest:** bilberry, cowberry, chickweed, wintergreen, twinflower and creeping ladies' tresses. In gardens: broom, gorse, primulas.
7 **Highland peat area:** bog asphodel, cross-leaved heath, sundews, dwarf birch. In peaty bog gardens: gentians, primulas, heathers, rhododendrons.
8 **Sea cliffs:** wild chives, goldilocks, rose root on lime cliffs; sea spleenwort, sea plantain gorse on acid. In gardens: whitlow-grass, stocks, bluebells.
9 **Rocky headlands:** fine short turf with sea pink, spring squill, sea campion. In gardens: red valerian, fuchsias, mesembryanthemums, hardy geraniums.
10 **Sand dunes:** marram grass, marsh helleborine, creeping willow. In gardens: red hot pokers, hebes, hydrangeas.
11 **Salt marsh:** glasswort, sea lavender, sea aster, spartina grass. Few gardens have such conditions.
12 **Sandy coastline:** sea holly, bloody cranesbill, burnet rose. In gardens: these plants plus those listed under sand dunes.
13 **Blanket peat:** cotton grass, tormentil, heath bedstraw, heathers. In gardens: these plus pernettya, Canadian dogwood, bearberry.

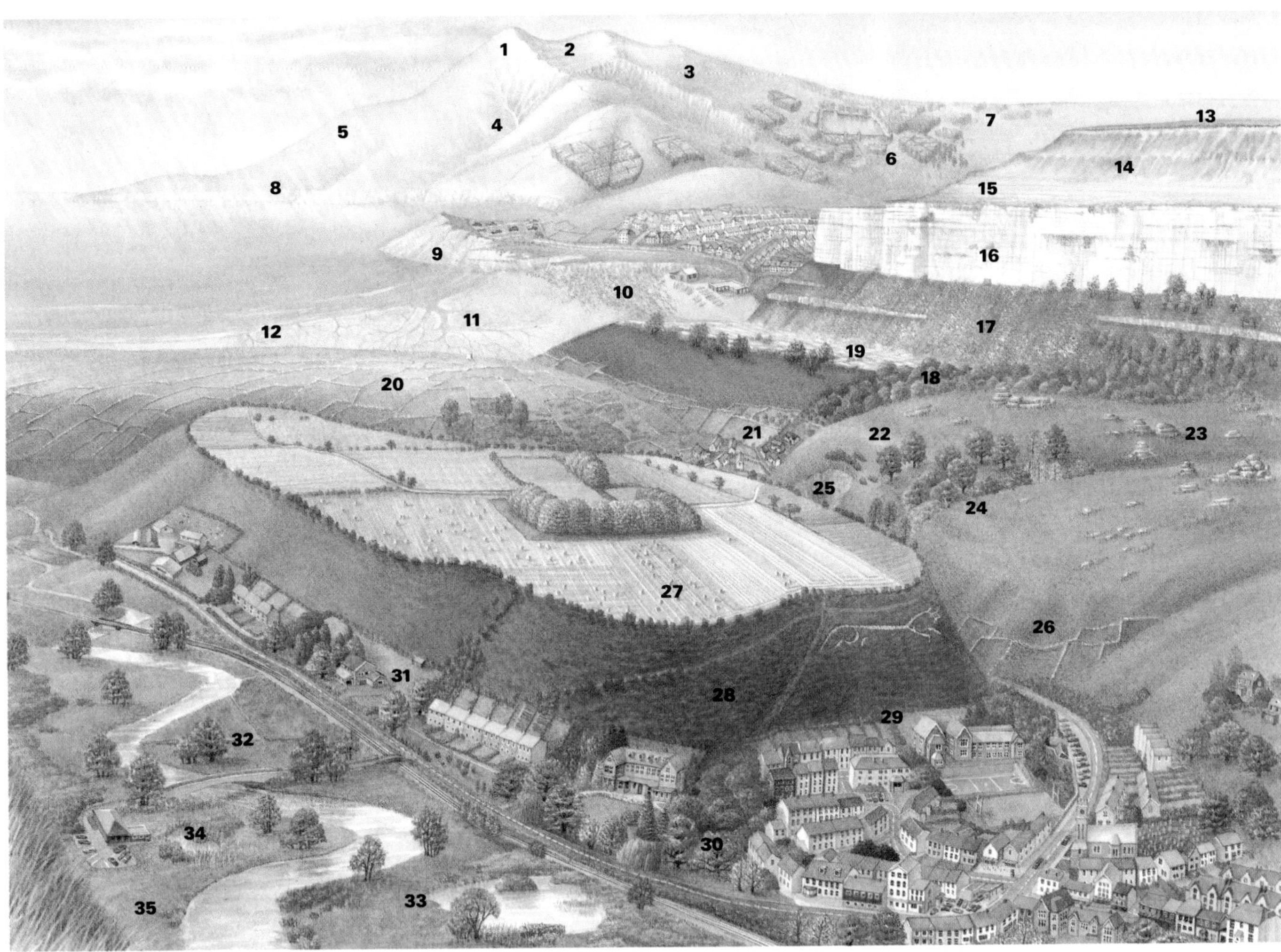

14 Gritstone scarp: bilberry, bell heather, crowberry, wild golden rod. In gardens: acid rockeries could also contain rhododendrons, azaleas, brooms.
15 Upland shales and limestones: purple saxifrage, sandworts, red campions. Few gardens offer similar conditions.
16 Limestone scar: Cheddar pink, hoary rockrose, spiked speedwell, ivy. In limestone rockeries: these plants plus daphnes, Hutchinsia, erinus, rockrose.
17 Limestone scree: Jacob's ladder, limestone polypody, lesser meadow-rue, dark red helleborine. In gardens: these all do well in lowland scree gardens.
18 Limestone woodland: lily of the valley, wood anemone, Solomon's seal, wild garlic, *Daphne mezereum*. In gardens: London pride, lilies, anemones, phlox.
19 Limestone pavement: baneberry, angular Solomon's seal, hartstongue fern, lily of the valley, hard shield fern. In gardens: these plus cinquefoils, campanulas, wild strawberry.
20 Exposed limestone pasture: rockrose, scabious, Nottingham catchfly. In gardens: these plus taller hardy geraniums, bistort, yarrows.
21 Lowland limestone pasture: meadow cranesbill, field clary, field scabious. In gardens: salvias, Jacob's ladder, lambs ears.
22 Exposed acid heath: gorse, petty whin, broom, milkwort, marsh gentian. In gardens: heathers, heaths.
23 Sandstone tor: wood sorrel, oak fern, filmy fern, on sheltered side. In gardens: all do well.
24 Acid woodland: sessile oak, golden male fern, foxglove, honeysuckle. In lightly shaded areas: skimmias, pieris, golden rod, calico bush.
25 Lowland acid rock outcrop (eg quarry): wood sage, buckler fern, black spleenwort. In gardens: rhododendrons, azaleas, foxgloves, palm trees.
26 Lowland acid pasture: hardheads, hedge bedstraw, dog rose, elderberry, wild daffodil. In gardens: hardy rhododendrons, azaleas, brooms and genistas.
27 Chalk woodland: beech, bluebells, hellebores, spurge laurel, orchids. In gardens: dogwoods, campanulas, butcher's broom.
28 Chalk scarp: wild candytuft, pasque flower, clustered bellflower, juniper, dogwood, wild clematis seed heads. In gardens: buddleia, weigela, rockroses, pinks, bellflowers, cowslips.
29 Sheltered springline: forget-me-not, devil's-bit scabious, sedges. In gardens: astilbes, hemerocallis, hostas.
30 Clay woodland: pedunculate oak, wild cherry, woodrush, campion, oxslip. In gardens: hamamelis, choisya, philadelphus.
31 Damp cold clay vale: figwort, meadowsweet, valerian, guelder rose. In gardens: pyracantha, kerria, chaenomeles.
32 Alluvial silts: ragged robin, common meadow-rue, fritillary soapwort, crab apple, blackthorn. In gardens: lupins, delphiniums, phlox, hollyhocks, indian poppies, irises, michaelmas daisies.
33 Valley bottom bog: cranberry, bog rosemary, royal fern, sundew, bog myrtle. In gardens: candelabra primulas, irises, lobelias, bog bean.
34 Ponds: flag iris, rush, watermint, water forget-me-not, marsh marigold, willows. In gardens: Arum lily, sweet flag, dogwoods, kingcups, swamp cypress.
35 Riverside: water avens, marsh woundwort, globe flower, loosestrife, alder and hazel. In gardens: gunneras, rogersias, astilbes, rheums.

1988, for example, average temperatures were a remarkable 2 to 3 deg C higher than normal, and crocuses were blooming in the East Midlands.

The average climate anywhere is the sum of a host of different factors – total rain and snowfall, the number of frost-free days, mean temperatures for each month, the strength and direction of winds, and so on. Failure to understand local climate can result in poor seed germination, frost-damaged plants or growing days needlessly lost. Any northern or Midland gardener who worked to a Cornish calendar would be courting disaster. Roughly speaking, the growing season for hardy plants is the period during which the temperature remains above 6 deg C. In the Scottish Highlands and in Snowdonia, the season lasts only four months; over most of the British uplands it extends to five or six months and in most lowland areas, seven to eight months. In the very mildest coastal areas of the south-west, it continues from between nine to almost twelve months.

Britain enjoys an oceanic climate intensified by the warmth of the Gulf Stream. The sea gains and loses heat much more slowly than the land does, with the result that the extremities of temperature in our islands are much reduced. Birmingham is roughly on the same latitude as Barnaul in Siberia, where temperatures of −5 deg C are recorded in winter and 25 deg C is common in summer. Compare the *normal* Barnaul winter with the *record* low of −27 deg C recorded 340m above Braemar in the Cairngorms in 1895. Barnaul has an extremely continental climate, while sea-girt Britain is just large enough to produce its own minor continental effects. On many a winter or spring night, for example, Midland counties will have a degree or two of frost while the English coastal counties stay frost-free. Over the country as a whole conditions vary enormously – and the differences are not just those of north and south. The warmth of the Gulf Stream, for example, allows sub-tropical plants to flourish in the famous Inverewe Gardens in the Western Highlands – plants which certainly could never succeed in inland or eastern gardens more than 100 miles further south.

Rainfall is just as variable as temperature. Most of our rain is brought by cyclones from the Atlantic and much of it is intercepted by mountains and uplands before it reaches the lowlands to the east. The Scottish Highlands, Lakeland, the high plateaux of the Pennines and the Welsh mountains receive more than 150cm of rain or snow a year, with a few exposed places getting twice as much. The East Midlands, by contrast, generally receive only 50 to 60cm of rainfall.

But it isn't rainfall alone that determines the moisture-content of the soil. The soil-type itself is crucially important. Free-draining sands lose water more quickly than clays; steep slopes increase the rate of surface run-off; and the position of the water-table (the junction between the dry and saturated soil levels) creates

CHARTING THE CHILL

For more than 1000 years the vine has served as a unique indicator of the switchback curve of relative cold and heat in the British climate. Meteorologists have estimated average temperatures from documentary evidence to before AD1000, and the success of viticulture provides strong corroborative evidence of when Britain was warming

By Gareth Huw Davies

It was almost certainly the Romans who brought the vine north, but probably not until well into their 400-year occupation. Tacitus in the first century AD found the British climate unsuitable for growing vines, due to "excessive rains and general moistness".

There is evidence of unsuccessful vine cultivation at North Thoresby, Lincolnshire, around AD280. The remains of a vine at a villa in Hertfordshire dating from the later Roman period is one of the first tangible proofs of viticulture in Britain.

Bede mentions vineyards planted in the first half of the eighth century, probably in the newly established monasteries, such as Ely, later named the Île des Vignes by the Normans.

By late Saxon times rising summer temperatures encouraged further planting in Britain. The golden age of the British vineyard, according to F. A. Roach in *Cultivated Fruits of Britain* (Blackwell, 1985), coincided with a prolonged period of favourable weather from the mid-11th to the early 14th century, with peak warmth in the 12th and 13th centuries: higher summer temperatures to ripen the grape and, crucially, warmer springs with a low risk of May frosts.

Domesday Book (1086) records 38 vineyards in southern England. In 1125 Gloucestershire boasted more vineyards than any other county. The vine flourished throughout Kent, and was planted in Worcestershire, Derbyshire and Northamptonshire. Many vineyards were attached to monasteries in East Anglia.

In the 14th and 15th centuries the weather in Britain deteriorated. There were frequent severe winters and colder springs: this harsher regime lasted into the 17th century, culminating in the Little Ice Age in the late 1600s. The weather and rural decline partly caused by the Black Death in 1348 brought an end to commercial vine growing in Britain.

The monasteries, the only place where vines were likely to survive, were dissolved in 1536. By 1580 the country's vineyards had almost disappeared, and not for lack of a market. "The one benefit which our nation wanteth . . . is wine," noted a writer in 1580.

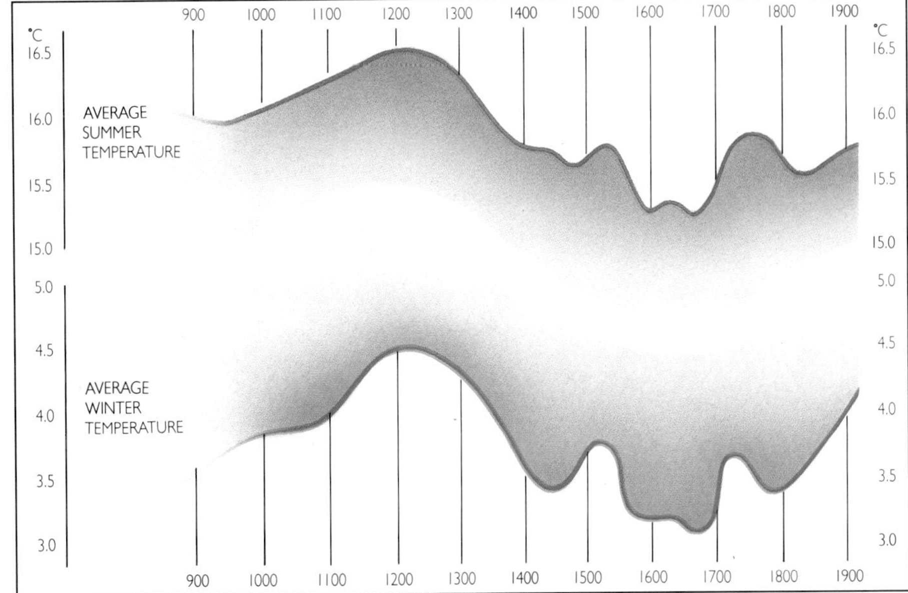

Noblemen coaxed French experts across to re-establish the vines around 1629, but the weather was too harsh. By 1650 average temperatures were probably at their lowest for two millennia.

Vineyards were recorded on south-facing sites on light soil during a warmer spell in the 18th century, at Bitton near Bath in 1726, at Hoxton, Rotherhithe and at Painshill in the 1740s onwards. For the next 100 years dessert grapes were grown under glass or against walls, but few of the small number of vineyards were profitable – it was a period of renewed cold.

In 1875 the Marquis of Bute established successful vineyards in Glamorganshire. The renaissance of the British vineyard since the mid-1940s is due in part to warmer weather, but in the main to the dedication of better informed, enthusiastic growers planting carefully chosen stock. Unlike the serene 12th-century growers, they still dread the May frost and the damp cloudy summer.

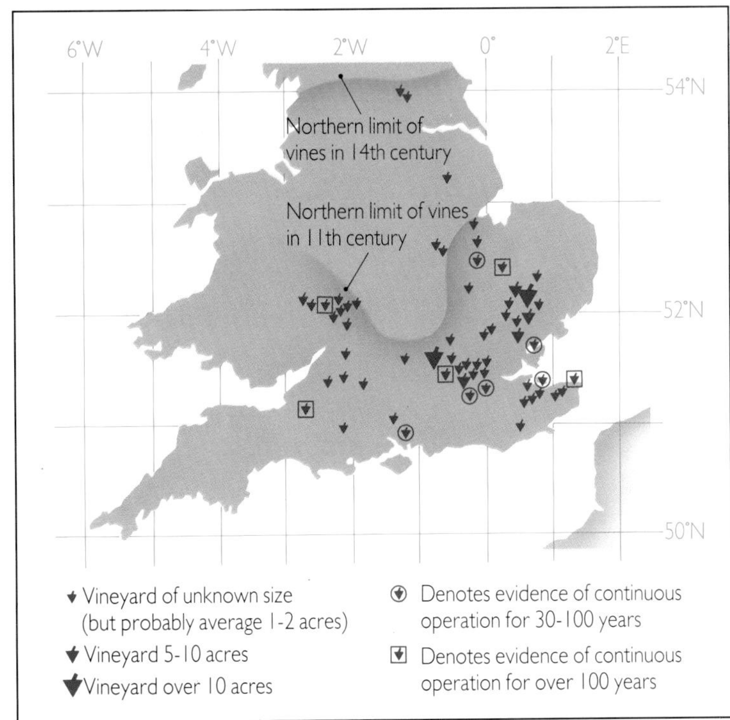

Historical grape-zones (right) present a vivid picture of climatic variation. The graph (top) shows 1000 years of constant change – summer and winter average temperatures from 900 to 1900

Opposite: relic of a more formal, earlier age – floral parterres at Garsington Manor, Oxfordshire

significant local differences. The water-table itself is mobile, rising with the winter rains and falling in summer. Irrigation and drainage are the most important correctives to excessively dry or wet conditions, but they are not the whole answer. On dry ground, spreading a mulch of peat or compost will help to reduce the loss of water through evaporation; on heavy ground liming and incorporating peat can improve the flow of water through the soil.

Light is another important variable. The driest places in Britain are not necessarily the brightest. The Channel shores of England receive around 63 to 75cm of rain or snow each year, but top the sunshine league with an average of 4.5 to 5 hours of sunshine per day. Pembrokeshire is both damp and sunny, receiving 100 to 150cm of rain and snow but enjoying a daily ration of 4 to 4.5 hours of sunshine; and the Scottish Highlands average less than three hours of sunshine a day. No year is entirely typical. In the cool wet summer of 1987, most parts of northern England received only 95 per cent of the sunshine they expected. The results, exacerbated by a mild autumn, were curiously disorientating. My *Schizostylis coccinea,* which should have flowered in October, was struggling to bloom in late January.

Britain is a windy country, with the prevailing winds coming from the west. Destructive gales are normally associated with unusually deep and fast-moving Atlantic depressions, but other winds can be very unwelcome to the gardener. In winter and spring, north-east winds from the frozen heart of Scandinavia or easterlies from the frigid interior of the continent can threaten all but the hardiest of plants. Less frequently threatening are the occasional hot southern summer winds from the Sahara, which can parch crops and dry out the soil very quickly. Exposure to wind varies enormously from place to place. In some parts of northern England, the supposedly tender passion flower flourishes in places well shielded from the wind chill of the easterlies. Strategically-placed hedges and other windbreaks can be used to protect plants from a particularly troublesome wind, though they can create new problems of their own, such as shading. Devotees of the island border claim that tall border plants which grow leggy and need staking when grown in conventional hedge-backed borders are sturdy and self-supporting when exposed to the more open and bracing environment of an island bed.

Exposure to the elements has been a problem faced by all those who have gardened on flat upland plateaux or featureless windswept plains. It can also make difficulties for coastal gardeners, who receive the full blast of the wind from the sea. Northern and western coasts generally have about 20 to 30 days of gales each year; eastern and south-eastern coasts have 5 to 15 days. Onshore gales contain their own particular menace in the form of salt spray, and seaside gardeners in the worst affected places may be restricted in their choice of plants. *Senecio laxifolius* is

MEN OF THE SOIL

If it's not too wet, it's too dry. If it's not too heavy, it's too light. In a gardener's mind, there is no such thing as the perfect environment. For as long as he has grown plants, man has been looking for new ways to improve the fertility of his soil

By Graham Rose

The only time a gardener ever stops complaining that he has too little rain on his crops is when he has too much – which, in Britain, is quite often.

Though our showers are rarely torrential, they are regular and persistent. As a result, vital nutrients and calcium carbonate (essential to neutralise the acidity of rainwater) are leached from the soil, carrying them far beyond the reach of the plant roots. On heavier soils, too, the particles of solid matter are compacted by rain, excluding air and hampering drainage. It is probable that more plants have perished as a result of their roots rotting in waterlogged soils than from any other cause. Two of the greatest garden preoccupations therefore have a frustrating kind of symmetry – on the one hand, irrigation to overcome a shortage of water; on the other, drainage to overcome a surplus.

Very little is known for certain about the earliest husbandmen, but it can't have been long before they learned the value of digging open drainage furrows. There is plenty of evidence to suggest they fully understood the benefits of dressing the soil with animal manure, human night soil or domestic refuse and wood ash. Similarly, as great growers of peas and beans, the Romans must have been aware of the usefulness of these crops in boosting the fertility of the land, and employed them to help following crops of non-nitrogen-fixing plants like cabbage. They are also credited with the invention of an underground drainage system. They also had leather buckets which they may have used for irrigation, and they probably watered each plant individually with an earthenware beaker or iron ladle.

By the late 14th century, gardeners fully understood the value of burnt limestone (quicklime) to neutralise soil, and late medieval gardeners knew how to build longer-lasting drains with rock. They also appreciated the value of organic manures, such as the feather-rich droppings from poultry houses and dovecotes. Irrigation was by means of iron- or withy-bound staved barrels, mounted on barrows.

Covered, stone-lined drains were still regularly used at the close of the 17th century and in most gardens water was still barrowed about in barrels or buckets.

In the early years of the 17th century, Francis Bacon had praised the value of "nitre" as a soil additive, and by the end of the century it was

IRON AGE *The early growers were simple but effective husbandmen. They would have learned from bitter experience that waterlogged ground resulted in heavy crop-losses, and soon understood the value of open drainage ditches (diagram below). Their soil was enriched with both animal and human sewage, and organic refuse. Unknowingly, they also dressed their land with an effective potash fertiliser when they dug in the wood-ash from burned forest clearings. As their crops were mostly cereals, they probably knew and cared little about irrigation*

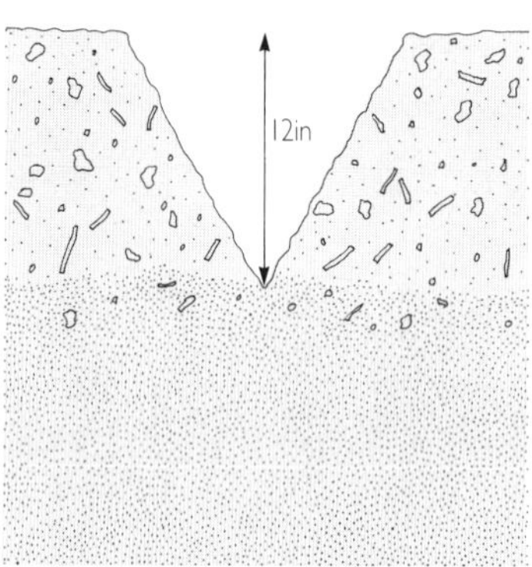

THE ROMANS *The conquerors brought with them many new plants. They fully understood the value of good underground land drains (below), which they made by filling a deep furrow with gravel, topped with brushwood and earth. They spread marl to neutralise acid soils, and used household refuse to make compost. Peas and beans were grown to release nitrogen into the soil for the benefit of other crops – a technique learned from observation rather than any true understanding of the chemistry. Irrigation was by means of terracotta jars or leather buckets, from which they scooped the water with beakers or ladles*

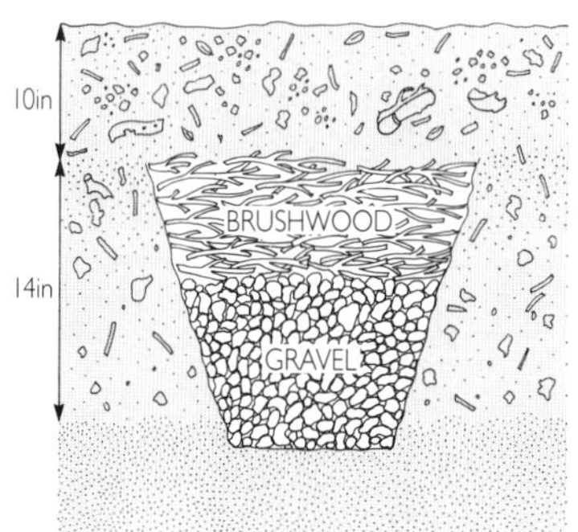

MIDDLE-AGES *By the late 14th century, drains (below) were of more durable construction – rock-lined, with a topping of stone slabs. Quicklime was used to neutralise the soil, and organic fertiliser to enrich it. Water was brought to the garden in barrels mounted on barrows*

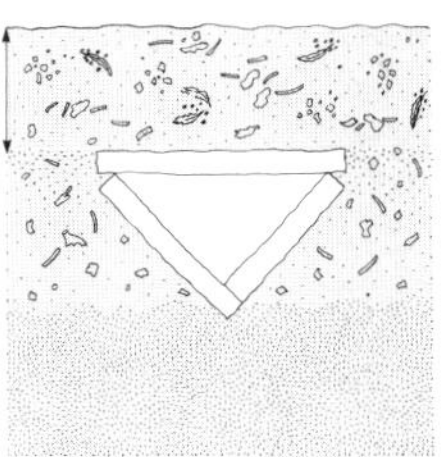

17TH CENTURY *Leaf-mould was now recognised as a useful additive to improve the water-retentive qualities of the topsoil, though nobody yet understood the value of organic material breaking down into humus. More efficient drainage was introduced (below), with open tubular tiles laid end-to-end in deep trenches covered with gravel and soil. A particularly favoured soil additive was 'nitre' – crystalline deposits of potassium nitrate which built up in drying animal dung. Bones were also used, and were a valuable source of phosphates. The first watering 'cans' appeared at this time, made of pottery with rose spouts*

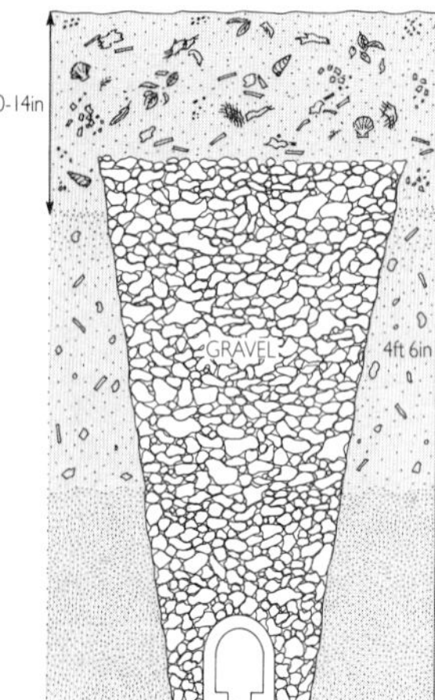

THE VICTORIANS *Many new plant varieties appeared, imposing new challenges to the gardener. Improved irrigation systems, included hoses, sprinklers and metal watering cans; and the problem of run-off was met by improved tile-drains (below). Superphosphate fertilisers were also developed*

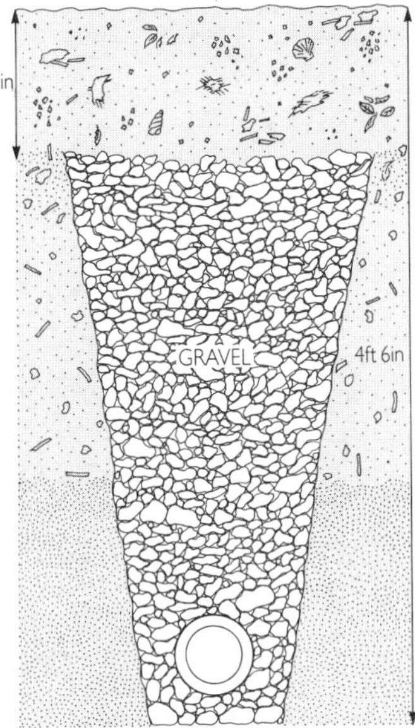

20TH CENTURY *Granulated, liquid and slow-release fertilisers have transformed the ease and accuracy with which the modern gardener can enrich his soil. Irrigation, too, can be precisely controlled by means of small-bore drip irrigators, and sprinkler systems with electronically-controlled taps. Water-retention is enhanced by dressings of peat, and drainage made simple by easy-to-lay plastic conduits (below), consisting of a polyethylene core wrapped in permeable polyethylene fabric. In terms of technology it's a very long way from the Iron Age; in terms of basic principles no distance at all*

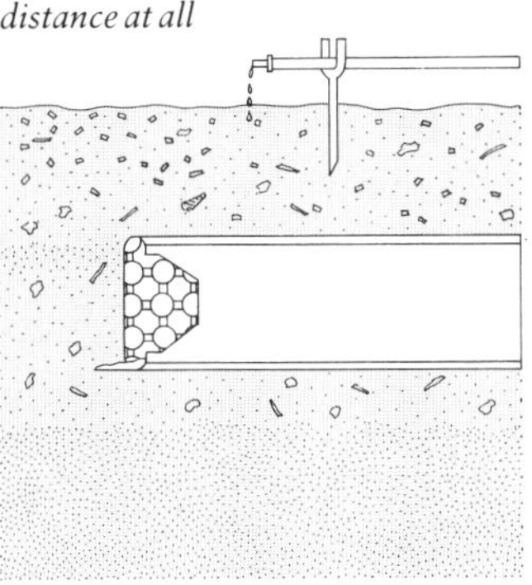

eagerly sought. "Nitre" was the light-coloured crystalline deposit of potassium nitrate which built up in layers of animal dung as it fermented and dried out. Other gardeners similarly extolled the virtues of sand, seaweed, seashells, saltpetre (potassium nitrate again), bones, dried blood and animal remains, leather cuttings and shoddy.

One of the advances in the late 17th century was the introduction of efficient tile drainage. Water percolated into the pipes through the joints, and ran away into ditches. Drains of this type were able to cope with the much-increased volumes of water which 19th-century gardeners were able to lavish on their plants with the aid of their new hoses, sprinklers and large metal watering cans.

In the first quarter of the 20th century, precisely-formulated, factory-made mineral fertilisers heralded another era of spectacularly-improved plant performance.

The era of fertiliser manufacture had begun in the 1840s, when John Lawes and Joseph Gilbert began to experiment at Rothamsted with what later became known as superphosphate. This was made by dissolving bone ash in sulphuric acid – a process which made the phosphates much more soluble in water and thus more immediately available to plants.

The next major development was the fixing of nitrogen from the air to form ammonia, which could be used to make cheaply, sulphate of ammonia, ammonium nitrate and nitrochalk. The process of synthesising the ammonia was first used in Germany in 1913, and developed in the 1920s by John Brunner and Alfred Mond at Billingham – an enterprise which led to the foundation of ICI.

A great problem with the early fertilisers was their tendency to become sticky when exposed to atmospheric moisture, and then to set like rock in their bags. This problem eased when they were compounded into granules, and was finally overcome after the Second World War when first heavy-grade treated papers and later plastics replaced hessian in the bags.

The most significant recent development has been stable resin-coated slow-release fertilisers.

The process of watering, too, has been greatly simplified. Easily-moved sprinkle irrigators with reciprocating mechanisms driven by the pressure of the water, with electronically-controlled taps, can now be bought in every garden centre. And controlled doses can be administered through cheap plastic small-bore drip irrigators. The conservation of water within the soil, too, has been greatly improved by the application of peat and special products like heat-expanded mineral particles.

Below ground, plastics play their part in the latest BTR Landrainer conduits, which consist of a corrugated high-density polyethylene core wrapped in permeable woven polyethylene fabric. These can be set in very narrow trenches with only minimum disruption to the garden.

A favourable microclimate can sustain plants which normally would flourish only much further south. These palms could be in the south of France, or Malaysia – in fact they are in a corner of the Abbotsbury sub-tropical garden in Dorset

resistant to windblown salt, and heathers, cotoneaster, tamarisk and yucca all do well in seaside settings.

Altitude similarly has an effect on gardening possibilities, with temperatures dropping as height increases. In hilly areas exposure can be a more serious challenge, though deep winding valleys are often sheltered from winds. Such valleys, however, are particularly vulnerable to frost as cold dense air sinks down the hillsides. When most of Britain is still enjoying the last warm days of summer, thoughts of winter are awakened by forecasters announcing frosts in the sheltered valleys of the Scottish Highlands.

The British climate is not only unpredictable on a year-by-year basis but is also changeable over large timespans. Before around 1200 BC, for example, Dartmoor was well-populated farmland. Then the climate shifted into a cooler and wetter phase, a blanket of acid peat spread across the pasture and the farmers withdrew to the valleys. The relics of their abandoned farms are still there on the moor today and you can't ramble far without stumbling across the remains of Bronze Age dwellings and field walls.

Another severe climatic deterioration took place in the 14th century, with scores of coastal villages perishing in ferocious sea storms. Settlements on poorer lands were deserted, and many farmers living on cold heavy clays switched from mixed farming to livestock. Forecasters now are talking of "minor perturbations" but are reluctant to predict the future course of our climate.

One of the most important factors determining the impact of climate on your garden is that of aspect. In the countryside, south-facing slopes receive far more direct sunlight than north-facing ones. From my south-facing study window I can see the midwinter sun creeping along the skyline, and my north-facing neighbours have their sunset an hour or two earlier than mine. In towns, the question of aspect is complicated by the effects of buildings. While a nearby house to the east or north may offer protection from chilling winds, one to the south will rob you of warmth and sunlight. Urban climates are generally a degree or two warmer than those of the surrounding countryside, and most gardens are more sheltered. On the debit side, the gaps between tall buildings can act as wind-tunnels, and shading by buildings and fences can limit gardening possibilities.

Each garden has its own particular micro-climates. Each side of the house, for example, favours different wall plants. In their walled gardens Victorian gardeners grew sun-loving peaches and apricots on the south-facing wall and the shade-tolerant morello cherry on the north. Aspects and obstructions like fences and hedges will determine the positions of shady spots where ferns might grow or salad vegetables stay cool and fresh, and sunny places which most vegetables and flowers will prefer. If the garden undulates there may be dells which act as frost hollows, and a solid wall or fence at the foot of a slope might also trap and hold cold, sinking air. Such places must be avoided when siting tender plants. Plants themselves create micro-climates which can be exploited. For instance, I underplant my old-fashioned shrub roses with dwarf daffodils and polyanthus. The foliage of the roses protects the shade-loving polyanthus from summer sun, while the combination provides colour all the way through from March to October. If one imagines that the garden is composed of a host of little climatic zones, and understands the characteristics of each micro-climate and plants in sympathy, then the resources of the garden for growing plants are exploited to the full.

Modern gardeners are becoming increasingly sympathetic to the requirements of nature, realising that an understanding of the natural order can be of benefit to man and wildlife alike. Around 7000 years ago, most of our gardened areas existed as broadleaf forest. Throughout most of England, lime had become the dominant tree and stands of oak, elm and ash were common. Trees like holly and hazel grew in the "understorey", while in lighter glades, or at the woodland margins, shrubs like bird cherry or guelder rose were flourishing. After about 5000 BC, farmers began to fell the wildwood to create farmland. The brown forest earths were not particularly fertile but the burning of timber produced wood ash which gave an initial boost to fertility. The creation of hedged fields produced artificial environments with trees and shrubs colonising and flourishing in the hedgerows.

Several of our native shrubs – guelder rose, bird cherry, gean wild cherry, wayfaring tree, rowan, silver birch and field maple – are extremely attractive as garden specimens. The wildlife-conscious gardener who is torn between native or exotic trees or shrubs should consider that oak supports 284 indigenous species of insect; birch, 229; hawthorn, 149; and hazel, 73. Imported trees support few native insects, so those who wish to see masses of insect-eating birds and watch butterflies in their gardens are well advised to include some native shrubs and flowering plants in their schemes, taking care to buy only subjects of guaranteed British stock. My own garden includes a hedgerow packed with a dozen native trees and shrubs, grown on a hedgebank of native grasses and wildflowers which I mow like an old hay meadow after the seed has shed, plus a couple of alien plants, the buddleia and the iceplant, which always attract throngs of butterflies. In addition, a pond provides essential water for birds and animals and a breeding place for frogs, toads and newts.

Some plants flourish particularly in disturbed ground. When the first farmers began digging and ploughing they created environments in which these could multiply, so that archaeologists can often identify areas of early cultivation by the discovery of ancient plantain pollen. As arable farms expanded, so charlock, fat hen and black bindweed became abundant, along with other weeds of cultivation which are now only too eager to take up residence in our gardens. Ironically, the development of modern herbicides has led to the virtual eradication of many of the old field weeds, so that conservation-minded gardeners now reserve a patch for corncockle, cornflower, corn marigold and field poppy, their seeds being commonly displayed in garden centres.

For thousands of years, farmers enriched their ploughlands with manure. We know this because broken pots, thrown out on the dunghill and spread with muck, still survive in fragments in the soil. Your garden is likely to contain pot fragments of many ages – lots of blue-and-white 19th-century ware, probably some medieval shards and quite possibly Roman and Iron Age pieces too.

The history of the lawn and the pasture is stranger than most people imagine. On the global scale, grasslands are normally associated with areas too dry to support dense tree cover. One can imagine that once the first British farmers had harvested a

LEVELS OF EXCELLENCE

Sloping sites would be of little practical – or aesthetic – use to gardeners without the adoption of the ancient land-engineering technique of stepped terraces

By Christopher Thacker

The origin of the garden terrace is agricultural, a response to the question: how do you grow things on sloping ground? Answer: cut the slope into a series of level plots, each divided and supported by a wall – a process we now call "terracing". This development is therefore linked – physically as well as historically – with that of steps, which began as a way of helping us climb mountainous slopes. The terrace also has a military origin in the development of sentry walks along fortress-walls.

In gardens, terraces enable us to make maximum use of slopes; to prevent good topsoil from being soaked and washed downhill; to vary the planting from level to level; to divide the garden into different sections; and sometimes to gain both privacy and an element of surprise by concealing the upper levels from the viewer below. If there is water, we can add the delights of cascades and tumbling streams. Above all, we can enjoy varying views, either within the garden itself, looking up or down, or out beyond it to the countryside or neighbour's garden.

Remembering the military aspect of the terrace, we may note the similarity of the watch-tower and the garden pavilion, gazebo or belvedere – all, for their very different reasons, places designed to provide a view.

In Europe, terraces on a grand scale were first developed on steep hillside sites in Renaissance Italy. The most extravagant and spectacular of these is at the Villa d'Este at Tivoli, created in the 1560s. It is no accident that it is outstanding both as a sequence of ornamented terraces and as a water garden, with streams, fountains, jets, sprays, cascades – at every level. Spacious views open out over the Campagna from the ends of the terraces, and from the garden summit.

Gardens like this – the Villa Lante near Viterbo, or the Villa Garzoni near Lucca – were quickly imitated in the British Isles, using the natural slopes around existing fortresses or mansions: Haddon Hall, in Derbyshire, in the 17th century; Powis Castle, near Welshpool, around 1700. Here the terraces below the castle are adorned with balustrades, steps, urns and statuary, and still have huge bulging hedges of clipped yew almost as old as the architecture. Yet most of the planting has been developed in this century – a brilliant combination of an ancient framework with modern shrubs and plants.

Artificial terraces were also made. At Northbourne Court in Kent, brick-walled

One of the most attractive adaptations of changing levels is the step cascade. This one is at Chatsworth

terraces (*c.*1616) rise up around three sides of a grassy enclosure facing the site of the mansion. As at Powis, this ancient structure has been given outstanding planting in the present century, with fine herbaceous and seasonal borders well-separated in the different terrace areas.

With the development of the landscape garden, the formal, architectural terrace was largely rejected in favour of a "natural" layout. Yet the need for changes in level, for variety of scene and viewpoint, remained as important as ever. In place of flights of steps and balustraded walks there were undulating grassy slopes with paths meandering across the rising ground. So at Stourhead in Wiltshire the paths around the lake are at several levels, and the upper ones – like those in the woodland behind the Temple of Flora, or higher up leading to the Temple of Apollo – are effectively terrace walks, giving ever-changing vistas of the lake below.

At Farnborough Hall in Warwickshire, the terrace winds, slightly serpentine, across the gently sloping park, with wonderful views of Edge Hill. Grandest of them all, in North Yorkshire, is the Rievaulx Terrace (*c.*1758). Along a high, wooded ridge more than half a mile of curving walk has been levelled out, with a temple at each end. The ground falls steeply to the west, and as we follow this perfect sweep of grass we glimpse, far below us, ever-changing vistas of the ruins of Rievaulx Abbey.

Formality returned to gardens in the 19th century, bringing back "Italianate" terrace schemes. Sometimes they were modest – as when Charles Barry restored a firm "platform" between the house and Capability Brown's parkland at Kiddington, Oxfordshire (*c.*1850). Elsewhere they were grandiose, rivalling their Italian ancestors – like Barry's complex terraces at Shrubland, in Suffolk, with a main staircase of 137 steps, and further stairs beyond (1848–52); or Thomas Cubitt's terraces for Prince Albert, at Osborne in the Isle of Wight (1847–54). In contrast are the terrace walks outside the rugged, medieval walls of Berkeley Castle in Gloucestershire, planted in the 1880s and early 1900s, and praised by Gertrude Jekyll.

By the end of the century the terrace was recognised as essential to garden design, whether conceived as "architecture", as a part of "nature", or simply as a means of achieving a useful division and variety. Superb examples can be found all over the country – Bodnant, in North Wales, where each of the splendidly architectural terraces contains a separate garden; Renishaw, in Derbyshire, where steps, statuary, fountains and clipped yew hedges echo the Renaissance schemes loved by Sir George Sitwell; Iford, in Wiltshire, by Harold Peto, with architectural and sculptural features rising *up* the hillside behind the house; Port Lympne, in Kent, by Sir Philip Sassoon and Philip Tilden, sited on the escarpment and with the calm, vast prospect of Romney Marsh and the Channel beyond; Dartington Hall in Devon, where the Tournament Ground is enclosed on three sides by the grassy levels of the amphitheatre, linked by broad flights of steps; and East Lambrook Manor, in Somerset, where Marjorie Fish's crowded planting is given space and freedom by means of changing levels and low stone walls – in short, by terraces.

Bull's-eye precision: the house and garden at Llanerch, Derbyshire, painted by an unknown artist in 1662

few cereal crops from among the charred stumps of the retreating wildwood, their livestock would have grazed the exhausted clearings. Grazing would nip off seedlings and prevent the regeneration of woodland. In many places a mixed farming system was adopted, with worn-out ploughland recovering its fertility under pasture. Some extensive areas became permanent pasture and severe problems were encountered when the farmers eventually decided to plough and sow a cereal crop. The turf was so robust that a new type of plough, known as a "rip ard" was developed to cut the sod. Many ancient pastures became infested with bracken and this may explain the apparent popularity of pig-keeping in the third millennium BC. Pigs were the only animals which, by rooting and trampling, could keep the invasion in check. Pasture is not a natural form of vegetation throughout most of Britain, and this may explain why the lawn often seems to be the most time-consuming and vulnerable part of the garden. Any lawn which is poorly drained, thinly grassed, underfed and too closely cut is a real ecological disaster area.

The garden can be viewed as a collection of resources – soil, climate, water and plants – which are exploited and orchestrated by human ideas about what a garden should be like. Prehistoric peasants probably found beauty a-plenty in the unspoilt and townless countryside of Britain; their only "gardens" were small vegetable plots beside their dwellings. The relics of these can still be seen as earthworks beside the Romano-British houses preserved at Chysauster in Cornwall. The Roman concept of gardening was transplanted directly from the Mediterranean, with the gardens forming courtyards attached to villas. Fishbourne Palace gardens in West Sussex, for example, have been revealed by excavation. Here the four ranges of the Roman palace were set around a rectangular garden 75 × 100m. This was surrounded and bisected by paths which appear to have been edged by low box hedges. On the eastern side of the garden a backdrop of flowering or fruiting trees or shrubs seems to have been supported by a timber framework, while water pipes following the outer pathways may have served fountains or raised basins set in recesses. This very formal arrangement was complemented by a less-formalised terraced garden to the south of the palace with a pond, stream, fountain and randomly planted trees and shrubs.

Imperial grandeur: the Roman gardens at Fishbourne Palace in West Sussex have been excavated and restored

No genuine medieval gardens survive, but their appearance can be recreated from contemporary records and paintings. They were small, secluded places set within high walls or hedges. Stone or gravel pathways ran between lawns (in which small flowers grew freely) and beds, and the gardens were situated so that they could be seen and enjoyed from the private apartments of the castle or manor house. The medieval enthusiasm for practical water engineering, which produced moats, mill ponds, mill races, water meadows and ingenious fishponds, was applied to the

Long in the tooth: the common dog-rose, Rosa canina, is the hedgerow ancestor of many modern hybrids

garden, where streams, pools and moated islands were popular. Gardens of a specialised kind were cultivated by herbalists, whose potions may have been more effective than was previously thought, and who set the science of botany in motion.

The medieval realm also contained recreational landscapes of a very different kind. At the time of *Domesday Book* in 1086, about 25 Royal Forests had been established, and during the reign of Henry II (1154–89) more than a quarter of the realm was subject to the Forest Law which protected the deer. Within each forest, a core of woodland cover was surrounded by commons and working farmland. Deer parks were far smaller than forests and provided ditch- and bank-girt sanctuaries where deer were confined to provide a reliable source of meat and sport. At the peak of their popularity around 1300, England may have contained more than 3000 deer parks. Most were around 150 to 200 acres in area and generally existed as grassland stippled with lollipop-like pollarded trees. Deer-park countryside must have resembled the wood pasture of *Silva pastilis* – the association of trees and grassland which was very common in Domesday England covering, for instance, about a quarter of the county of Derbyshire. Neither the wood pasture nor the deer park was regarded as a garden and by the close of the Middle Ages wood pasture was greatly reduced

Swards of Honour

It's hard to imagine a British garden without a patch of grass, and hard to imagine any garden element so demanding in time and energy as the lawn. But what is the source of this peculiar addiction to greensward? The story begins with a Persian carpet

By Gareth Huw Davies

There are few areas of horticultural excellence which suburban gardeners can convincingly replicate in their postage-stamp plot. But while the rich scale of Kew or Wisley is beyond the most ambitious small gardener, even the unskilled can recreate in microcosm Wembley Stadium or the Lord's outfield.

The origins of the lawn, the universally attainable gardening challenge, can be speculatively traced to the Persians in 500 BC or so. King Cyrus, keen to try any good idea, may have grown some kind of low beds of short, cropped shrubs or flowers in his well-watered gardens, from the supporting evidence in carpets. The Greeks, who copied Persian gardens, may have established similar flower lawns. But it was Pliny the Younger who made one of the first references to the lawn in *pratulum* – little meadow in the garden.

This decorative concept may have endured in British villas. The Celtic "lann" and Old English "laund" signify an enclosure or waste. An alternative origin might be the French town Laon, which gave its name to lawn, a smooth cloth. By the Middle Ages the lawn had become the cropped grass in an orchard, or "pleasaunce", a pleasure garden planted with fruit trees, flowers, sweet herbs and containing a maze, knot garden and sundial.

This was Chaucer's "verray paradys", where he sat at sunrise in his little arbour on the raised turf seats planted with camomile, violets and daisies. The lawn, folded into a seat, received its highest celebration from Shakespeare in Titania's "bank whereon the wild thyme grows".

The medieval lawn, fashioned from flower-filled meadow turfs, would have been any naturalist's delight. Early 15th-century paintings show worthies promenading on luxuriant swards, pied with daisies and camomile. The lawn at the Villa Palmieri near Florence, given dubious fame in Boccaccio's *Decameron*, was just such an example of the abundant natural meadow "starred with 1000 flowers" and set around with orange and cedar trees.

John Evelyn's gardening calendar (1669) extolled the camomile lawn's virtues: a thick year-round pile of deep green, which became as smooth as grass. The branching stems thickened into a firm sward and its leaves, bruised when trodden on, gave an aromatic fragrance. There is a camomile lawn today at Buckingham Palace.

The earliest kind of grassed enclosure in the British landscape was the Domesday wood pasture

The 18th-century landscaped park developed the idea of grass as a "natural" form of ornament

Heath Robinson (below and far right) gently mocked the manufacturers' emphasis on the recreational value of the lawnmower

Close-grazed turf became exclusively a rich man's preserve to the palisaded medieval deer-park

In the modern age, the lawn has become an extension of living space

Lawn preparation was a complex labour. The writer Magnus advised that the ground be first flattened, thoroughly scoured of roots, and doused with boiling water to suppress weed seeds. "Turves from good meadow grass . . . [must be] beaten down with wooden mallets and stamped down well with the feet." Thereafter it was important to compress the turf "to avoid luxuriance and bursting forth into seed".

The lawn was found in monastery cloister, university precinct and royal estate. Henry II had a lawn laid outside his bedchamber window. The use of grass as a sports surface contributed to the development of the perfect lawn. Bowls and club ball, precursor of cricket, might at first have been played on a sandy, gravelly surface when first recorded in the 13th century. And Drake may have played his famous bowls game on a camomile lawn. But by the 17th and 18th centuries the bowling green as a close-cut surface was a standard in the great houses. At Chatsworth the bowling green was the garden's central feature. At Cassiobury in 1706 there was a green "incompassed with great trees".

Lawn care taxed the resources of even the biggest estate. In 1721 the Duke of Chandos's lawns were mown twice or thrice weekly, and weeded daily by teams of "weederwomen". Scything could achieve a good clean cut, down to an inch. "Very nearly as smooth and even as the piece of green cloth I'm writing on," noted William Cobbett.

Victorian ingenuity eventually liberated the gardener from the most gruelling of chores. In 1830 Edwin Budding, foreman in a textile factory, adapted a process for shearing the nap from the cloth and designed the first lawn mower (see page 34), manufactured by Ransome of Ipswich. Every size of mower was swiftly mechanised. Shank's donkey- and horse-drawn mowers (animals' boots extra) followed in 1842, the petrol mower in 1900 and the gang mower in 1914. The revolution was completed with the introduction of the rotary mower in the 1940s and the hover mower in the early 1960s.

There was an equally rapid development in grass seed. Early propagators used hay-loft sweepings for seeds, then the grass of "clean upland pastures" – fine-leaved species such as bents. The seedsmen Suttons and others developed purer seeds, thus opening lawn preparation to the masses, in one of the world's most favourable climates. However, the "sodding over seeding" argument still awaits final resolution.

A CONVENIENT MOTOR MOWER FITTED WITH ASH TRAY AND ATTACHMENT FOR LIGHT READING WHEN MOWING

It only remained to defeat nature's principal opponents of the perfect sward: invasive weeds like the resourceful *Bellis perennis* (daisy) and the various strains of ranunculus (buttercup).

The weedless lawn became the horticultural advertiser's equivalent of the cleaner shirt. Today total chemical rout is within the power of any gardener who tours the garden centre's shelves.

But the shining sward, "green like Genoa velvet", taken to its unnatural extreme in the bowling green, laid over a raft of quick-draining porous material, will always have its detractors. W. H. Hudson, naturalist, wrote heretically: "I would rather see daisies in their thousands, ground ivy and even the ugly plantain with tall stems, and dandelions with splendid flowers and fairy down, than the too-well tended lawn."

Grasscutting, according to the advertisers, was a leisurely pursuit – and so simple that even women could do it

and most deer parks had gone. During the great post-medieval vogue for landscaped parkland, however, these archaic forms of countryside were revived. The naturalised park of the 18th century had much in common with the medieval deer park, though by this time the deer were included only for ornament and for "lawn-mowing" duties.

Examples of changing perceptions of the ideal landscape and garden abound. As the fashion for Romanticism gathered strength in the middle of the 18th century, so natural flowing arrangements replaced the formal order imposed on older landscaped parks. The disciplined floral gardens planted beside great houses were swept away, allowing "nature" to advance right up to the walls of the mansion. One of the most interesting and expensive attempts to reconstruct a lost formal order can be seen at Het Loo palace near Deventer in The Netherlands. Here a late 17th-century intricate French garden has been excavated and replanted, having been entombed until recently beneath a garden including geometrical avenues of around 1800, a slightly later "English" landscaped garden and an exotic tree collection dating from the 19th century.

Gardeners have always been keen to exploit the opportunities of their age. Techniques borrowed from civil water engineering were applied to create wonders like the crescent-shaped lake containing islands representing a ship, a fort and a spiral mount specially built at Elvetham in Hampshire by Edward Seymour, Earl of Hertford, in 1591 – and abandoned after three days of spectacular water pageant, staged for Queen Elizabeth I. At Chatsworth in Derbyshire a formal garden in the Derwent valley with canals and fountains was created from 1685 onwards, but here the summit of achievement is the Emperor Fountain with its 90m-high jet, created by Joseph Paxton in 1843–4. In the 19th century the expansion of the British Empire stimulated collectors and botanists to explore a wealth of hitherto mysterious parts of the world, creating a great demand for exotic plants and transforming the face of Victorian gardens.

The modern gardener still exploits the age-old resources of soil, climate, water and topography. He or she inherits facets of the environment created long ago by the colonisers of the wildwood and their successors, while at his or her disposal is a remarkable portfolio of ideas about garden design. The medieval deer park, the Victorian arboretum, the cottage garden in its many guises, the enclosed terrace gardens of the early 17th century and a multitude of other design themes have each left a legacy of ideas, so that now the gardener can experiment with a wealth of different idioms. Although our visions of perfection change and change again, the delightful garden still remains a harmonious marriage of good ideas with an understanding of the resources which each environment offers.

To Weed and Hoe and Rake and Sow

The digging tool was invented by an early man who picked up a stick. Iron and steel have since added qualities of precision and durability, but traditions are slow to change.

By Ted Collins

The main types of garden hand tool in use in Britain today are of great antiquity. Some are descended from the primitive stone axes and hoes developed by the first farmers in the 3rd millennium BC and used to clear and break open the ground for growing arable crops. Most of those we know, however, date from Roman times, while many of the more specialised tools were introduced in the later 16th and 17th centuries. Indeed, so comprehensive was the range established then that the Victorians, for all their inventiveness, added little that was fundamentally new.

GARDEN TOOLS THROUGH THE AGES
1 *Roman scythe (facsimile)* **2** *Metal-clad wooden spade of type used by Romans* **3** *19th-century scythe* **4** *19th-century turfing spade/turfing irons* **5** *19th-century turf-stripper/breast plough* **6** *19th-century iron fork* **7** *19th-century hoe* **8** *19th-century border spade* **9** *19th-century border fork* **10** *19th-century Cornish shovel* **11** *19th-century steel rake* **12** *A variety of late 19th-century billhooks showing regional variation* **13** *Three sizes of 19th-century trenching spade* **14** *Early 20th-century bent shanked Cornish shovel* **15** *Early 20th-century*

long-handled "dibber" **16** *Early 20th-century bulb planter* **17** *Early 20th-century twig besom* **18** *Three early 20th-century variants on the hoe* **19** *19th-century fine sieve* **20** *Early 20th-century turfing spade/turfing iron* **21** *Early 20th-century long-handled "parrot beak" secateurs* **22** *Early and late 20th-century reaping hooks* **23** *Mid-20th-century brass spot weeder* **24** *19th century pesticide syringe* **25** *Late 20th-century Qualcast strimmer* **26** *Early 20th-century hand lawn clipper* **27** *Wilkinson Sword late 20th-century stainless border spade.* **28** *Wilkinson Sword late 20th-century stainless border fork* **29** *Wolf late 20th-century cultivator* **30** *Wolf late 20th-century springtime rake* **31** *Wolf late 20th-century soil miller* **32** *Bolens 829E ride-on mower* **33** *Parkes Winstanley narrow trenching spade for inserting BTR land-drainer pipe* **34** *Wilkinson Sword stainless garden rake* **35** *Wilkinson Sword stainless lawn edging knife* **36** *Wilkinson Sword stainless long-handled fork* **37** *Wilkinson Sword stainless "Swoe" hoe* **38** *Wolf Terrex Auto Spade* **39** *Merry Tiller "Cadet" Rotavator* **40** *Simplicity 4212 Tractor-Mower* **41** *Hayter "Hunter" rotary mower* **42** *Ransomes, Sims & Jefferies "Marquess" cylinder mower* **43** *Qualcast Concorde XR35 electric cylinder mower* **44** *Flymo "Sprintmaster" – Hover/collector mower* **45** *Prototype Flymo Hover mower* **46** *Prototype Hayter rotary mower* **47** *Early 20th-century hand-operated reciprocating hedge-clipper* **48** *Qualcast electric hedge-clipper* **49** *Wilkinson Sword "Professional" pruner* **50** *Wilkinson Sword adjustable super shear* **51** *Wilkinson Sword stainless hand trowel* **52** *Wilkinson Sword stainless hand fork* **53** *Ransomes, Sims & Jefferies petrol cylinder mower* **54** *1880s Budding cylinder mower* **55** *19th-century moleskin jacket*

Gardeners in Roman Britain used a wide range of tools drawn from many parts of the empire. The substitution of iron for wood and bone improved strength and durability, and one of the greatest achievements of the Romano-British smith was his ability to forge-weld iron and steel together to form a sharp, durable cutting edge.

Among the important new tools introduced during the Roman occupation were the iron-shod spade, the turf-cutter, weeding hook, various designs of digging hoe, the long-handled scythe, and a variety of pruning and grafting tools. The most interesting of these was the iron-shod spade. Found only in north-west Europe, it differed from Mediterranean spades, with their long handles and shield-shaped or triangular blades made wholly of iron. Wooden spades and shovels had probably existed before the Romans, but the encasing of the cutting edge and sides in an iron sheath or shoe was an important innovation, and this successful combination of materials continued for spades right up until the 18th century.

Much of the actual breaking-up of the soil was done by the heavy hoe or mattock wielded in the manner of a pickaxe. Lighter types of hoe were used for weeding and loosening the soil, and rakes, with wooden or iron tines for preparing the seed bed. Grass and weeds were controlled by means of a variety of hooks and, in the later Roman period, possibly by long-handled scythes, of which a number of impressive examples, some more than 5ft long, have been discovered in Britain. The cultivation of fruit and vines necessitated the use of various pruning knives and hooks and, for heavy work, the billhook, one of the few tools to have achieved a definitive form in the pre-Roman period.

Although ornamental gardening almost certainly ceased with the decline of Roman civilisation in Britain, various garden tools appear to have survived but were probably used for agricultural purposes. Little is known about gardening in Anglo-Saxon or medieval times but in the 9th and 10th centuries fruits, vegetables and medicinal herbs were certainly cultivated, chiefly by monasteries.

By the 14th century aesthetic as well as economic gardening had become fashionable in castles and manor houses. Illuminated manuscripts depict gardeners using iron-shod spades with short handles and T-shaped grips, and different types of digging hoe – the two-pronged, single-bladed and double-ended – but not as yet the digging fork, nor the hand trowel. The *Luttrell Psalter* (*c.*1340) shows a number of hand weeding tools, including a hook, spud and wooden tongs used to pull out docks and similar deep-rooted perennial weeds. There is little evidence for the use of the modern weeding hoe. Later medieval gardens contained areas of grass which would have been cut either by smooth-bladed hooks, or by scythes, the latter with a shorter, wider blade than in the 19th century, and similar to the hammered steel scythe with a straight handle still in use in mainland Europe.

Illuminated manuscripts depict for the first time the trimming of hedges using a hook, smaller and more open than the modern grass hook, which remained the standard tool until the development of shears in the 17th century. A notable invention during the late medieval period was the wheelbarrow.

The next most innovative phase after the Romans came with an upsurge in interest in gardening in the late 16th and 17th centuries. Pleasure gardening became a genteel pursuit while fruit and vegetables became staple items of diet. The European influence was crucial. Plant material, garden designs and tools and techniques were introduced from Italy, France and the Low Countries. During this period the evolutionary paths of garden and agricultural tools began to diverge. As the scale and variety of garden tasks increased, so technical standards became more exacting, and gardeners began to demand more sophisticated tools. Improvements in metal-working techniques and a cheaper, more abundant supply of iron and steel helped tool manufacturers to meet this need.

The considerable progress achieved in the design of gardening tools can be seen in the sketches made around 1650 by the botanist and aboriculturist John Evelyn for his unpublished *Elysium Britanicum.*

In the mid-17th century, however, the predominant digging and soil-breaking tools – the iron-shod spade and the heavy hoe – were little changed from those in use in the Middle Ages. The increase in flowers created a demand for a lighter class of cultivating tool for weeding and loosening the soil, which was met by the development of a range of push-and-pull hoes with varying blade widths.

By the early 17th century, closely-cut lawns and bowling greens were an integral feature of garden designs and maintaining them was one of the most demanding of garden tasks. The long narrow-bladed scythe with an S-shaped handle, specially adapted for mowing lawns, the stone garden roller, edging irons and besom broom were essential items of equipment. Similarly, the interest in trees, ornamental hedging and topiary created a demand for more refined pruning, trimming and grafting tools. New tools developed in this period include the hand trowel, watering-can and transplanter.

A study of manufacturers' catalogues testifies to the enormous energy and virtuosity of the Victorians in tool design, although they added little that was radically new apart from in the areas of lawn care and irrigation.

The maintenance of large areas of lawn would have been impossible but for the timely invention of grass-cutting machines in place of the scythe. The cylindrical lawn-mower was unquestionably the single most important new item of gardening equipment to emerge from the Industrial Revolution. This indispensable tool was patented in 1830 by Edward Beard Budding, a foreman carpenter, who adapted the spiral cylinder used in textile mills for trimming the nap of cloth to the cutting of grass. Designed originally to be operated by one man, machines were also powered by donkeys, ponies and horses. A lawn edger, constructed on the same principle, was developed in the 1860s.

The Victorians were also much preoccupied with the problem of watering. Primitive pumps had existed from the 17th century, although in

A plan for all seasons: the Victorians (above, left and above right) aimed at the "all-purpose" gardening tool

most gardens buckets and barrels were used for the conduit and transport of water, and perforated clay pots and watering-cans for applying it. The all-important breakthrough was made in the 1840s with the introduction of the pressure hose made of gutta-percha, or India rubber, and later of rubber overspun with canvas. There were important improvements in the design and manufacture of pumps, ranging from the small stirrup pump for local use to the elaborate aquajet systems used in the late 19th century for irrigating large areas. The invention of galvanised iron helped in the manufacture of watering-cans, water barrows and mobile pumping engines. Larger numbers of greenhouses, and the availability of various washes to control diseases and pests, prompted the development of a useful variety of syringes and sprays.

Iron and steel were used lavishly by the Victorians. The all-iron spade, a comparative rarity in the 17th century, had almost entirely superseded the iron-shod types by the 1820s. Similarly, garden rollers were now made of cast iron, in two sections. Steel was progressively substituted for iron in the manufacture of edge tools. The modern cast-steel fork with elastic tines was patented by Parkes of Birmingham in the 1840s.

A remarkable feature of Victorian gardening and agricultural hand tools was the vast number of local and regional patterns. A study of local tool patterns shows that between 1850 and 1930, leading manufacturers produced 14 local patterns of axe, 18 spades, 26 scythes, 27 hoes, 106 reaping and grass hooks and 136 billhooks. Particularly interesting are the several local patterns of spade – treaded blades and D-shaped handles being commonest in the east and south, T-shaped handles in the north and west, and pointed blades and long-poled handles, similar to the Mediterranean *pala*, in the Celtic lands and extreme south-west.

The 20th century is remarkable chiefly for the introduction of power tools. The first steam mower was produced by a small firm of Lancashire blacksmiths, the forerunner of British Leyland, in 1895; the first motor mower powered by internal combustion engine soon after 1900, and the first electric mains mower in 1926. The post-war era has seen in rapid succession innovatory designs of mower – the rotary, air-cushioned Flymo and nylon line-strimmer and, for the more affluent gardener, the ride-on mower and lawn tractor, first developed in the USA. Power has been applied to other tasks, from sawing and hedge-cutting to cultivating and hoeing.

Standardisation began in the 1950s. Most of the tools now in use are little different from the turn of the century, except that they are made principally of steel, often stainless steel, and, as a result of changes in manufacturing techniques, are in some cases of a different construction. Attempts to remodel traditional tools have made only partial headway in the face of innate conservatism, or lack of interest. Some of the most successful innovations have been adaptations of agricultural tools, such as the tined-cultivator and soil miller, to gardening purposes, and miniaturised versions of traditional Mediterranean tools, such as the double-headed hoe, the *ascia rastrum* of Roman times. The Romano-British gardener, in short, would not feel out of place in the tool section of a modern garden centre.

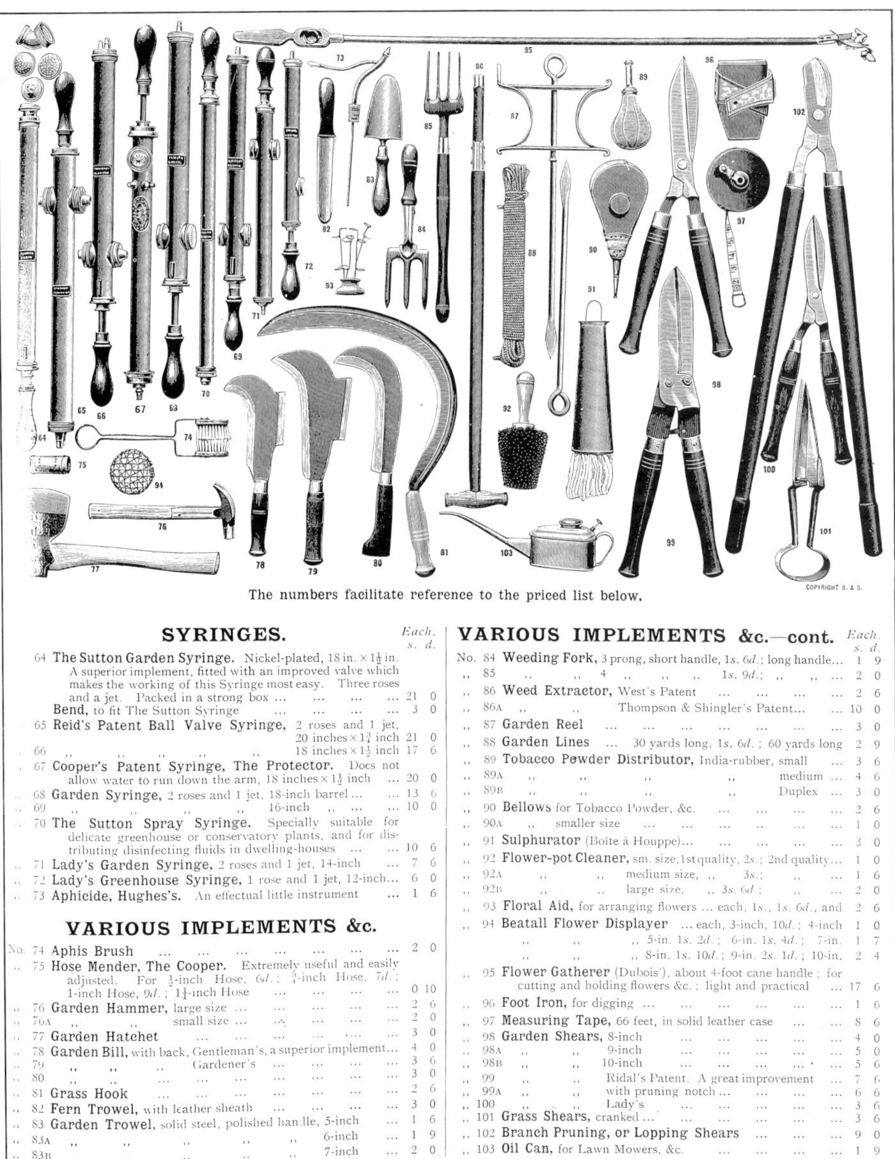

The numbers facilitate reference to the priced list below.

COPYRIGHT S. & S.

SYRINGES.

No.		Each. s.	d.
64	**The Sutton Garden Syringe.** Nickel-plated, 18 in. × 1½ in. A superior implement, fitted with an improved valve which makes the working of this Syringe most easy. Three roses and a jet. Packed in a strong box	21	0
	Bend, to fit The Sutton Syringe	3	0
65	**Reid's Patent Ball Valve Syringe,** 2 roses and 1 jet, 20 inches × 1¾ inch	21	0
,, 66	,, ,, ,, ,, ,, 18 inches × 1½ inch	17	6
,, 67	**Cooper's Patent Syringe, The Protector.** Does not allow water to run down the arm, 18 inches × 1½ inch ...	20	0
,, 68	**Garden Syringe,** 2 roses and 1 jet, 18-inch barrel	13	6
,, 69	,, ,, ,, ,, 16-inch ,, ...	10	0
,, 70	**The Sutton Spray Syringe.** Specially suitable for delicate greenhouse or conservatory plants, and for distributing disinfecting fluids in dwelling-houses	10	6
,, 71	**Lady's Garden Syringe,** 2 roses and 1 jet, 14-inch ...	7	6
,, 72	**Lady's Greenhouse Syringe,** 1 rose and 1 jet, 12-inch...	6	0
,, 73	**Aphicide, Hughes's.** An effectual little instrument ...	1	6

VARIOUS IMPLEMENTS &c.

No.		s.	d.
No. 74	**Aphis Brush**	2	0
,, 75	**Hose Mender, The Cooper.** Extremely useful and easily adjusted. For ½-inch Hose, 6*d.*; ¾-inch Hose, 7*d.*; 1-inch Hose, 9*d.*; 1¼-inch Hose	0	10
,, 76	**Garden Hammer,** large size	2	6
,, 76A	,, ,, small size	2	0
,, 77	**Garden Hatchet**	3	0
,, 78	**Garden Bill,** with back, Gentleman's, a superior implement...	4	0
,, 79	,, ,, ,, Gardener's	3	6
,, 80	,, ,, ...	3	0
,, 81	**Grass Hook**	2	6
,, 82	**Fern Trowel,** with leather sheath	3	0
,, 83	**Garden Trowel,** solid steel, polished handle, 5-inch ...	1	6
,, 83A	,, ,, ,, ,, ,, 6-inch ...	1	9
,, 83B	,, ,, ,, ,, ,, 7-inch ...	2	0

VARIOUS IMPLEMENTS &c.—cont.

No.		Each. s.	d.
No. 84	**Weeding Fork,** 3 prong, short handle, 1*s.* 6*d.*; long handle...	1	9
,, 85	,, ,, 4 ,, ,, ,, 1*s.* 9*d.*; ,, ,, ...	2	0
,, 86	**Weed Extractor,** West's Patent	2	6
,, 86A	,, ,, Thompson & Shingler's Patent... ...	10	0
,, 87	**Garden Reel**	3	0
,, 88	**Garden Lines** ... 30 yards long, 1*s.* 6*d.*; 60 yards long	2	9
,, 89	**Tobacco Powder Distributor,** India-rubber, small ...	3	6
,, 89A	,, ,, ,, ,, medium ...	4	6
,, 89B	,, ,, ,, ,, Duplex ...	3	0
,, 90	**Bellows** for Tobacco Powder, &c.	2	6
,, 90A	,, smaller size	1	0
,, 91	**Sulphurator** (Boite à Houppe)...	3	0
,, 92	**Flower-pot Cleaner,** sm. size, 1st quality, 2*s.*; 2nd quality...	1	0
,, 92A	,, ,, medium size, ,, 3*s.*; ,, ...	1	6
,, 92B	,, ,, large size, ,, 3*s.* 6*d.*; ,, ...	2	0
,, 93	**Floral Aid,** for arranging flowers ... each, 1*s.*, 1*s.* 6*d.*, and	2	6
,, 94	**Beatall Flower Displayer** ... each, 3-inch, 10*d.*; 4-inch	1	0
	,, ,, ,, 5-in. 1*s.* 2*d.*; 6-in. 1*s.* 4*d.*; 7-in.	1	7
	,, ,, ,, 8-in. 1*s.* 10*d.*; 9-in. 2*s.* 1*d.*; 10-in.	2	4
,, 95	**Flower Gatherer** (Dubois'), about 4-foot cane handle; for cutting and holding flowers &c.; light and practical ...	17	6
,, 96	**Foot Iron,** for digging	1	6
,, 97	**Measuring Tape,** 66 feet, in solid leather case	8	6
,, 98	**Garden Shears,** 8-inch	4	0
,, 98A	,, ,, 9-inch	5	0
,, 98B	,, ,, 10-inch	5	6
,, 99	,, ,, Ridal's Patent. A great improvement ...	7	6
,, 99A	,, ,, with pruning notch	6	6
,, 100	,, ,, Lady's	3	6
,, 101	**Grass Shears,** cranked	3	6
,, 102	**Branch Pruning, or Lopping Shears**	9	0
,, 103	**Oil Can,** for Lawn Mowers, &c.	1	9

Victorian ingenuity. Some ideas caught on – others did not

II

Magic, Medicine and Broth

By Richard Mabey

Edible plants have been the gardener's mainstay for more than 2000 years. Their properties at various times in history have been held to include the magical as well as the medicinal, the ornamental as well as the edible. Often it was only by accident or afterthought that they found their way into the soup. Surprisingly few of them owe their wild origins to Britain. From the mountains of South America to the high tundra of northern Europe and Asia, they have reached our gardens – often by circuitous routes which disguised their parenthood – from all over the world.

Where the practical meets the aesthetic: the formal kitchen garden at Barnsley House, Gloucestershire

FRUITS OF THE EARTH

Few places are more cosmopolitan than an English kitchen garden. Our favourite vegetables and fruits are all derived from wild species with their origins scattered across the globe

By Stefan Buczacki

Our map shows the native ranges of some of the commonest garden species, though in many cases it is not easy to be precise. One problem is that many cultivated edible plants descend from species which occur over a very wide area. The blackcurrant, for example, originates from *Ribes nigrum*, which ranges naturally from Scandinavia to eastern France, through the Italian Alps and then on through Bulgaria into central and northern Asia as far east as the Himalayas. But, as it was probably cultivated first in northern Europe and Siberia, these are the regions indicated on the map.

Other cultivated plants are derived from more than one wild species – the plum from two, for example, and modern apples from three. Sometimes the distribution of one may be better known than the others, and in a few cases – the raspberry and the strawberry, for instance – the different species originate from widely separate parts of the world, and the crosses could have occurred only in cultivation. In other cases, including apples and plums, it seems that the original hybridisation was natural, and that its location can be reasonably proposed as a region where both parents and the hybrid commonly occur together. The Caucasus in particular is a favoured area for many plants.

In other cases again, the plants may have been cultivated since ancient times over much of their natural range, and it is now impossible to know where their cultivation first took place. This problem is exacerbated in plants such as the radish, which have been in cultivation so long that their wild ancestors are now unknown. In such cases we have selected the most *likely* wild candidate and shown its range. For the radish, this is *Raphanus raphanistrum*, which occurs throughout temperate Europe and Asia. A related problem with plants such as the asparagus is that they have been cultivated for so long that their natural distribution is unknown. Asparagus can be found apparently wild along the Mediterranean and Atlantic coasts of Europe, but it is impossible to know the extent to which these plants are truly wild or descended from garden escapes.

To complicate matters still further, some plants have geographical origins different from the origin of the form now cultivated. The cabbage and its allies are examples of this, for almost all of the group commonly called brassicas are derived from the wild cabbage, *Brassica oleracea*, from the Mediterranean and Atlantic coasts of Europe. But such diverse cultivated forms as kohl-rabi, cauliflower and Brussels sprouts can no longer be traced to the wild stock and, while cabbages were cultivated by the Romans wherever they went, Brussels sprouts seem to have been developed in the Low Countries, calabrese in Italy and other types in other areas. Finally, it should always be borne in mind that many plants now grown for food were originally cultivated for some other purpose – usually medicinal, though in the cases of tomatoes and runner beans, ornamental.

Greenland
CHIVES
RASPBERRY
BLACK CURRANT
CHIVES
RASPBERRY
CARROT
Siberia
RHUBARB
Iceland
Scandinavia
TURNIP & GOOSEBERRY
CARROT
CHIVES
Ocean
BLACK CURRANT
Asia
RASPBERRY
RADISH
Russia
LETTUCE
GARLIC
MINT
THYME
TURNIP
Denmark
CELERY
PARSNIP
Belgium
RED CURRANT
RADISH
Germany
GLOBE ARTICHOKE
SPROUT & BROCCOLI
CABBAGE & CAULIFLOWER
ASPARAGUS
France
FENNEL
SWEDE
MINT
SAGE
THYME
RASPBERRY
GOOSEBERRY
Portugal
CHIVES
ROSEMARY
Italy
GOOSEBERRY
RASPBERRY
Spain
ONION
China
CELERY
MULBERRY
PARSNIP
APPLE
PLUM
PEAR
LEEK
Caucasus Mts.
ROSEMARY
SPROUT
BROCCOLI
CABBAGE
CAULI-FLOWER
LEEK
PEA
LETTUCE
PEACH & NECTARINE
APRICOT
Nepal
CHIVES
Mt. Everest
CHIVES
Japan
CELERY
CUCUMBER
BROAD BEAN
PARSLEY
Greece
Asia Minor
Mediterranean Sea
PEA
Morocco
GOOSEBERRY
ASPARAGUS
CARROT
Canary Is.
LEEK
MARJORAM
BROAD BEAN
BASIL
CARROT
India
East Indies
RED CURRANT
Africa
BASIL
CUCUMBER
Indian Ocean
Australia
CELERY
South Africa
Herbs
Fruits
New Zealand
tables
A.S.

When the Irish monk Manchan of Liath set down his personal vision of paradise in the 10th century, it was, more or less, a plan for a self-sufficient cottage retreat. In a clearing hacked out of the wilderness would be a cell, a chapel and a little kitchen garden. Manchan knew exactly what he would grow and eat: "This is the housekeeping I would undertake," he dreamed, "hens, speckled salmon, bees," adding, with undisguised worldly relish, "fresh fragrant leeks."

Domestic gardening has never been just a matter of hand-to-mouth subsistence. Even during the privations of the Dark Ages, kitchen gardeners had the familiar stamp of the enthusiast about them. They swapped growing tips, bragged about huge and extravagant fruitings, defended the virtues of the home-grown and dreamed of those special moments – way beyond the needs of survival – when crop, season and pure pleasure merged into a delicious whole.

For another medieval monk, Walafrid Strabo, the greatest joy was cutting melons in high summer: "When the iron blade strikes to its guts, the melon throws out gushing streams of juice and many seeds. The cheerful guest then divides its bent

A feast to behold: the publishers of seed catalogues have always understood the value of eye-appeal

back into many slices. He tastes the delightful succulence of gardens. Its pure taste charms his throat."

Reading these early accounts of European kitchen gardening one is struck not by their ignorance or strangeness but by how little its rewards and preoccupations have changed over the last 1000 years. More perhaps than any other branch of gardening, it has been part of a common culture, and a uniquely sociable business.

The leek has been a central component and, in a way, a symbol of this whole history. Ever since the Romans brought it here as an antidote to the chill northern climate, it has been a festive vegetable, transcending class and language barriers, outlasting fashions and whole centuries of disdain and cocking a snook at utilitarianism. The Anglo-Saxons thought so highly of it that the *leac-ton*, the leek patch, became the generic term for kitchen gardens. They grew at least two sorts, including a sophisticated "unset" variety which was cut repeatedly, like giant chives. But the Celts laid claim to it as well. They called it "green purity", and it became the Welsh national emblem after King Cadwallader's victory over the Saxons in AD 640. Just before the battle, the Welsh had gathered leeks from nearby gardens, and stuck them into their hats for solidarity and mutual recognition.

Leeks passed out of fashion during the 18th and 19th centuries as part of the general hostility to all things oniony. But echoes of the old affections survived, not just on St David's Day, but in the yard-bred "Miners' Leeks" that helped many poor families through the Depression, and in the leek competitions of the north-east. Now the leek is returning to mainstream gardening and cooking, encouraged, exactly as it was 2000 years ago, by a fascination with the cultures of the warm south.

Fruit and vegetable growing, closely tied to the necessities of health and existence, seem to be more firmly anchored to unchanging principles than other branches of gardening. Their history, consequently, is not so much a simple march of new species and refined techniques as something cyclical, a continual rediscovery of old values. It can even bring basic raw materials of kitchen gardening repeatedly in and out of commission. Plants like fat hen, for instance, introduced to this country by neolithic settlers, could become leaf crops in the Iron Age, be reduced to despised weeds by the 16th century, and then be revived as an exotic green for latter-day foragers and specialist gardeners. Even the land on which fruit and vegetables are grown moves in and out of cultivation according to fashion and circumstance.

In times of land hunger (much of our history) opportunities for growing food have been snatched way beyond the perimeter of the garden itself. Fruit trees were planted in hedges and in the headlands that separated the medieval open fields. Staple crops were grown on the edges of commons and on seaweed-rich beaches – and later, and more legally, in the municipal allotments that were meant to replace lost common land. During the Second World War even the railway embankments were taken into cultivation. Some of these lineside beds still survive, and the tangles of naturalised asparagus and loganberries that often poke through their undergrowth are one of the clearest testaments that British kitchen gardeners are hedonists even when their backs are against the wall.

In fact, something resembling kitchen gardening began long before there was anything as clearly defined as a kitchen garden, and a little poking about in the mud behind the hut was probably a crucial intermediate stage between hunter-gathering and communal farming.

It is easy to guess but impossible to prove what fruit and vegetables Ancient Britons picked and ate before the arrival of the first farmers from the Mediterranean about 3500 BC. The earliest physical evidence dates from about 1000 years later and was unearthed in the remains of various neolithic "Lake Villages" in northern Europe. Deep in the ancient waste pits, often stuck to fragments of crockery, were the seeds of a host of wild fruits and vegetables: raspberries, crab apples, wild plums and cherries, hazelnuts, acorns, strawberries, parsnips and carrots. There were also the seeds of plants like fat hen, orach and blackberry, that flourish in nitrogen-rich waste ground. It is fair to assume that, even if these species were originally gathered from the wild, they would sprout on the settlements' middens, from discarded plants or from seeds passed in faeces, and would thrive in all that manure. Perhaps these happenstance forcing-beds even spawned the idea of deliberate cultivation.

What is certainly beyond question is that manuring – and maybe some minimal tending to reduce competition – are the basic procedures of primordial gardening and can make perceptible differences to the cropping of many plants. Wild sorrel, dandelion and chicory were all "fattened" like this during the 15th and 16th centuries, and until the American wood strawberry was introduced in about 1600, it was the sole way of increasing the size and yield of European wild strawberries.

Yet as soon as any kind of special consideration began to be given to certain species or individual plants, the processes of selection, transplantation, and occasional cross-breeding would automatically have been set in motion. Even gathering from the wild would have led to the selection of superior strains, from the simple fact of fruits and seeds being picked from the most prolific and tasty plants.

By the last few centuries BC quite new crops had joined the improved strains of wildings in the prehistoric garden. Iron Age villagers at Glastonbury, for example, grew field peas, a small Celtic or "tic" bean, linseed, emmer wheat and oats – all originally from southern Europe or the Middle East. Crops like these were introduced by successive waves of immigrants, and later as trophies by returning British explorers, and the flow has barely slowed down since.

Spring preview: pear and apple blossom offer extravagant promises of things to come

The Romans brought with them an array of gourmet fruit and vegetables, including figs, quince, a versatile green called alexanders (now naturalised in coastal areas) and a battery of medicinal herbs to cope with their dietary excesses, including ground elder (for gout) and fennel (for indigestion).

During the Dark Ages the European Christian community kept up the traffic in new plants. Many monasteries and abbeys became centres for the growing and study of herbs. Some of the more potent and recondite species, like birthwort and peony, were virtually restricted to these sites.

The Renaissance brought as significant an expansion of opportunities for gardening as it did in other fields of enterprise, and there was a surge of new and improved varieties of vegetables into Britain from mainland Europe. Savoy cabbages and endives came from the already highly skilled Dutch nurserymen; asparagus, red beetroot and several new kinds of lettuce from Italy. Later in the 16th and 17th centuries it was the turn of the New World, which supplied not just potatoes and tomatoes but maize, Jerusalem artichokes, wild rice and runner beans.

If the varieties of fruit and vegetable cultivated in Britain increased steadily, the gardens which accommodated them scarcely changed at all. For much of the late medieval period there were essentially just two sorts of garden: the large, semi-commercial estates of the monasteries, infirmaries and a few large manor houses; and the small back-yards of just about everyone else. They differed in structure and in the kinds of produce they grew, but when it came to the techniques of cultivation

COOKERS AND EATERS

In the beginning there were two wild apple species. Now, after well over eight centuries of development, Britain's national collection at Brogdale in Kent maintains around 2000 different apple varieties

By Stefan Buczacki

The apple undoubtedly has been the most popular fruit in temperate regions since early pre-history. Remains of fruits dating from 6500 BC have been found on sites in Anatolia.

Two species in particular have been significant in the development of the modern apple – *Malus silvestris*, the wild crab which occurs in Britain and more or less throughout Europe and western Asia; and the smaller *M. pumila*, which has a more restricted distribution around the Caucasus and Turkestan, where it grows in extensive mixed woods with *M. silvestris*. Natural hybrids here are common, and it is from some of these, plus the very hardy Siberian crab, *M. baccata*, that modern apple varieties are descended.

Selected forms of wild apple were spread through the Fertile Crescent and had reached Palestine by about 2000 BC; the Old Testament records Solomon asking, "Comfort me with apples, for I am sick of love". It was a short step from Palestine to Egypt, where apples are mentioned as temple offerings in writings from around 1200–1100 BC. Not surprisingly, both the Greeks and Romans appreciated apples, too. Homer refers in his *Odyssey* (900–800 BC) to apple orchards, and his compatriot Theophrastus described the techniques of budding and grafting.

Although remains of apples have been found at Neolithic sites in Britain, there is no suggestion that there was actual cultivation until the Romans arrived with some of their selected forms. Strangely, too, there is little direct evidence of the extent or importance of apple cultivation either during the Roman occupation or in the immediately following centuries.

After the Norman conquest, however, many varieties were brought over from France both for eating and for making cider, which joined ale and beer as major national drinks.

Subsequently, apple cultivation developed to become a major industry, and a large number of indigenous varieties were raised. Many of these have achieved international importance and, in the 20th century, the Merton and Malling rootstocks, bred to produce trees in a range of defined sizes, have revolutionised efficiency.

Apple varieties can be grouped loosely into three types, in ascending order of acidity – eating or dessert apples, cooking or culinary apples, and cider apples. Although a variety called Decio is thought to be a possible survivor from around the fifth century AD, the oldest authentically recognisable apple varieties still found in Britain date from the 13th century. Among them is the first named variety recorded in England, the pearmain – a pear-shaped apple that in one form or another was the principal dessert form until well into the 18th century.

The second of the great old English apples was the cooking variety costard, a name that survives in the word costermonger (originally, one who sold costards), although the apple itself seems to have disappeared early in the 18th century.

The pippins comprise a large group of dessert apples of the general form of large crabs, and derive their name from the old custom of raising them from pips. The first pippin trees seem to have been brought here from France by one Robert Harris, fruiterer to Henry VIII. Before then, the very best dessert fruit were almost all imported from the Continent.

Numerous other varieties were familiar to the Elizabethans. Shakespeare, in *Henry IV, Part I*, for instance, mentions the keeping variety Leathercoat. Another popular form, the Queening or Quoining, like the appropriately-named Catshead which still survives, was typical of a group of markedly angular apples which today would find little favour with supermarkets.

Codlins were originally small, green apples. The name survives through its attachment to varieties amenable to "coddling", or parboiling.

Many of our modern favourites are survivors from more-or-less chance finds of the 19th century – Bramley's Seedling, raised by an amateur in Southwell, Nottinghamshire, around 1810 (but not introduced to commerce until 1876), is still the best cooker; and Cox's Orange Pippin, raised from seed by the retired brewer Richard Cox in about 1825, remains the unrivalled English eating apple.

More concerted breeding programmes were undertaken in the early years of this century by the great fruit nurseries such as Laxton's, which produced Laxton's Early Crimson, Laxton's Fortune, Laxton's Superb and Lord Lambourne. Today breeding work in this country has largely been taken over by government-financed programmes, especially at the East Malling station of the Institute of Horticulture. From here have come Greensleeves, Redsleeves, Suntan and several other major commercial varieties. Fortunately both for apple breeders requiring old breeding material and for gardeners seeking old varieties to grow, the Ministry of Agriculture maintains a national collection at Brogdale in Kent of around 2000 apple varieties, including those still surviving from earlier times.

The apple has the longest recorded history of any cultivated fruit. The varieties illustrated all represent significant chapters in its long and illustrious story

Bramley's Seedling
Court Pendu Plat
Cox's Orange Pippin
Cat's-head
Crab
London Pippin
Winter Permain
bston Pippin
Bountiful
Fiesta

– digging, sowing, weeding, harvesting – they shared in what has been a common currency for much of gardening history. Alexander Neckham's list of tools, tasks and tribulations, written in 1178, would not be altered much for the next 800 years:

> *A fork, a wide blade, a spade or shovel, a knife . . . a seed basket for seed-time, a wheel barrow . . . a two-edged axe to uproot thorns, brambles, briars, prickles and unwanted shoots, and rushes and wood to mend hedges . . . timbers, palings, and stakes or hedging hurdles . . . he should have a knife hanging from his belt to graft trees and seedlings, mattocks with which to uproot nettles or vetch, darnel, thistle, sterile oate and weeds of this sort, and a hoe . . .*

The distinguishing feature of the big monastic gardens was not so much their size as their organisation. Partly because of the demands on their resources – they often had to serve the surrounding community as well as their incumbents – their different functions were separated in the interests of efficiency. There were beds for the growing of bulk quantities of staple vegetables, like broad beans, peas and cabbage, and beds with impressive ranges of medicinal and culinary herbs, many of whose favourites – rosemary, lavender, mint, comfrey, for example – are unchanged in herb gardens today.

Orchards formed another compartment. They were often simply walled plantations of fruit trees, but occasionally there were crops growing under the trees, or walks and arbours around them. In the Benedictine monastery of St Gall, the orchard doubled as a cemetery, and there were plots specifically marked for apples, pears, plums, service trees, quinces, almonds, hazelnuts, walnuts, chestnuts, bay trees, mulberries, peaches and figs. Other large settlements had vineyards, though these began to be abandoned from the 12th century, as French wine became more easily available and the climate deteriorated.

The improved communications of the late medieval period also saw the beginning of another characteristic feature of British kitchen gardening: the highly local fruit or vegetable speciality that became much more widely known and enjoyed.

Good advice for bad times: wartime economy plea

Blandurels apples, for instance (now known as Colville Blanc because of their almost pure white colour), first appeared in Aquitaine. Edward I's queen, Eleanor of Castile, had grafts sent over to England and grew them on in her orchard at Langley Manor in 1280. They apparently thrived, as the royal fruiterer notes, 20 years after her death, in his accounts for 1310: "For the Queen, going to Canterbury on the Friday before the Nativity of St John (24 June) 800 Blandurels, price 6s." Many of the medieval apples seemed to last well into the summer following picking, provided they were stored under straw.

But the majority of kitchen gardens had nothing as grand as these productive orchards and *herbiers*. They were simply small enclosed yards. *Domesday Book* (1086) lists thousands of these *garths*, of all sizes from a few square yards to a couple of acres, and attached to both peasant cottages and town houses. But they have one essential feature in common. Everything – herbs, vegetables, fruit trees and most probably hens and bees – were raised together, lettuces cheek by jowl with lilies and cabbages next to king-cups. This was not just a result of the pressure of space, or of an uncivilised lack of order. In the common medieval view of the vegetable world there was simply no real dividing line between plants grown for food or medicine and plants grown for pleasure. Damsons, for instance, were enjoyed as an appetiser, a dessert and, according to the Anglo-Saxon *Leech Book of Bald*, as a remedy for loose bowels. The ubiquitous leek was not only a warming pot-vegetable and a catarrh cure, but an all-purpose domestic purifier. Leek seeds and juice were made into a kind of toothpaste; skins were used for bleaching the hair.

The variety of plant uses was as much a product of the medieval philosophy of nature as of the necessary frugality of the times. The *mana* of plants was believed to permeate all their parts, and to be connected at one extreme with how they grew in the earth, and at the other with how they affected the body. One finds, consequently, a unified set of ideas governing the way that fruit and vegetables were cultivated and how they were used in the kitchen. At their heart were the doctrines of sympathetic magic which, in essence, decreed that the workings of the natural world could be predicted – and therefore controlled – by analogy and association. Like would repel like – though sometimes attract it. Exterior similarities of shape were clues to interior resemblances. Processes of clear cause and effect in the visible world – burning, cutting, withering – could generate analogous processes deep inside living things. So, ground-up crayfish could be used as a deterrent to similarly shaped "noisome insects". Parsley seeds could be made to sprout more strongly and quickly if watered with Aquavit, or to produce crinkled and "frayed" leaves if bound up in a cloth and hammered with a stick. Onions could be sweetened by growing them among melons and cherries reddened by scalding the trees' roots with quicklime.

The notion that mere physical proximity could cause chemical and maybe even genetic change in plants was widely believed up until the 17th century. Even though the practical techniques of fruit grafting, for instance, had been well understood and practised in Europe for more than 1000 years, the production of hybrid fruit was still thought to be a possibility. As late as 1685 John Baptista Porta wrote that the intimate grafting of different species could make them "intermingle" and generate "new compounded fruit". The trees "are joined together as it were, by carnal copulation, to the end that the fruit thereof might contain in it all the excellencies of both the parents: and the same trees were garnished with two sorts of leaves, and nourished with two sorts of juices, and the fruit had a double relish, according to both the kinds whence it was compounded."

Sympathetic magic also guided pest control. The muddled plantings of the typical medieval garden meant that insect pests would have been much less trouble than in modern highly cultivated and over-specialised plots. But gardeners were bothered by birds and mice, and many of the prescribed deterrents relied on counteracting the pest with the *mana* of a predator – by burying an owl's heart among the cabbages, for instance. Sympathies and antipathies could also help with the weather. Firing a gun or ringing a bell could disperse a thunderstorm. The grey pelt of a seal or crocodile, hung at the entrance to the garden, would keep louring rain clouds away. Failing that, the clouds' own image could be reflected back at them with "a mighty glass". More farcically, lentils – notorious even then for their windiness – were sown around young plants to protect them from gale damage.

It is easy for us to mock these beliefs as gullible and superstitious nonsense. But they were at least based on a conviction of the indivisibility of the natural world that was to be lost for many centuries – until, indeed, the growth of ecology in the last few decades. And some of the most apparently far-fetched beliefs are now known to have at least some basis in fact. "Companion planting", for instance – the physical juxtaposition of plants so that one might assist the growth of the other – is now recognised as being genuinely effective with certain species because of the insecticidal effect of their root secretions. Work in Holland, for example, has shown that African marigolds can kill potato eel worms up to a metre away from their roots.

For most of the medieval period all garden wisdom was passed around by word of mouth, and its more extravagant advice was tempered by a good deal of hard-won experience. But in 1577, the first full-length popular gardening manual in English, Thomas Hill's *The Gardener's Labyrinth,* was published, and was enough of a success for a new edition to be issued the following year.

It was an apt moment for such a book to appear. The Elizabethan era was a time of national self-confidence and open-minded curiosity about the world. Discovery

Fashions in vegetable growing may come and go,
but the basic priority remains unchanged.
The countryman's packed garden (above) would have
won the approval of yield-conscious Victorians

Left: Brassica oleracea – ancestor of the modern cabbage and all its allies

THE ORIGINS OF FRUIT AND VEGETABLES

As the plant biographies on these pages reveal, many of the fruit and vegetable varieties common in our gardens have far from common backgrounds

By Stefan Buczacki

PEAR (Pyrus communis)
There is little evidence of pears being used as a food in prehistoric times – the wild pear is hard and unappetising. Modern cultivated pears are thought to be hybrids between *Pyrus communis* and other species from the Caucasus and Turkestan. They spread across Europe in the same way as apples, through the Fertile Crescent to Greece and Rome. The earliest reference to British cultivation is post-Norman Conquest; although old pear trees were mentioned as boundary markers in *Domesday Book*. Genetically, pears are very variable and no old varieties survive.

PLUM (Prunus domestica)
Considered a cross between blackthorn, *Prunus spinosa* (green/blue fruits) and myrobalan, *P. cerasifera* (yellow/red fruits), plums probably arose first in the Caucasus where both hybridise naturally. The fruit is enormously variable, but greengages (round, mainly green or yellow), yellow egg (ovoid yellow fruit) and prunes (dark purple with high sugar content) are among the most characteristic groups. Plums were well known to Romans, and in Britain stones have been excavated on late Iron Age sites. Since myrobalan is not native to Britain the domestic plum must have been introduced to the country in pre-Roman times.

STRAWBERRY (Fragaria spp.)
The first record of strawberry cultivation in Britain was in 1328, but until the 17th century the fruits were little different from the small, wild European wood strawberry *Fragaria vesca*. This survives as the Alpine strawberry, but other modern types in Britain are complex hybrids derived mainly from the North American *Fragaria virginiana* and the pan-American *Fragaria chiloensis*. Of special importance in the development of modern large-fruited types was the Pine, bred in France from *Fragaria chiloensis*.

RASPBERRY (Rubus idaeus)
Wild *Rubus idaeus* is native to many temperate regions, including Britain, and the fruit was collected in prehistoric times. The Greeks and Romans used it mainly for medicinal purposes. It was probably not cultivated in Britain until the 16th century and was known as raspis, because of the thorns. Improved in the 18th century – especially the large-fruited Yellow Antwerp – and by the early 19th century, 23 varieties were recorded. In the early 20th century many new varieties like Lloyd George and Norfolk Giant were chance findings. Modern heavy cropping types are derived from crosses with several North American species.

GOOSEBERRY (Ribes grossularia)
Although the wild plant occurs in many parts of Europe and North Africa it is probably not native to Britain. Little is known of the gooseberry's early history, and the first reference to its cultivation in Britain was in 1275. By the 17th century, several varieties were grown for edible fruit, juice, wine-making, medicinal purposes and also for the young leaves, used as a salad. The main types are pale green and dark red, each in a range of sizes and shapes. By the 18th century, competitive gooseberry clubs were formed and championships held. Varieties like Golden Drop and Warrington survive from this time, but modern varieties have been bred from crosses with other ribes species for disease and pest resistance, and for freedom from spines.

RED AND WHITE CURRANTS (Ribes spp.)
Currants were not cultivated in ancient times, although several species occur throughout Europe and at least three have contributed to modern red and white currants. The first references to cultivation were in the 16th century, and by 1568 they were grown in England – mainly imported from Holland where they have long been popular. But they were difficult to raise true to type so there have never been many named varieties. Most of the types grown today are fairly old: Red Lake (USA, 1920) and White Versailles (France, 1835), for instance.

BLACKCURRANT (Ribes nigrum)
Ribes nigrum is a fairly common plant throughout much of Europe and central Asia, especially in the north. Apparently the wild plants in Britain are almost certainly escapes from cultivation. Like other currants, the blackcurrant was not mentioned by either the Greeks or Romans, but it had probably been long collected and cultivated by northern Europeans. The first reference in Britain was in the Middle Ages when it was used to flavour wine. It was not described as a garden plant until 1611 when it was imported from Holland to Hatfield House. Few named varieties existed until the 19th century when Boskoop Giant and Baldwin originated. Most of the currants we know today are more recent hybrids between *Ribes nigrum* and other ribes species.

CABBAGES AND ALLIES (Brassica oleracea)
Wild cabbage-like plants occur in coastal regions of the Mediterranean and also along the Atlantic coast of western Europe, including Britain, but they may not all belong to the same species. Theophrastus mentioned kale-type plants, while Roman authors clearly knew both kales and headed cabbages, but it is not known which forms are the ancestors of the modern types. Some forms have been grown and eaten in Britain since Roman times. Variations with swollen flower heads, such as cauliflowers and broccoli, probably originated in southern Europe; those with swollen stems (kohl-rabi) came from more northerly regions; and those with swollen lateral buds (Brussels sprout) are the most recent types and originated in the Low Countries.

TURNIP (Brassica campestris=rapa)
This is a complicated species which includes the swollen rooted turnip, and is closely related to the leafy Chinese cabbage types and some oil-seed crops. Forms of the species without swollen roots occur in the wild in Britain and throughout Europe, North Africa, western Asia and China. Turnips have been cultivated since prehistoric times in Europe and have always formed a major food for livestock. Although in Britain the roots alone are eaten, the young leaves are useful, too. Roots may be spherical, cylindrical or flattened in shape, and some are green or purple at the top.

Pyrus communis – the wild ancestor of the pear, found in British hedgerows

Cucumis sativus – the wild cucumber

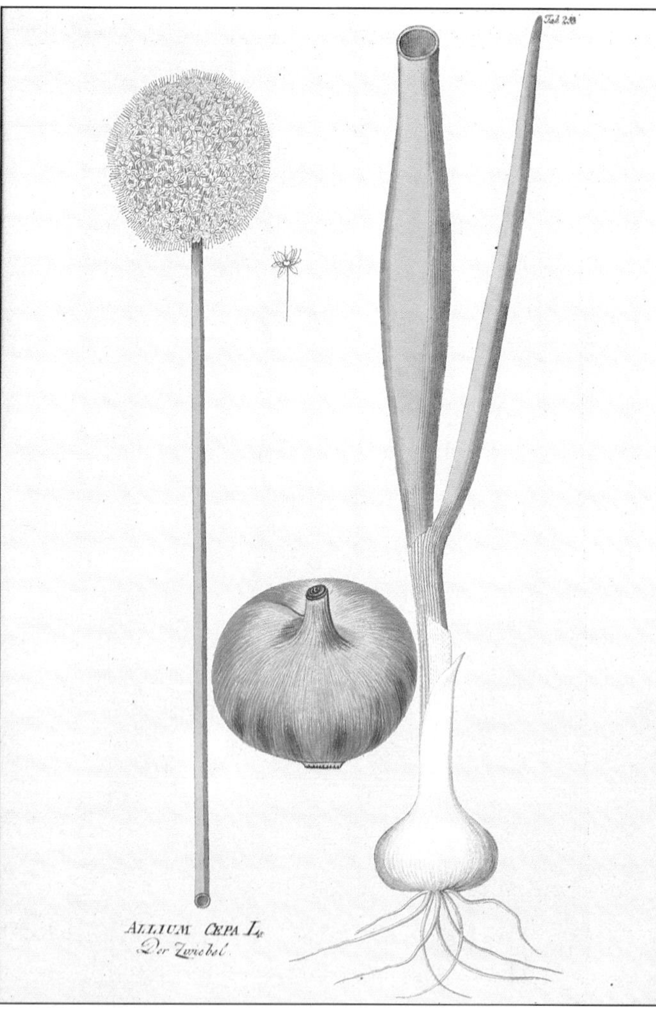

Allium cepa – the onion

LETTUCE (Lactuca sativa)
The lettuce has been cultivated since antiquity, and it is thought it might have originated in south-west Asia and Siberia. The cultivated species probably derived from *Lactuca serriola* (widely distributed and native to Britain). It seems to have been cultivated in part for medicinal purposes, but the lettuce was used as a food in prehistoric times and was well known to both Greeks and Romans. All early lettuce types were leafy, and hearted forms did not occur before the 16th century. Now lettuces are divided into smooth-leaved or butterhead, crisp-head and the more upright cos types. Varying degrees of reddish pigmentation occur to produce the red lettuce.

CARROT (Daucus carota)
The wild carrot is distributed widely throughout Europe and Asia, although its original range is unknown. Naturally it is a plant of dry, sandy places near the sea. Its early cultivation history is often confused with that of the parsnip, because wild carrots have pale coloured or white roots. Most modern British garden carrots have red or orange roots, although pale-rooted forms are grown elsewhere. They were cultivated by the 10th century in Europe, but probably not until the 16th century in Britain. Among the modern varieties there is a considerable range in root length and shape, and in earliness of maturity. Autumn King types are hardiest.

ONION (Allium cepa)
The onion probably no longer exists in the wild, but it seems to have originated in Iran and Pakistan, possibly from *Allium oschaninii*. It was grown and eaten extensively in Egypt, and onions are often found with mummies. The Greeks and Romans described many medicinal uses for the onion but the date of its introduction into western countries is uncertain, although it is known that onions were being cultivated by the Middle Ages.

PEA (Pisum sativum)
The pea may have originated from natural crosses with *Pisum elatius*, a common weed in Europe and Asia, but it does not occur in the wild. It was first cultivated in south-west Asia and reached Ancient Greece through the Black Sea, spreading through the Himalayas to India and China. Peas were important in many parts of Africa long before European invasions. But it was not until the 16th century that green peas were eaten, as opposed to ripe, dry seeds. There is a wide range of types, varying in height, hardiness and sweetness. Among recent developments are the semi-leafless varieties and the appreciation of edible pods such as mangetout.

BROAD BEAN (Vicia faba)
This is probably the oldest cultivated plant. It is not known in the wild but the cultivated *Vicia faba* is very similar to *Vicia pliniana* from Algeria. The broad bean can be subdivided by seed size, the modern bean having larger seeds than the field bean, horse bean or tick pea; and being larger than prehistoric seed remains found on sites in Britain. All ancient western civilisations grew this species; it was the only

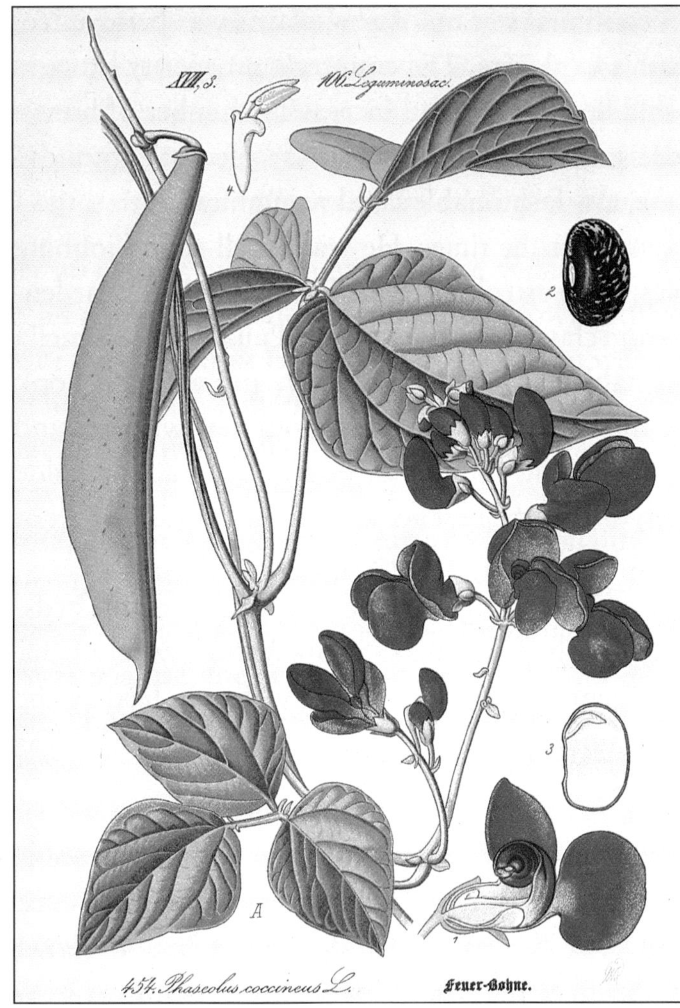

Phaseolus coccineus – the runner bean

Prunus domestica – the plum

edible bean known in Europe in pre-Columbian times, and was introduced to the New World after 1492. The broad bean reached western Asia and China early in its history. Some forms, represented by the garden variety Aquadulce, are winter hardy.

RUNNER BEAN (Scarlet Runner) (Phaseolus coccineus)
The runner bean occurs in the wild at around 2000m in the Guatemalan Highlands, and in neighbouring parts of Central America where perennial forms have long been cultivated. Wild collected beans were probably eaten in Mexico around 5000 to 7000 BC, although by 200 BC it was cultivated at Tehuacan. The runner bean was introduced to Europe as a climbing ornamental plant and reached Britain in 1633, but it was not grown seriously as a food crop until the 18th century. It is the only perennial bean grown in British gardens, and succeeds well as it is a long-day species; but it is not frost hardy. Roots can be stored over winter for a small early crop.

TOMATO (Lycopersicon esculentum)
Native to the Andes, the tomato was cultivated extensively in South and Central America before being introduced to Europe around 1554. For some time it was grown only as an ornamental fruit. It was known by several names: love-apple, because it was often thought to be an aphrodisiac; and golden apple, because the wild forms are golden fruited. The species is variable, but most garden tomatoes are derived from *var.* cerasiforme (cherry tomato). Modern types include the bush and cordon varieties; within the latter are potato-leaved types (including most garden yellow-fruited forms), large-fruited Marmande, pear-shaped and sweet small-fruited types such as Sweet 100 and Gardener's Delight.

POTATO (Solanum tuberosum)
The potato has been widely cultivated (together with related tuberous *Solanum* species) by South American Indians since ancient times, especially in Peru and Bolivia. Late-maturing knobbly forms from the Andes were brought to Spain around 1570 and to England around 1590. Despite popular legend, it is unlikely that Drake and Raleigh played any part in the introduction, although the latter may have planted them on his Irish estates. The potato was grown first as a curiosity, but eaten as a delicacy at the court of King James I. It was not grown as a field crop in England until the mid-18th century which was probably later than in Ireland.

CUCUMBER (Cucumis sativus)
The cucumber is thought to have originated in tropical or sub-tropical Africa or Asia. It has long been cultivated in India and a similar species, *Cucumis hardwickii*, is found near the Himalayas, although this may be a relict of an ancient escape from cultivation. It came from India to the West and was well known to Greeks and Romans. There are two main groups: long types for cultivation in greenhouses and shorter, outdoor or ridge varieties. Indoor types require no fertilisation and male flowers must be removed to prevent it happening (it results in a bitter taste). Some modern indoor types are all-female, and thus avoid the problem.

It was a challenge which Gilbert White could not resist. Each year, as he began the ritual of preparing the hot-beds and nursing the temperamental seedlings, he seemed to be throwing down a gauntlet to the vagaries of the 18th-century climate. The hot-beds themselves (referred to grandly as "the melon ground" and still something of a novelty in British gardens) were 15 yards long, and had up to 30 cart-loads of dung dug into them every year. On it the young melon plants were cosseted in what amounted to precursors of the cloche: "lights" – usually rough shelters of oiled paper stretched on frames, or the bell-jars ("glasses") that had been in use for raising tender plants since the early years of the 18th century. As the hot-bed heated up during the summer, White experimented with different ways of controlling the heat, topping the bed with bark to heat it up, or with earth to damp down the steam. In 1758 – long before the workings of the oxygen cycle in plants had been discovered – he built a ventilation system for one of the frames, to benefit the "plants in Hot-beds by preventing them from being stewed in the night-time in the exhalations that arise from dung, and their own leaves."

Yet at harvest-time, a more ancient and familiar figure emerged from behind the inquisitive scientist. On 12 September 1758, there is an entry in the *Kalendar* that could have come from Walafrid Strabo nine centuries before: "Held a Caltaleupe-feast at ye Hermitage. Cut-up a brace and a half of fruit among 14 people. Weather very fine ever since the ninth."

By the Victorian era, White's improvised arrangements of paper-covered frames and lead ventilation pipes had matured into the fully-fledged hot-house, or "stove". These were the centre-pieces of the great Victorian gardens, which must be counted as a kind of culmination of the arts and traditions of kitchen gardening.

The ready availability of cheap coal and skilled labour meant that a Victorian big house was able to produce fruit and vegetables on a scale and with a diversity that cannot be matched from any other period of our history. A three or four-acre walled garden could make the whole estate self-sufficient in vegetables throughout the year and generate a large surplus for market. It would employ up to 20 full-time gardeners who had responsibility for an awesome range of components: orchards, nutteries, vineries, cold-frames, hot-houses, potato and carrot clamps, rooms for storing fruit and washing vegetables, mushroom cellars and even ice-houses. The continuously running boiler-room would pipe heat to houses where seedlings could be raised, plants forced for early cropping, and tender fruits like pineapples, figs and peaches grown.

But the heating was about as far as the garden was industrialised. Even pest control was carried out by comparatively innocuous substances like lime-wash – or done by hand, in laborious leaf-by-leaf brushing and grooming. Labour-intensity

In the early 1900s, Ailsa Craig onions were grown on an island in the Thames and taken by punt to be stored. The grower, Mr Barber, claimed to have achieved a record single bulb of 8lb

was the secret of these gardens' success, and the reason why difficult fruits like nectarines could be given what amounted to intensive care throughout the year: pruned, trained and tagged to the walls afresh each year, pollinated with a rabbit-tail brush and protected against frost and wind with curtains or layers of yew branches.

If nothing could match the big estate gardens for sheer output, they were not the sole repositories of gardening skill. The Victorian period was the heyday of cottage gardening, too. In small, crammed rural plots, in suburban allotments, even in the backyards of industrial cities (where "night-soil" often stood in for horse-manure) amateur gardeners grew an astonishing variety of vegetables, often raising their own local specialities by cross-breeding and careful selection.

The English Wonder Pea, for instance, was raised by Mr Tipping of Kenilworth in 1880. It was very dwarf, whereas the Altrincham carrot was huge, sometimes up to 20 inches long. The Stoke lettuce, an ancient, hardy variety of the Cos, was grown for centuries by one family in the Kent village of Stoke. As well as deliberate plant-breeding there was a good deal of opportunistic selection from chance sports and from the wild. The Keswick Codlin apple sprang from the rubbish tip at Ulverston Castle in Cumbria; the first Victoria plum was a naturalised seedling discovered in a Sussex wood.

MURDER MOST FOUL

The fight against pests and diseases over the centuries has called for some desperate remedies – a horse's head on a pole, bear's blood, burning crabs and the excommunication of fieldmice

By Graham Rose

It can't have taken early gardeners long to notice two striking coincidences: swarms of insects on their crops were always followed by blemished plants; and high-density weed-growth was always associated with reduced crop yields. They drew the obvious conclusions, and so began a war that has been going on ever since.

Plant diseases, however, were more of a mystery. It was not until the 19th century that the fungi responsible for most diseases were properly identified and understood. We have no idea what magic those early cultivators invoked to keep diseases at bay and have to move on to the Romans before we find any written record.

Pliny, for instance, bewailed the difficulty of ridding land of couch grass, and described a broad range of pests and blights which still afflict gardeners today. Identifying the pests was about the summit of the Romans' achievement, however, for there was precious little science in their attack. Pliny wasn't speaking just as an isolated and idiosyncratic moralist when he suggested that the remedy for cereal rust was for Romans to placate the gods: huge religious festivals were held to ward off the scourge, and ritual and magic nostrums proliferated.

To protect vines from grape moth, Cato recommended either wiping the pruning knife on a beaver skin or anointing the pruning cuts with bear's blood. Burning three live crabs upwind of the crop was thought to offer the best possible protection against bacterial blight of vines.

Yet not all Roman methods were so fantastic. Farmers and gardeners crushed laurel leaves and mixed them with their seed before sowing. The laurel released tiny amounts of hydrocyanic acid, which may have offered some protection against insects while the young plants established themselves. Laurel leaves are still used in the killing bottles of entomologists today.

Banding-grease, made by boiling down olive oil residues with bitumen and sulphur, was applied to the trunks of vines to trap leaf roller caterpillars. Smoke from burning galbanum resin (extracted from fennel) was used to repel gnats when people sat in their gardens. Some sinister narcotic baits were recorded – made by mixing seed with the liquor from boiled "Alum garlic" The scattered seeds were eaten by birds, which immediately collapsed unconscious. The gardener would then kill the ones he considered pests, leaving the others to recover and fly away.

There is plenty of evidence from the Continent to suggest that the only available remedy against pests and diseases was ecclesiastic law. In 1120, fieldmice and caterpillars were excommunicated by the Bishop of Leon. At Troyes in 1516, caterpillars were given six days to withdraw from the crops or face excommunication.

Equally bizarre advice was still being offered at the end of the 17th century. To banish the flies that destroyed cabbages, for example, gardeners were advised to mount a horse's head on a pole. The practice of trapping earwigs beneath upturned pots and damp rags, and then treading on them, is still in use today. And technology was beginning to take a hand. An improved understanding of hydraulics had produced hand-operated syringes and pumps. At that early date, too, some very precise chemical formulations were recommended: for example, wool impregnated with honey and arsenic as a control for wasps and ants.

By the 19th century, biologists in Europe and America produced precise descriptions of pest and disease organisms, and unravelled the mysteries of their life cycles to reveal the stages at which they would be most susceptible to control. Chemists, too, had learned much about the extraction and synthesis of effective pesticides. The 19th century also saw the first attempts at biological control. Seagulls with clipped wings, for example, were loosed in gardens to eat the caterpillars of cabbage white butterfly.

By the 1860s, flowers of sulphur was being applied as a powder to control powdery mildew diseases, and not long afterwards the more effective lime sulphur was being used at Versailles. Highly poisonous nicotine preparations, extracted from tobacco sweepings from cigarette and cigar factories, were sprayed to control aphids; and pyrethrum powder was being made from daisies grown in Dalmatia.

By 1882, the other great class of pathogenic fungi – the downy mildews – was being controlled on crops like potatoes and tomatoes with "Bordeaux mixture", a blend of copper sulphate and lime. And frightening stomach poisons like London Purple, an arsenical residue from the manufacture of magenta dye, were used to kill caterpillars and other leaf-eating pests. Murderous chemicals began to pour in from all over the world. The ground-up roots of the Jamaican quassia tree, mixed with soap, were used to control aphids on hops. Derris root – the nerve-poison still used by many gardeners – was imported from Malaysia. Biological methods advanced when citrus scale in America was controlled by a ladybird introduced from Australia.

In the first quarter of the current century, progress was relatively slow. Mercurial and iron salts were introduced as a control for weeds and moss in lawns. Phenolic and cresolic washes, by-products of the gas industry, were used to control insect eggs and over-wintering adults on dormant fruit trees.

It was the discovery of the effectiveness of DDT during the Second World War that heralded the modern chemical era in the garden. After DDT came a long list of synthetic pesticides, among which the highly selective organo-phosphorus materials are perhaps the most remarkable. Improved fungicides, able to eradicate established diseases as well as giving protection to healthy plants, have also been enthusiastically received. For lawns, probably the greatest boon was the discovery of hormone weedkillers which do no harm to grass.

Today, the most promising research projects have followed from genetic engineers discovering how to insert DNA from disease- or pest-resistant plants into garden varieties, carrying the resistance over. This, combined with the development of fungi and bacteria which will fatally attack insect pests, suggest that gardeners in future will rely mainly on biotechnology rather than on chemistry.

Light numerals on facing picture denote degree of magnification from life size.

TOP TEN PESTS OF VEGETABLES

Main bird pest is the pigeon, which eats young seedlings and sown seeds

1 *Peach potato aphid (sucks young shoots and leaves)*
2 *Cutworms turnip moth (larvae eat roots)*
3 *Wireworms click beetle (larvae burrow into potato tubers)*
4 *Carrot fly*
5 *Small white butterfly caterpillar (attacks many green veg.)*
6 *Large white butterfly (larvae eat leaves of cabbage and greens)*
7 *Cabbage aphid*
8 *Whitefly (attacks leafy veg.)*
9 *Cabbage moth*
10 *Cabbage root fly*

TOP TEN PESTS OF FRUIT

Main bird pest is the bullfinch, which eats the buds

1 *Raspberry beetle (the maggots eat the fruit)*
2 *Winter moth (eats apple leaves)*
3 *Rosy apple aphid (attacks young shoots and leaves)*
4 *Apple sawfly (eats the leaves)*
5 *Tortrix moth (attacks the leaves of apples and pears)*
6 *Pear sucker (attacks young shoots and buds)*
7 *Coddling moth (bores inside apples and pears)*
8 *Red spider mite (attacks underside of apple and soft fruit leaves)*
9 *Pear bedstraw aphid (attacks young shoots and buds)*
10 *Big bud mite (attacks the buds on blackcurrant)*

1×4
2
3×2½
4×4
5
6
7×4
8×4
9
10×1½
1×4 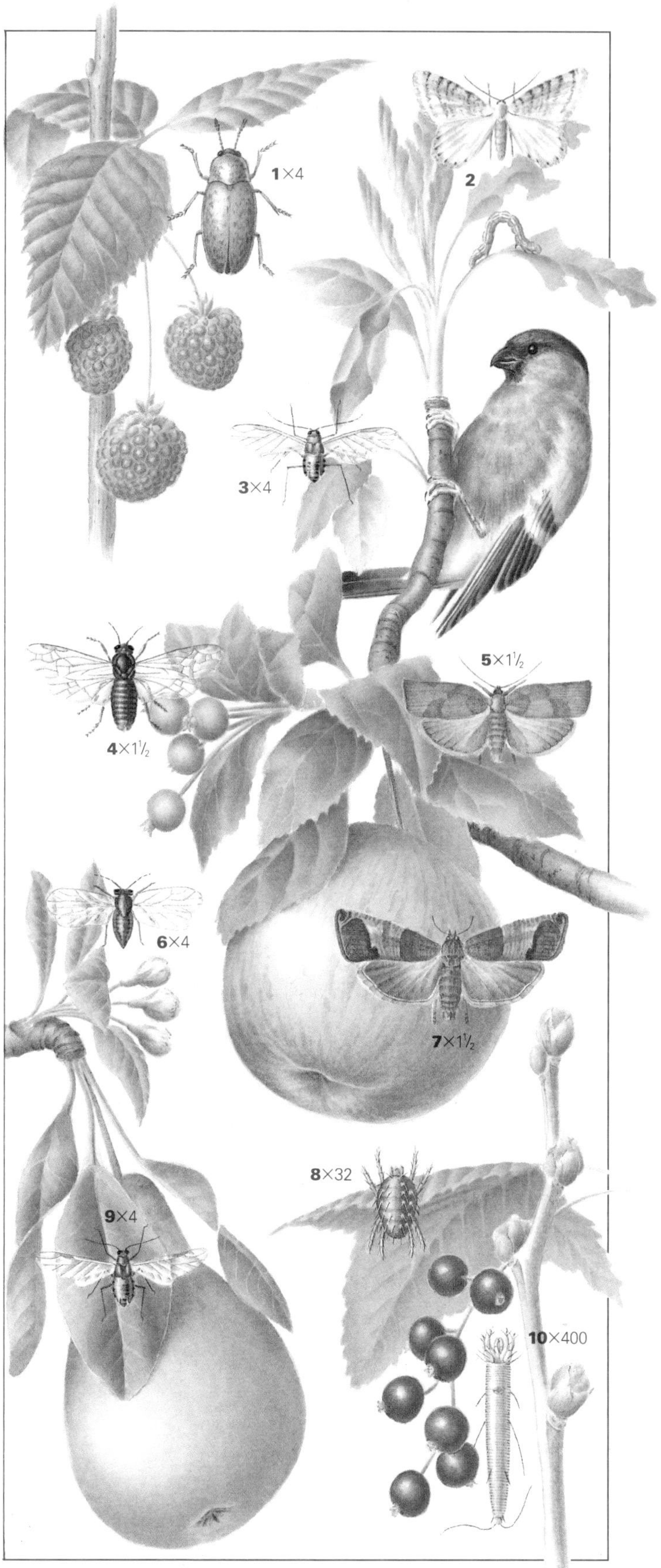
2
3×4
4×1½
5×1½
6×4
7×1½
8×32
9×4
10×400

Perhaps the most remarkable story of cottage industry in plant breeding is the transformation of the gooseberry from a humble and rather sharp wild berry to a sumptuous dessert fruit. There is no record in Britain of the introduction of any cultivated varieties of gooseberry, nor much in the way of cultivation itself before the 16th century. Yet by the end of the Victorian period more than 2000 named varieties were in circulation.

What happened during these three centuries was that gooseberry growing became a cult among cottagers in the industrial north and the Midlands. They were the perfect fruit for these small back-to-back gardens, growing easily from seed and needing very little space, and they became the focus of an elaborate and festive local tradition, in which competition and co-operation played equal roles. The berries, in an immense array of sizes, colours and flavours produced by rule-of-thumb crossing and seedling selection, were entered for annual shows, in which they were matched, weight for weight, against others of the same kind.

Gooseberry shows, a mixture of solemn weighings and high-spirited gardening gossip, are still held in August in a few Cheshire villages, and often it is old Victorian varieties like London, Leveller and Hero of the Nile that take the prizes. But new varieties are still being raised and, though competition is fierce, cuttings from successful new varieties are freely exchanged.

The fate of the dessert gooseberry since the Victorian period could stand as a symbol for what has happened to kitchen gardening in the 20th century. Home-grown fruit began to be challenged by mass-marketed produce; the number of varieties

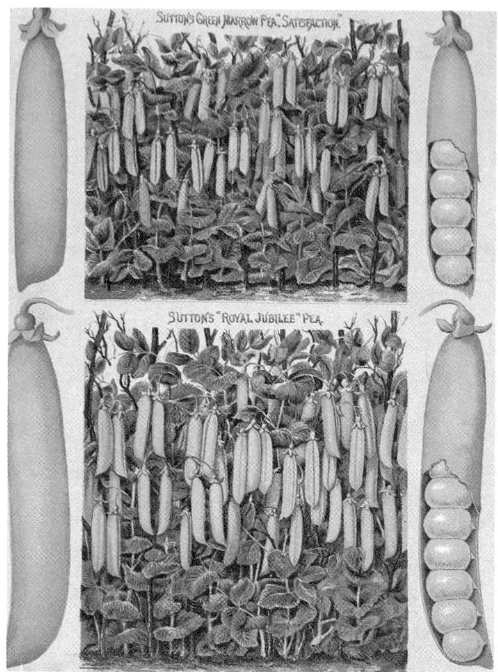

Picker's paradise: peas and lettuce from the Sutton's seed catalogue of 1887

grown declined, and the public understanding and expectation of diversity dwindled. With demand spiralling downwards the 2000 varieties has rapidly slumped to a couple of hundred, mostly grown in special collections, or in the few remaining Midlands gooseberry-show villages. Elsewhere the dessert gooseberry is extinct.

The same contraction has occurred with almost every kind of fruit or vegetable, and it would be over-simplifying the issue to look for a single cause. The overall decline in the size of gardens and in available labour was no doubt one factor, as were changes in taste and fashion. Damsons, medlars and sorb apples, for example, probably declined in popularity largely because of their small, sourish and easily-damaged fruit.

There is no doubt that the single overriding influence was the transformation of the structure of the food growing and marketing businesses. For the first time in its long history kitchen gardening began to mimic farming. All the changes that had characterised the rise of industrialised farming were reflected in the kitchen garden: the standardisation of crops, the ironing out of regional flavours, the regularisation of size and colour, regardless of taste; the reduction of choice; the massive use of chemicals.

An ironic and near-terminal acceleration was given to the decline by the EEC, when it prohibited the marketing of any vegetable variety that had not been properly registered. It was a well-meaning enactment, designed to guarantee quality. But because of the elaborate and expensive procedure of registration, its practical effect was finally to drive from the market all those varieties that were not amenable to mass cultivation and marketing. So, after centuries of good service, favourites like Ragged Jack Kale (dark-leaved and prolific in even the hardest winters) and Wood's Early Frame Radish (described by Vilmorin-Andrieux in 1885 as "very white, firm, juicy, very crisp, fresh and pleasant to the taste"), were banished from the trade and so from most kitchen gardens.

But the great tradition of cottage gardening in Britain had not entirely died out, and many of these now rare fruit and vegetable varieties were still being grown on, sometimes just in single villages or even single gardens. Early in the 1970s – largely through the efforts of Lawrence Hill, of the Henry Doubleday Research Association – it became clear that the extinction of these ancient varieties amounted to an irreversible genetic loss, which boded ill for us in the future. Hills mounted a nationwide appeal for gardeners to send him seed of the old varieties, and used them to start a "seed library" scheme, which neatly bypassed the EEC rules against commercial trade. Seeds are "lent out" by the association to gardeners, who grow them on, save the seed, and then at the end of the season return some of this to the library together with notes on how well the variety has performed.

The scheme has been exceptionally successful, and many old vegetables have been rescued from the brink. A number of "vegetable sanctuaries" have also been set up – notably the Seed Bank at the National Vegetable Research Station at Wellesbourne in Warwickshire (financed chiefly by Oxfam). This is a sophisticated cold store which will eventually house the seeds of 15,000 vegetable varieties. The purpose is to guarantee the survival of the widest possible genetic spread of vegetable characteristics, as an insurance policy against, say, changes in climate or the rise of new insect pests – or just a return of more diversified markets.

Some varieties have already proved so encouraging that they may well be brought back into commerce, or at least into the breeding lines. Pen-y-Byd ("Top o' the World") marrow, is a very ancient Welsh marrow with pale, round fruit that is able to grow in cold, wet conditions. Evesham Brussels sprouts were grown for centuries before the development of insecticides, and appear to have a degree of natural insect resistance which has been lost in the new hybrids.

The wild precursors of cultivated fruit and vegetables are also being brought back into the breeding line. Tomatoes are being crossed with their small wild South American ancestors to try and regain flavour and vitamin content, and globe artichokes with their Middle-Eastern ancestors, to promote choke formation at a more regular height.

It looks as if the tide may at last be turning in modern kitchen gardening. With the increasing popularity of flavoursome varieties and organic cultivation methods, the craft is beginning to rejoin its ancient traditions. Ingenuity and festivity are back in favour, as is the ancient conviction that styles of cultivation and the "vitality" of food are inseparable. Even the layout of kitchen gardens is reverting, and a typical north-country cottage plot, with strawberries growing in the paths, clematis climbing up the clothes-line, and carrots and dahlias planted in companionable rows, is as marvellously assorted as a medieval garth.

Not that innovation is frowned on any more now than then, just so long as it brings gardeners closer to each other and to their plants – provided that it does not drive an inanimate wedge between the two. Tomato grow-bags and "poly-tunnels" would have been approved by Tudor gardeners as canny developments of their wheeled fruit-tubs and "tabernacle" seedling-frames (often made out of old sailcloth or paintings). So would many of the new crops that have been introduced, prompted partly as a result of the increasing interest in Oriental cuisine. Various Chinese and Japanese cabbages, used for stir-frying, are proving very viable in British gardens. And in the Midlands, a number of community gardens have been started for the cultivation of exotic vegetables and herbs, such as coriander, okra and fenugreek.

Summer seduction: strawberry "Royal Sovereign" and raspberry "Superlative", from Commercial Gardening, 1913

But it is the return of the sheer fun and imaginative gusto of earlier kitchen gardening that is the most heartening trend. Seed catalogues are increasingly figuring plants and devices that could have come straight out of Thomas Hill in his most impishly inventive mood: vegetable bath sponges (the original *Luffa* gourd), pre-spawned oyster fungus logs, salad seed mixtures, ornamental lettuces, "burpless" cucumbers, self-blanching celery (and self-wrapping cauliflowers), vegetable spaghetti, frost-resistant tomatoes, comfrey to be grown as "green manure" and "Vegiforms", plastic moulds that can shape marrows and cucumbers into hearts, faces, and no doubt "strange figures", too.

By the end of the century, when statistics suggest that at least 10 per cent of Britons will be wholly vegetarian, kitchen gardening may have entered one of its periodic Golden Ages. In the final chapter of his book *Future Cook*, Colin Tudge imagined a possible 21st-century vegetable-based banquet. One of the centrepieces was a revived Tudor vegetable, but it could equally well have been a monster version of those "fresh fragrant leeks":

> *Interest focuses mainly upon ... a massive but delicately aromatic salsify, carved reverentially, like a goose. Outstanding among the fruits are the three shades of apricot, grown hydroponically on miniature but artfully formed rootstock like old-fashioned bonsai, and served on the tree. The little pyramids of climbing strawberries are good too, especially the golden ones, but they have become commonplace.*

HEAVYWEIGHT CHAMPIONS

When the human urge to cultivate is combined with the urge to compete, the record-breaking results can often be spectacularly improbable

By Peter Seabrook

Winning acclaim for growing exceptional plants is the gardening equivalent of climbing Mount Everest. Ask growers why they grow 8lb onions and 444lb pumpkins and the immediate response is, because the challenge is there and, like Roger Bannister's four-minute mile, the impossible becomes possible and is then beaten yet again.

Growing plants is for the most part a solitary fight with nature. Protection from all excesses of heat and cold, rain and drought have to be provided for plants round the clock for their whole life cycle. A constant battle, too, is waged to prevent any damage from wind, hail, frost, pest and disease.

Gardeners get immense satisfaction from seeing plants grow to fruition but they need a scale of standard measurements against which to compare their skills. The first exhibit of the Horticultural Society, now the Royal Horticultural Society (formed at the offices of Mr Hatchard, bookseller of Piccadilly, on March 7, 1804), was a potato grown by a Mr Minier. "Its tubers form so late in the season and have so thin a skin that they may be used through the winter like young potatoes."

Much of the society's early work covered fruit and vegetables, and there was great competition between members to produce the biggest and most succulent fruit for their annual anniversary dinner. The Marquis of Hertford's gardener, Thomas Baldwin, sent four pineapples in 1822, the largest weighing 8lb 14oz.

The London-based Horticultural Society idea spread. A Belgian, for example, who attended these meetings, arranged similar events in Ghent which later developed into the internationally renowned Floralies, held once every five years.

While at the end of the 18th century there were agricultural societies for the improvement of agriculture in most counties, the local horticultural societies came later. There were, however, annual parades, pageants and festivals dating back to the 14th century, where the various guilds "took stock of their portable possessions". By all accounts these occasions could often become rowdy scenes of drunkenness, debauchery and the selling of young girls into service.

The 19th century saw a move towards more genteel public gatherings: in July 1836 a Carnation and Gooseberry Show was held by the Salop Horticultural Society, and a similar show was held at the Compasses Inn, Frankwell, Shrewsbury, organised by the Shropshire Union Florists' Society – forerunners of the Shrewsbury Flower Show which has just celebrated its centenary.

UK record tomato, 5lb 9½oz: Reg Burrows, 1987

UK record pot leek, 12lb 2oz: Paul Harrigan, 1987

The competition to grow the largest gooseberry still continues in Derbyshire, where individual berries are accurately weighed one against the other on jeweller's scales. At one time more than 2000 different cultivars were grown for their size, colour, season of ripening and flavour. More than 200 are still for sale today.

Inns, pubs and brewers have close connections with show and giant-sized fruits and vegetables. Working men's clubs in the North-east are the centre of competitions for short, thick "Pot Leeks". The first recorded leek show was at the house of Thomas Anderson who ran a pub at Swalwell on November 21, 1846. Bill Made had the best three leeks at 7lb 8oz and won a prize copper kettle. Up to £1200 can now be won at a single show for prize leeks. In the warmer south it is giant pumpkins.

Village shows became the annual event for the locality in the late 19th and early to mid-20th centuries. Everything was shown, from the prettiest baby to the best chicken and plate of boiled potatoes, but flowers, fruits and vegetables were the foundation. Most shows had their hero who regularly triumphed and swept the prize board.

UK record pumpkin, 444lb: Ron Butcher, 1984

UK record onion, 8lb 13½oz: Ivor Mace, 1987

World's longest carrot, 135½in: Ken Ayliffe, 1987

Class provides no barriers when it comes to growing the biggest and best fruits and vegetables. Which is not to say that there isn't some nobbling; whole leek crops have been slashed and vandalised where substantial prizes were on offer in the North-east. At shows like Shrewsbury the tables of fruit, with delicious bunches of grapes, plates of melons, nectarines, peaches, pears and plums, were netted around to keep off marauding fingers. Head gardeners have been known to pluck a grape to prevent a good bunch being shown a second time.

Most of the competition was within a locality; it took the editor John Bloom and his colleague Ray Wells on the then flat-capped gardener's new tabloid *Garden News* to set the national pace. In 1959 and 1960 they started the *Garden News* Giant Fruit and Vegetable Competition to boost circulation. At once weights and sizes leap-frogged. Now *Garden News* is the largest circulation weekly gardening paper.

Listing the record breakers in the *Guinness Book of Records* brought universal acceptance of these backyard Olympians. It took Unwins, the Cambridge seed firm, to bring in stocks of Atlantic Giant Pumpkin and set UK growers against their North American contemporaries. Now the race for giants is international.

When John Bloom sought gardening broadcaster Fred Loads's advice on the likely top weight for a single onion they set the figure at 3lb. In no time a grower from Kent appeared with a 5lb specimen. Tom Fenton capped that with a 6lb 3oz onion, and then for several years the Scots reigned supreme with bulbs over 7lb. Last autumn Ivor Mace from Wales weighed in with an 8lb 13½oz bulb of the Kelsae strain that won prizes worth nearly £5000.

Contrary to common belief, the normally strongly flavoured onions and leeks grown quickly and with great skill are very succulent and delicious to eat.

III

BRANCHES THROUGHOUT THE WORLD

By Hugh Johnson

The character of the British landscape depends on trees and hedges – a character which has always been reflected in the English way of gardening. It is no accident that our favourite garden flower, the rose, owes its wild origins to the hedgerow; nor that the most reckless passion of plant-hunters – often pursued at risk to their lives – has been to plunder the most inaccessible and hostile valleys of the Himalayas, and the lost interior of China, to send home new species to adorn the British shrubbery.

Ultimate formality: part of the great parterre at Drummond Castle, Perthshire, whose overall plan is in the form of a St Andrew's cross

All the world's a shrubbery: even an ordinary British garden, with a hedge, a couple of dwarf conifers and a rose-bed, is like a chapter from a botanical encyclopaedia of the world. Our map shows the native origins of the wild species from which most of our popular tree and shrub species derive

The plant-explorer George Forrest: he ransacked the jungle north of Burma and collected 300 new rhododendron species

If there had been a Pliocene gardener (two million years ago) his patch in Britain would or could have contained as rich a collection of woody plants as modern Kew: wild magnolias, sequoias, ginkgos, rhododendrons, camellias would all have made a nuisance of themselves.

What we think of today as our native trees and shrubs were here too, but in a glorious medley with species that are now exotic. Not that the climate was necessarily very different from today's. What put an end to this ubiquitous Garden of Eden was the cooling of the earth's climate that led to the Ice Ages: four of them, over a period of nearly two million years. Gunz, Mindel, Riss and Würm, to give them their stage-villain German names, froze off the glorious variety that had evolved over millions of years from the first primitive forests of ferns. The poles froze and the subsequent survival or extinction of any of the countless species of plants depended on two questions. Could it withstand long winters of freezing weather? And did it have an escape route: new country to colonise as the temperate zone moved south and closer to the tropics?

Physical geography was against the retreat of plants from Northern Europe. The Mediterranean, the Alps and the Pyrenees formed a barrier of sea and ice drawn directly across their retreat to more temperate lands. Over thousands of centuries the great majority of "our" trees and shrubs died out, leaving a scanty rearguard of their toughest members to recolonise northwards as the glaciers of Würm thawed, only 10,000 years before our era.

These are the oaks and ashes, birches and alders, beeches and willows, elders and dogwoods, hawthorn and hazel, yew, whitebeam, wayfaring tree, rowan, field-maple, dog-rose . . . (the complete list comes to only 60-odd woody plants) which botanists today classify as "native" to Britain. Other continents were more fortunate. The landmasses of North America and China beyond the Himalayas have no uncrossable east–west barriers to hinder plant migration to healthier climes.

These migrations actively promoted the diversification of species. They stimulated genetic mixtures, favoured mutations that would have been suppressed under more stable conditions. The net effect of the Ice Ages was a great acceleration of evolution, leading to far more species than before. All this activity accounts for the same trees and shrubs, lost to Europe, turning up in many different specific forms in North America and Eastern Asia. America's great glossy evergreen magnolia and China's beautiful "Yulan" (parent of some of our favourite magnolias) are surviving cousins in a family whose European relations were frozen to death a million years ago.

Opposite: the laburnum walk at Barnsley House, Gloucestershire

So the natives of the English greenwood are essentially survivors; winterproof and in gardeners' language "hardy". The vast majority of them take refuge from the

Acer palmatum atropurpureum is an elegant feature on acid soils

winter by letting their leaves go in autumn: we have only two or three native evergreen trees.

The ultimate gauge of hardiness is the lowest temperature a plant will stand without ice destroying its fabric by rupturing its cells. One really sharp frost and a coconut palm, for instance, is done for. All the trees of the temperate forest pass that test. The much trickier test that gives gardeners sleepless nights is the question of timing. Britain's seasons are absurdly unspecific. We have just had a winter almost without frost, following a summer almost without sun.

Think of the dilemma of (let's say) a Siberian larch. Leafless, its buds dormant, no temperature is too cold for it. In Siberia it stands bare until the onrush of spring in June. Already in February 1988 the thermometer told it that spring was here. It exposed its tender new leaves, only to find that March nights can be extremely nippy. If it loses its new leaves, not once but regularly, year after year, that tree is not "hardy" here.

These then are the conditions that govern what trees and shrubs can grow in this country, and the historical reason for our depleted indigenous flora. Together they form a paradox: we have few trees and shrubs of our own, but the chance to grow a vast range from the whole temperate world.

The relative softness of our climate tempts us out of doors all the year round. From the plants' point of view, our island climate is even more special: it combines the temperate effects of the Gulf Stream with a situation so far north that our midsummer days last almost 20 hours. With rain evenly spaced through the growing season, a better environment for temperate plants could scarcely be imagined.

Whether the Romans, settling in their northernmost colony, saw the great forest of Albion in such a rosy light we may well doubt. Oak covered almost all the deep lowland soils which held most promise for agriculture. It is unlikely that the Romans made very much impression on the immense, largely monotonous, forest. But certainly they brought some of their own trees for use and beauty. Many botanists suggest that the sycamore, the walnut, possibly the sweet chestnut, even perhaps the "English" elm were introduced (or re-introduced) to these islands during the three and a half centuries of Roman rule. We know that such popular garden shrubs as bay, box, rosemary, various roses, grape vines and all sorts of fruit trees (including the black mulberry) came over to decorate villa gardens. The palace of Cogidubnus at Fishbourne, Sussex, shows us the scale and formality of Roman gardening in Britain, and at least some of its plants.

Throughout the Dark and Middle Ages the dominant tree of the English greenwood continued to be the oak. *Domesday Book* reckoned woodland not by the number or size of the trees, but by the number of swine that could fatten on their acorns. Oak seemed an inexhaustible resource. Indeed, it was so managed that this was perfectly true. The felling of full-grown trees was the exception. They were not needed for normal building and they were far harder to saw up and use than smaller trunks, which were produced by the simple expedient of coppicing to give a new crop of ideal building materials every 20 years or so. When really big pieces of timber were needed (as for the roof of the new Westminster Hall in 1397) a special search was made for ideal specimens, preferably growing not far from a river so that they could be floated to the building site.

Tinged leaf-margins and spectacular berries make Sorbus commixta a popular choice for gardeners

Meanwhile in gardens the only trees that it would have occurred to anyone to grow were fruit trees: apples, pears, cherries, plums, medlars and quinces, just as the contents of the beds and borders were nearly all either edible or medicinal or both. Vineyards, whose produce combined both virtues with a third, the raising of the spirits, were common. Abbeys and monasteries had the best-organised gardens and presumably the most skilful gardeners.

This was the state of affairs until Henry VIII's reign, when the Northumberland-born apothecary William Turner turned his curious eye on the plants around him and became the progenitor of the endless stream of gardening writers that forms one of the minor glories of English literature. Turner studied at Cambridge and in Italy, where the University of Padua had just created Europe's first botanical garden. It is a fact to provoke all sorts of speculation that Turner's own garden was at Kew.

The early English herbals are perched somewhere between classical pedantry and a lovely freshness of vision that is purely Elizabethan. The apothecaries knew their classics better than they knew their plants. The ancient physician Dioscorides, or Galen, or Theophrastus, had prescribed a certain plant for fever or the ague. Turner's and his successors' concern was to identify which plant was meant. Many, of course, did not grow here: it entailed a voyage to the eastern Mediterranean to go further into the matter. And just then the eastern Mediterranean had fallen into the hands of the garden-loving Turks.

The middle of the 16th century marks the turning-point when the introduction of new plants started to cause excitement among gardeners. They came from the east, often via Constantinople. The horse-chestnut reached Europe at about this time. And they came from Spain's new empire in the Americas. The plants that were announced in *Joyfulle Newes out of the Newe Founde Worlde,* translated from the Spanish in 1577, were the crops of Mexico and Central America: potatoes, tomatoes, sunflowers, marrows and tobacco. As soon as the colonisation of North America began, a generation later, there were trees and shrubs to add to the list.

Overleaf: pleached lime trees surrounding a rectangular lily-pond add a note of Mughal mystery to the Victorian garden at Knebworth House in Hertfordshire

Meanwhile the Tudors had begun to find that even the apparently inexhaustible supply of timber from our woods was being depleted at a worrying rate. The

The Tradescant family is credited with having been the first to travel abroad from England to collect plants in the 17th century. John the Elder (above) brought oranges, cypresses, oleanders, myrtles, figs and brooms. John the Younger (opposite) brought the tulip tree, swamp cypress, Virginia creeper, thuja and Robinia "acacia"

charcoal-burners were using up the Wealden forest for the iron-foundries of Sussex. The once-mighty Caledonian forest (the only place where the "Scots firr", as it was called, grew wild in Britain) was described as "utterly destroyed". The notion of planting trees, rather than just letting them grow, entered our national consciousness. And the voyages and adventures of Tudor seamen brought another extravagant but vital use for oak: the building of our first navy.

Lord Burghley, Queen Elizabeth's chancellor, promoted the planting of acorns with future warships in mind. His system was to intersperse the acorns with holly-berries, to raise a "nurse-crop" of holly to protect the young oaks. The ideal tree was the common or pedunculate oak, not grown in close woodland but widely spaced to encourage its branches to spread wide and produce their characteristic sharp angles: brackets of immense strength to hold a man-of-war rigid in heavy seas and under fire. Thus military necessity had its effect on the way our commonest tree was grown – and ultimately on the appearance of England's parks and landscape.

John Evelyn, whose *Sylva* of 1662 was the first paper to be presented to the newly-formed Royal Society, set out the principles. His French contemporary Jean-Baptiste Colbert, minister of finance and the navy, was meanwhile planting the forests of north-central France with straight-growing or sessile oaks – trees that can still be seen, titanic pillars of perfect rectitude, in the Tronçais forest. Whether the final result at Trafalgar had anything to do with their sylviculture one can only conjecture. Evelyn's *Sylva* is a great stock-taking of the trees reckoned significant in England in the middle of the 16th century. The list of newcomers since 1600 is remarkable: acacia, cypress, cedar of Lebanon, celtis, cork oak, silver fir, spruce, larch, Weymouth pine, umbrella pine, gleditschia, alaternus, phillyrea, myrtle, pomegranate, swamp cypress, thuja, manna ash, plane and tulip tree.

Credit is usually given to the distinguished family of Tradescant for being the first to travel abroad from England on purpose to collect plants in the 17th century. John Tradescant the elder visited nurseries in Holland, Brussels and Paris where he bought orange trees, cypresses, oleanders, myrtles, figs, brooms and many other plants. He seized the chance of a visit to Spain and North Africa on a ship sent to pursue pirates. Apricots and lilacs were among his baggage when he came home. John Tradescant junior appears to have been the first gardener/botanist to visit the new "plantations" in Virginia. He is thought to have brought home at least the tulip tree, swamp cypress, Virginia creeper, thuja, and Robinia "acacia".

The botanising of North America in the second half of the 17th century was organised by Henry Compton, Bishop of London, whose diocese included North America. He appointed missionaries with sound botanical training who coupled

preaching with plant-collecting. His garden at Fulham Palace filled up with trees and shrubs never seen before, inspiring the collector's instinct in a new generation who put plant-hunting on a more business-like footing. With the start of the 18th century the professional plant-hunter makes his appearance.

The turn of the 17th century is a key date in the exploration of the world of plants. Louis XIV sent a well-equipped expedition under Joseph de Tournefort to scour the Near and Middle East, from Greece to Persia, for the plants that formed the basis of the famous Persian, Arab and Turkish gardens. More momentously, Europe got its first toe-hold in the forbidden land of China, the "mother of gardens", and the even more mysterious islands of Japan. For centuries the Chinese and the Japanese had been nurturing the most ornamental plants in their fabulous flora. In cultivated China a wild plant was nowhere to be seen. When John Cunningham, a surgeon in the East India Company, landed at Chusan near Shanghai, he discovered nurseries where peonies, camellias and chrysanthemums were cultivated in infinite variety.

An even more overwhelming sight greeted Engelbert Kaempfer, a surgeon in the Dutch East India Company, when he went ashore in Japan. The nurseries overflowed with plants unknown in Europe, from the prehistoric conifer, the ginkgo, to hydrangeas, azaleas, tree-peonies, magnolias and the first ornamental flowering cherries ever seen by western eyes. His money ran out as he deliberated which of these wonders to send home to Holland, and it was 80 years before another European, the Swede Carl Thunberg, had a similar opportunity.

It was one thing to buy plants in the Far East, but quite another to get them home alive. Months at sea, through the tropics, through Atlantic storms, short of fresh water, either starved of light or blasted by sea-winds, a large proportion perished. Many more died as European gardeners took wild guesses at how to cultivate them, often killing them with kindness on the supposition that such exotic rarities must be tender. It was not until the present century that camellias were found to be perfectly hardy out of doors in Britain.

At this pivotal period gardening in the old-fashioned sense (we might call it production gardening) had been developed to the highest possible pitch. The great textbook of the time, by Jean de la Quintinie, who ran the *potager* at Versailles, listed hundreds of varieties of apples, pears and the rest, illustrated scores of ways of making formal patterns with them, and carried the arts of grafting and pruning as far as they could go.

La Quintinie was widely consulted in England. The grandest gardens, led by Hampton Court, were remodelled in the French style, following (if not actually designed by) Le Nôtre. The Dutch style, equally formal, also invaded England in the reign of William and Mary, and can still be seen in front of Kensington Palace. But

HEARTS OF OAK

Many men suffered in the making of the English garden – and none more so than the plant-hunters who risked injury, disease and even death in their resolute search for new species

By Charles Lyte

In the early 19th century a technological breakthrough which was to revolutionise plant-hunting was discovered by accident by a keen naturalist, Nathaniel Bagshaw Ward. He had collected the pupa of a moth in a lump of soil and put it in a stoppered glass bottle. A little while later he noticed that some grass and a fern were growing in the soil. Thus was the Wardian case conceived – a sealed, portable glasshouse that gave plants complete protection and a stable environment on board ship.

The plants were set in damp soil or compost and the case was sealed. Natural transpiration through the foliage of the plant prevented them from drying out. The collector had to be careful not to over-water, otherwise the plants would rot. The environment within the case remained stable and clean and the plants were unaffected by changes in temperature during a voyage. They were still in use in the 1960s.

Joseph Hooker's expedition to Sikkim and the Himalayas in 1848 yielded many rhododendrons, including 'R. falconeri'

Before the Wardian case, live plants shipped home were kept in the fetid conditions below decks. When they were brought into the air inevitably they were damaged.

One of the first to enjoy the benefit of the cases was Robert Fortune, who was sent to China in 1843 by the Royal Horticultural Society with a formidable collecting list. In between coping with robbers, pirates, gangs and bandits and the hostility of the Chinese towards foreigners, Fortune fulfilled his commission with great brilliance. To this day, plants such as *Weigela rosea, Jasminum nudiflorum, Dicentra spectablis, Platycodon grandiflorum, Lonicera fragrantissima, Rhododendron fortunei* and *Mahonia bealei* remain firm favourites.

In 1903 Arthur Kilpin Bulley, the founder of Bees nursery, invited George Forrest, to leave the herbarium at the Royal Botanic garden in Edinburgh and go to China. Forrest introduced a positive deluge of rhododendrons, acers, berberis, conifers, daphnes, camellias, buddleias, lilies, irises, primulas and alpines.

His career came close to a violent end in 1905. The Tibetan lamas had risen against the Chinese, who were also threatening foreign missions – including the one at Tzekou where Forrest had established his base. The two priests in charge fled with their converts to a village garrisoned by Chinese troops, and Forrest went with them.

They left at night, but the following day were intercepted and cut off. Father Bourdonnec was felled by poisoned arrows and hacked to pieces, while Father Dubernard was dragged back to the mission and tortured to death. Forrest was among a handful of the party who escaped. For nine days he was hunted by trackers, walking barefoot so that his distinctive boot-prints would not stand out. Caked with mud, torn, bruised and cut, starving and in rags, he decided to hold up a village – he had a heavy revolver and a Winchester rifle – and demand food and shelter. In fact the villagers were friendly, took him in, and guided him to safety.

Four years earlier the nurserymen, Veitch and Son, had sent Ernest Henry Wilson to Yunnan. The gathering of *Lilium regale* very nearly cost Wilson his life, and left him slightly crippled – "my lily limp", he called it – when a rock slide hit his sedan chair in a remote valley in Tibet.

Professional plant-hunting is not at an end, but the method and style has changed out of all recognition. No longer does the botanical explorer have to trek for months on end on foot with his equipment being carried by native porters, yaks or mules.

The Wardian case transformed the collecting of living plants, but most of the new introductions actually arrived as seed. These were very carefully dried and cleaned in the wild, then packaged and stored in wooden or metal boxes. In 1921, Frank Kingdon-Ward experimented with a technique of packing seeds in a bath of CO_2 (carbon dioxide). The seeds

were put in a close-fitting tin, a Sparklet was used to introduce the gas, and the container was soldered shut. The seeds germinated well, but then so did the rest of the consignment packed conventionally so the experiment was inconclusive.

Bulbs, tubers and orchids with their pseudo-bulbs, were often packed in locally-woven cane baskets in the soil or compost in which they were found growing. Collectors would establish small gardens at their base camps to grow on plants for transportation.

The treatment of herbarium material has changed little. The plants are still dried in presses, with frequent changes of paper. The greatest hazard in the past was insects with a voracious appetite for paper and dried plants.

These days living plants can be whisked from the wild to their new homes in little more than hours. The modern explorer, supported by universities, botanic gardens, or a relatively small number of private sponsors, travels by scheduled airlines, public transport, and is wafted to his mountain destination in a helicopter. But his chances of finding anything new are much slimmer, and he is often more concerned with reintroduction than with discovery. The danger from hostile tribes and bandits is less, but because of war and political restrictions accessibility is greatly reduced. Conservation and plant health regulations mean that the huge collections of the past are no longer possible.

However, the job of the plant collector is just as important now, if only to rescue plants from extinction as industrialisation feeds ever more hungrily on the world's diminishing wilderness.

The Wardian case (left background) transformed the 19th-century plant-explorer's life, providing a hermetic environment in which plans survived the voyage home. Other material was brought back in baskets and flower presses (right foreground)

where in this scheme of things, where trees belonged in avenues and arbours, or were trimmed as topiary, was there room for the unpredictable shapes, sizes and behaviour of newly imported trees and shrubs?

The answer was in a new sort of garden, involving a whole landscape. A new breed of plant collectors made it their business. A small group of friends in and around London, led by a Quaker, Peter Collinson, who gardened on Mill Hill, employed America's first home-grown botanist, John Bartram (1699–1777), to collect for them all over the scarcely-known, Indian-haunted east of North America.

With courage matched only by his industry and botanical acumen, Bartram totted up more than 200 new species of plants and delivered to his patrons (among trees alone) the pines, birches, maples and oaks, the ash, elm and lime of the New World. Perhaps his most spectacular contribution to English gardens was the evergreen *Magnolia grandiflora* whose huge waxy flowers drop perfume from the south wall of almost every manor and old rectory in the country. He also sent us our first rhododendron, *R. maximum*.

It was not Bartram's fault that few of the trees of eastern America really like our climate. Their natural habitat has powerful extremes of summer and winter very different from our mingled seasons. Moreover, most of the soils of the east coast are acid, which limits the places where we can experiment with them.

Britain's far-ranging plant-explorers brought back trees, shrubs and flowering plants of all kinds. The examples on these pages are (left to right): Primula sikkimesis, collected by Sir Joseph Hooker; Iris milesii, by George Forrest; Kolkwitzia amabilis, by E. H. "Chinese" Wilson; Gladiolus byzantinus, by John Tradescant the Elder; and Liriodendron tulipifera, by Tradescant the Younger

Among the subscribers to Bartram's 30 years of collecting were several of the English nobility, including Frederick, Prince of Wales, the father of King George III, who with his wife Augusta dabbled in gardening at Kew House on the Thames just west of London. This royal patronage gave botany just the boost it needed. The Prince died in 1751; Princess Augusta swept on, encouraged by her friend Lord Bute, to appoint the first curator of the Royal Botanic Garden (another Scot, William Aiton) and to commission Sir William Chambers to adorn the grounds.

The great symbol of Kew Gardens is Chambers's 10-storey pagoda. American plants had taken second place in public interest to the increasing number from China, sent (in the main) by the ingenious French Jesuit missionary Father Pierre d'Incarville. D'Incarville's method was to offer the Chinese craftsmen skills that they lacked (engineering, clock-making and glass-blowing). He and his missionary colleagues, Benoit and Castiglione, designed a "Little Versailles" for the emperor. In exchange he was made welcome in the Forbidden City, where he lived for 15 years from 1742, sending home not only plants – the tree of heaven, the koelreuteria, the sophora, the Chinese thuja and juniper – but accounts and illustrations of Chinese life that created a European rage for chinoiserie.

The period that followed has rightly been christened the Botany Boom. Not a ship left for "the Indies" without commissions to buy and bring home as many Chinese and other plants as possible. In Perthshire the dukes of Atholl are said to have planted 17 million larches on the bare hills around Dunkeld. Lord Weymouth planted so many of the white pines of New England (recommended by Evelyn for ships' masts) at Longleat that they are still called the Weymouth pine.

Then "Capability" Brown set out on his career. Brown was the most effective anti-gardener in history. He was a genius with water, with (gentle) hills and valleys, with clumps of trees in telling situations. But as far as he was concerned there was no room for any except the most exceptional exotic in English parkland – the cedar of Lebanon. Many have mourned the ancient gardens (and many new French-style ones as well) that Brown destroyed. He could not abide straight lines and felled ancient avenues of elm or lime by the score. At the same time he caused to be planted more of our native trees than any other individual in history. In one midland park alone he was responsible for planting 100,000 trees, most of them oaks.

Brown's ideas were irreconcilable with the boom in botanical curiosity. The young Sir Joseph Banks set sail with Captain Cook to Australia with six naturalists and botanical artists on his personal staff. The *Endeavour* called at Tierra del Fuego, Tahiti and New Zealand on the way to what became Botany Bay, and at the Cape on the way back. Safe home, with illustrations of thousands of new plants (but pitifully few specimens) Banks rapidly despatched collectors to follow up his travels: most notably Francis Masson to South Africa, from where he sent home quantities of our best garden and greenhouse plants – among them the pelargonium. To Australia Banks sent David Nelson, whose collections included mimosa, the first eucalyptus, and New Zealand flax. Nelson's next voyage was his last: he was given responsibility for the bread-fruit trees on the ill-fated voyage of the *Bounty*. To the mutineers he was the cause of their troubles. He was cast adrift with Bligh and died of exposure.

The Oregon Douglas fir Pseudotsuga taxifolia – one of the many species sent back from the American West by David Douglas

Banks's man in China was William Kerr from Kew. Chinese collecting continued to be more of a shopping expedition than a true exploration. Kerr's list included lilies, begonias, *Pieris japonica* and the Banksian rose. More important, in the long run, were the freelance efforts of East India captains who shipped home towards the turn of the 18th century the roses now known as "the four stud chinas": the first perpetual-flowering roses and the ancestors of almost all our modern roses.

Modern gardening starts here. There must have been thousands of gardeners too modest to "landscape" their grounds who breathed a sigh of relief. There was no need to confine flowers to the kitchen garden. The flower garden was respectable again, and new plants in the nurseries at every season demanded that it be joined by a "shrubbery", by flowering trees, and by more specialised garden areas based on the character, needs and scale of the plants.

The (now Royal) Horticultural Society was founded in 1804 by, among others, Sir Joseph Banks. Its early meetings looked both backwards to the ancient skills of horticulture and forwards to the harvest of new plants that was coming in with every ship. The society sent its own man to China. In 1824 it made its most momentous move: it sent David Douglas to explore the American West.

No expedition has ever changed the gardens and the landscape of Britain as much as those of Douglas and his successors Nuttall, Hartweg, Jeffrey and Lobb. For Western America was the greatest retreat of the conifers from the Ice Ages. The Douglas fir and Sitka spruce, the prickly monster that will grow to over 100ft on the very beaches of British Columbia, and now causes tantrums among Highland conservationists, have revolutionised British forestry. The lodgepole pine, almost equally successful, is rather less aggressively exotic. Transported from California, where only a pathetic huddle was left, the Monterey pine now grows by the billion at an almost threatening speed in Australia and New Zealand.

Of more concern for gardeners were the cypresses of the west. The Lawson cypress has a genetic instability that leads it to produce all sorts of different forms and colours from a single sowing of its seed. Nursery catalogues list scores of named forms. The Monterey cypress was in its day the fastest-growing windbreak we could buy. But this year we celebrate the centenary of its marriage, in Wales, with a distant cousin, the Alaskan Nootka cypress. Their offspring is the Leyland cypress, certainly the most significant and popular conifer ever introduced to our gardens, and the tree which will, judging by its progress not only in gardens but on farmland (often planted as gamecover), totally transform our lowland landscape within the next half-century. There is no reason to suppose it will stop at 100ft. Where the occasional centenarian Wellingtonia now stands rocket-like above some vicarage garden, Leylands will tower in their millions in country and town alike. The soft domes of our native trees will give place to a skyline of jagged black.

All our botanists' hunting grounds up to this time had been reachable (if with difficulty) by sea. The toughest proposition still waited: the Himalayas. Expeditions had nibbled at their foothills since 1800. Wallich, the Danish director of the Calcutta Botanic Garden, had landed, in the form of the blood-red *Rhododendron arboreum*, enough evidence to excite the director of Kew. His son, the redoubtable Joseph Hooker, set off for Sikkim in 1847 and came back three years later with 43 new rhododendron species of great beauty.

The snag was that our climate lured them into flower too early: they came from icy regions but were not "hardy". The nursery trade, already a booming industry, went into long and secret session to cross these wonderful flowers with the more pedestrian, later-flowering kinds. A whole new style of gardening came into being,

Overleaf: a seamless join with nature. The woodland garden at Hascombe Court, near Godalming, was heavily influenced by the designs of Gertrude Jekyll

The Game of the Rose

More and more rose varieties, with more and more improbable names, are added to the catalogues every year. But, for all their differences in shape, size, colour and scent, they all share a common ancestry. The blooms on these pages are typical of the major groups in the family tree of the rose

By Hazel Le Rougetel

Our garden roses sprang originally from wild ones found across Europe, Asia and North America (none grew naturally in the southern hemisphere). Some were used to adorn medieval fences and arbours, and the sweet briar was particularly cherished for its fragrant foliage.

When Robert Herrick wrote in the 17th century, "Gather ye rosebuds while ye may," he was referring to the six-week season around midsummer when the old roses would fill the gardens with fragrant flowers ranging from white through every shade of pink from blush to magenta. These were Gallicas, Albas, Damasks, Centifolias (or cabbage roses) and a few of the earliest Mosses. One Gallica, the "Apothecary's Rose", was grown commercially in Europe for medicinal and culinary uses, while Damasks had for long been used to make perfume in the Middle East and India.

The West owes a particular debt to the Chinese. Trading ships called at Canton, providing an opportunity for their officers and passengers to visit the nearby *Fa Tee* (Flowery Land) nurseries, where they must have been amazed to find roses still flowering in the autumn. Because the plants were pot-grown, many survived the long sea voyage home.

Between 1793 and 1824 four important China garden hybrids arrived in England. Crossed with the summer-flowerers of the West, they produced a wealth of new roses in the 19th century, with blooms that would linger into autumn. The "Portland Rose" and a Bourbon, "Mme Isaac Pereire", are examples of those bred from the China roses called, after their growers here, "Slater's Crimson" and "Parsons's Pink". The latter, synonymous with "Old Blush China" of today, crossed the Atlantic and was used with the ancient Musk Rose, *R. moschata*, to produce "Champneys' Pink Cluster", the first of a class of Noisettes – remontant and sweetly-scented climbing roses, among which "Alister Stella Gray" is a reliable yellow.

By mid-century, breeders were amalgamating the best of these new roses to produce another class – Hybrid Perpetual. These became the most favoured roses of the Victorians, and "Général Jacqueminot", outstandingly handsome, gained admirers the world over. It

Rosa canina (1) *Fantin-Latour* (2)

Ferdinand Pichard (7) *Safrano* (8)

Peace (13) *Dorothy Perkins* (14)

OLD BLUSH CHINA (3) ROSA MOSCHATA (4) MME ISAAC PEREIRE (5) ALISTER STELLA GRAY (6)

ROSA WICHURAIANA (9) ROSA MULTIFLORA (10) ROSA FOETIDA (11) MME CAROLINE TESTOUT (12)

CÉCILE BRUNNER (15) BUFF BEAUTY (16) ICEBERG (17) GRAHAM THOMAS (18)

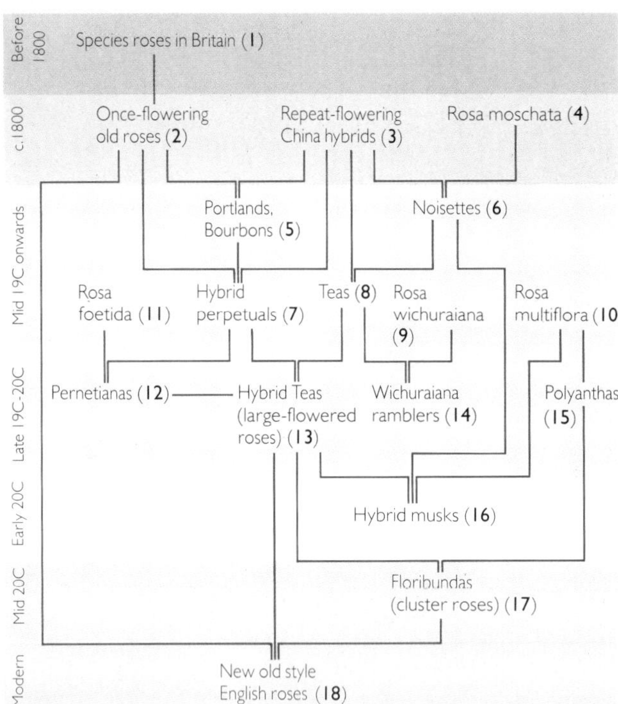

Left: simplified family tree to show the development of the modern rose

was said in 1892 that the dark crimson, velvety buds had slept on the bosom of every belle in New York. "Ferdinand Pichard" is a good example of a later variegated Hybrid Perpetual.

There was a parallel development from "Humes' Blush" and "Parks's Yellow". These tea-scented Chinas were the progenitors of Tea roses, of more delicate constitution than the robust Hybrid Perpetuals. Most were grown under glass and were sought by enthusiastic florists. Particularly favoured were those with new soft buff-yellow shades, like "Safrano" and the somewhat hardier "Gloire de Dijon".

These later Victorian roses were grown as much for the show bench as for the garden, for enthusiasm led to competition. Up and down the country growers vied to produce bigger and better blooms. An account by Dean Reynolds Hole (president of the National Rose Society, from 1877–1904) shows that these came not only from eminent nurserymen. When he was invited by a small group in Nottingham to judge roses on Easter Monday, he was in some doubt whether the journey could be justified. But his scepticism was quickly banished by a wonderful display of blooms grown by allotment owners who had stripped the blankets from their beds to insulate their tiny greenhouses against frost. This self-sacrificing dedication explained the superb Hybrid Perpetuals and Teas proudly shown in ginger-beer bottles so early in the year.

A marriage between these two classes produced the first Hybrid Tea, "La France", in 1867, and some 30 years later a true yellow, "Soleil d'Or", took its colour from the old "Persian Yellow" to establish the *Pernetiana* strain. This later appeared in new shades of orange and scarlet through the influence of *R. foetida*, although the more sober "Peace" won the greatest acclaim for a Hybrid Tea. "Pacquerette" led the development of small clustered roses known as Polyanthas, eminently suitable for pot-growth, bouquets and buttonholes. These in turn contributed to the creation of the first Floribundas in the middle of this century, "Iceberg" at one time being the most widely-grown rose throughout the world.

As with clothes, so it is with roses. Fashions change, and with the 20th century came a new trend in breeding from vigorous wild species. Crossed with the new garden varieties they produced Ramblers with dainty clusters on long, pliant stems – ideal for the lavish decorations in vogue during Edwardian times.

The emphasis now was on garden embellishment. Around pillar and pergola these versatile roses twined, and from tree and bank they tumbled. Nurserymen trained them into curious shapes and displayed pots of floriferous elephants, guns, ships or windmills at the shows.

The idea of growing roses as shrubs in mixed planting was not widely considered until after the Second World War, even though suitable roses – Hybrid Musks – had been produced by an Essex breeder 30 years earlier. Strains of Noisette, *R. multiflora* and current modern roses were used to develop strong bushes of good foliage with clusters of scented flowers repeating well in the autumn. Some were given the names of classical ladies ("Thisbe", "Penelope", "Cornelia") – apt for roses of delicate lemon, apricot and coral.

English roses are the most recent addition to the family. Moderns, crossed with summer-flowerers, have given us more graceful shrubs of new colour in old form, of which the golden "Graham Thomas" is a good example. Others have earlier associations: "Wise Portia" and "Wife of Bath" take us back to the days of Shakespeare and Chaucer, to the age of midsummer roses.

In recent years there has been a revival of interest in the subtle qualities of the old favourites, which for a time were overshadowed by their more flamboyant successors. Now they are back in the lists with their Chinese-influenced relatives, and from the vast family of roses we may select some for every situation, in any colour scheme. Be they "Rosa Mundi" or "Empress Josephine", "Reine des Violettes" or "Albertine", "The Fairy" or "The Bishop", "Whisky Mac" or "Queen Elizabeth", we may depend on a harmonious garden assembly. However, there is controversy among rose growers over the re-classification of Hybrid Teas and Floribundas as Large-flowered and Cluster roses. This has led to confusion over precise identification, although many amateurs have welcomed a general simplification.

During the last two decades there has been a surge of interest in additional rose qualities. Some of prostrate habit – "Nozomi", "Swany", "Snow Carpet", "Grouse" and "Partridge" – will provide underplanting of fine foliage and small flowers for many a rose border. Some are grown as graceful standards. "Patio roses" in pots supply a variety flowering over many months and hips extend colour into late autumn.

Given a year or two to become established, a single climbing rose can grow vigorously enough to decorate a whole house

based on the reconstruction, in the woods of Surrey and the forests of Argyll, of the Himalayan foothills where these plants produced the world's most sumptuous flowers. "Rhodoland" is still a fantasy world in which fanatics play for big stakes. By its very nature, the acid soil it needs and the overpowering presence of the rhododendron, it is almost impossible to combine it with traditional English gardening.

Still there were parts of the world to be ransacked. During the long Spanish domination of South America "spies" from other countries were not welcome. As these dominions freed themselves (Chile, for example, in 1817) English nurseries sent collectors to comb their flora for good garden plants. Chile's climate mirrored almost any conditions you could find in the northern hemisphere. Many berberis, embothriums (flame trees), fuchsias, abutilons, tropaeolums, eucryphias, nothofagus, Monkey Puzzles, gunneras, escallonias, orange-ball buddleias and lemon-scented lippias came from Chile, largely through the nursery of Veitch of Chelsea.

New Zealand had strange, down-beat flora, curiously drained of colour. Olearias, hebes and senecios are the most popular, though perhaps its most exquisite plants are tiny alpines from South Island, and tender tree ferns from the north.

The final and the toughest nut to crack was China behind the trading stations. The first man to slip through the curtain was another collector from the Horticultural Society, Robert Fortune, in 1843. His specific target was the teabush: his instructions, to introduce it into British India. How Fortune shaved his head and wore Chinese costume, how he smuggled the little camellias (that's what they are) on board a junk, and how his junk was attacked by pirates is one of horticulture's hairiest escapades. Fortune was on a bed of fever when the alarm was raised. He obviously enjoyed telling the story of his crawling on deck with his 12-bore, waiting for the junks to bump, then firing both barrels into the midst of the pirate crew.

Once more it was French missionaries who truly pioneered the exploration of China. David and Delavay are names familiar to gardeners for some of the most precious Chinese plants; they were among a dozen who dared push on westwards into the wild provinces of Yunnan and Szechwan. David is known for the *Davidia involucrata,* the handkerchief tree, which he discovered but did not introduce.

News of the extraordinary tree with white bracts the size of handkerchiefs reached the eager Veitch in Chelsea. He rapidly recruited a young man from Kew, E. H. Wilson, to trace the tree, guided only by David's recollections of a remote valley. Veitch cared for his men's well-being. He wrote to Wilson (already in China) "... always come up smiling and never allow yourself to think things are bad – rely on it, they could always be worse". With such encouragement Wilson not only found the tree, he went on to find more new ornamental plants for our gardens than any collector in history. The list, assembled by the RHS to mark the centenary of his

Growth of an Empire

Kew Gardens is the unofficial, but undisputed, world headquarters of botany, the scientific hub of the gardening wheel

By Gareth Huw Davies

Command of an empire confers great advantages on a nation's horticulturalists. They get the pick of the world's plants.

Kew Gardens prospered as Great Britain's explorers flourished. Surgeons, doubling as biologists on distant voyages of exploration, were detailed to look for commercially valuable plants. But before anything was done with it, the budding produce of the empire was sent to Kew, which rapidly became – and for 200 years has remained – the horticultural capital of the world.

The site, on a west London flood meadow, is a legacy of royal patronage. There had been royal links with Kew and Richmond since Norman times, and gardens around the palaces at Kew since George II's reign; but it was Augusta, Princess of Wales, who inaugurated the botanic garden at Kew, and who established its tradition of systematic botany when, in 1759, she recruited William Aiton from the Chelsea Physic Garden (founded in 1673).

Augusta developed the gardens with the Earl of Bute, whose close favours she enjoyed after her husband died. Bute, effectively Kew's first director, "raised hillocks to diversify the ground" and created nine acres of "exotick" gardens and "an arboretum of scientific interest".

The architect William Chambers threw up buildings in Classical, Gothic, Islamic and Chinese styles – including, in 1761, Europe's first

Sir Joseph Banks (above) found Banksia serrata (left) at Botany Bay on April 28, 1770

pagoda. The Great Stove, then the world's largest greenhouse, was built in the same year.

Augusta's envoys brought in *Robinia pseudoacacia* from North America, wistaria and ginkgo from the Far East, and *Pinus pinea* from the Mediterranean. By 1789, Kew's plant list had stretched to 5600 species.

When Augusta died in 1772, George III inherited his mother's riverside garden and joined it to the neighbouring garden which had belonged to George II: hence the "Botanic Gardens". Such is the commanding influence of Kew that the plural usage has been devoutly imitated throughout the world.

George III sustained the royal interest and appointed Sir Joseph Banks to take charge. Banks bought himself a place on Cook's *Endeavour* and plant-hunted his way up Australia's eastern seaboard. By royal appointment, Kew's collectors combed the world and brought back thousands of specimens never before seen.

In 1820 came a setback. George and Banks both died, the gardens fell into disrepair and there was even talk of putting up buildings on them. Twenty years of decline was halted in 1841, when the government took the gardens into state ownership.

The last royal contribution was made by the young Victoria, who donated the adjoining Queen's Cottage Grounds. Her stipulated condition was that they should be planted not with Kew's prevalent exotics but with British species – a condition which has been respected ever since in a special enclave to British trees and bluebells.

Under the gardens' first official director, William Hooker, nepotistically succeeded by his son Joseph and son-in-law William Thiselton-Dyer, the gardens grew to their present size of just over 300 acres. It was Sir Joseph Hooker who opened Kew's greatest era of acquisition by personally collecting 27 species of rhododendron from the Himalayas. Three million people a year took the horse tram to behold them.

Kew's collectors were never off duty. On one occasion the botanist Menzies, dining in Peru, was served with some fruits he did not recognise. He germinated the seeds on the voyage home, and grew them into Europe's first monkey puzzle trees. Their progeny still grow in the gardens. And so the conquest of the botanical world went on. Botanists trained at Kew went off to set up new gardens in far-flung countries, thus ensuring a continuing flow of material to the mother plot. Colonial administrators as well became leading amateur collectors.

Once having been logged and examined at Kew, valuable plants were passed on to be exploited in outposts of empire: the rubber tree from Brazil went to the Far East; quinine from Peru to India. The merely decorative, such as the eucalyptus and rhododendron, for example, were cleared for introduction into the humble British garden.

Built in 1761 by William Chambers, Kew's pagoda was the first in Europe

Kew grows specimens of 10 per cent of the world's flowering plants. "Nobody believes me, but we have such a good climate," says the present director, Professor Arthur Bell. "There is a relatively small fluctuation between maximum summer and minimum winter temperatures. The lack of extremes means we can grow a lot of things outside which may do better back home but at least don't die here."

Professor Bell concedes that Kew's situation, on the sand and gravel of the Thames flood plain terrace, is "terrible". The secret of success on such ground lies in rich feeding – high-quality manure procured from the royal stables and cavalry barracks.

Expansions and developments continue. In 1965 Kew acquired a satellite – the 462-acre Wakehurst Place estate in Sussex in whose deep soils are grown plants from South America and Australasia. And in 1987 it opened its largest and most technologically advanced greenhouse, the Princess of Wales Conservatory.

Kew is a rich feast to the visitors' senses, and a constant enricher of the British garden – part of the national fabric in a way which, for example, the New York botanic gardens never could be. Its reputation is such that, even today, collectors on expeditions from other gardens send unsolicited duplicate material to ensure their discoveries reach the collection.

Yet Kew is still primarily a scientific institution, where plants are studied for their potential benefits to mankind. The herbarium contains a basic reference of five million dried plants, increasing at a rate of 1000 a week. Researchers study the chemistry of plants for medicinal uses. Anti-viral compounds identified in plants may have an application, for example, in the development of drugs to combat the AIDS virus. Another department preserves seeds of potential economic value and sends them to the developing world.

Kew's skill in plant detective work is celebrated. Recently its scientists matched a sliver of wood from a sculpture Sotheby's was offering for sale against its library of 80,000 slides. Their conclusion that the sample came from a tree of the Pacific was a matter of great relief to the auctioneers, who were seeking support for their undisclosed belief that the sculpture was a work made by Gauguin in Tahiti.

Castanospermum australe (now used in AIDS research) – one of the strange and exotic plants which enchanted Banks

TRADE ROOTS

The professional nurseryman is to the garden what the casting director is to the cinema. His influence is all-pervasive, and yet too often taken for granted

By Peter Seabrook

The Veitch family firm sent more than 20 plant-hunters around the world, including E. H. "Chinese" Wilson

While famous plant-hunters travelling around the world get most of the credit for the wide variety of plants in British gardens, it is our nurserymen who are the unsung heroes, providing a large part of this great inheritance. An uncommon combination of qualities is needed to found and maintain a good nursery. Knowing about plants and how to grow them is but a fraction of what it takes. Even more important is having the business acumen, being able to recruit the right staff and foresee likely demands for specific plants years ahead.

Get all this right, as James Lee, the Veitches, the Slococks and the Hilliers surely did, and there still remains the question of the soil. Grow apples, any prunus, roses and the like year after year in the same soil and the quality of growth deteriorates because of what nurserymen now call "replant disease". As if it were not enough for second and subsequent generations to follow a remarkable founder, Krey also had the handicap of soil sickness, quelled to some extent by adding ever more manure.

The nursery industry as we know it today has its roots in the early part of the 16th century. Before then, surplus plants were sold by great estates and monasteries. With the dissolution of the monasteries by Henry VIII, however, a vacuum in the supply, especially of hedge plants, native and fruiting trees, was filled by commercial nurserymen.

There are three main groups of business given the title nursery: the tree and shrub nursery we are considering here, the florists who grow and trade in potted plants and flowers, and the seedsmen. Cramphorns, the Essex-based garden centre firm, can be traced back to seed and corn chandler trade in the East End of London in the 18th century.

Many early nurserymen were originally gardeners, and some managed to combine the roles of big estate gardener and independent nurseryman. Transport difficulties restricted development, and so London, the ports, the Fosse Way and canals influenced the siting of nurseries. The great concentration of them near Woking, Surrey, and the Hillier nursery at Winchester are in part due to the Basingstoke canal, bearing plants into London and carrying manure out.

Deciduous trees and shrubs were packed in straw with moss around the roots and where the journey would take eight days or more were often covered with honey and then moss.

Four London gardeners, Looker, Field, Cook and London, founded the Brompton Park Nurseries in 1681; the Victoria and Albert Museum now stands on part of the site. London, who studied plants from the Cape of Good Hope in Holland and visited France, formed a partnership with Wise, raised an incredible range of plants and designed gardens in all parts of the United Kingdom.

James Lee and Lewis Kennedy became partners in about 1745 at the Vineyard Nursery, Hammersmith, west London. The earliest surviving catalogue was produced by James Lee. He heard a sailor's wife in Wapping, east London, had a beautiful flowering fuchsia. He found her and offered her eight guineas, all the money he had in his pocket, and promised her replacement cuttings. The offer was reluctantly accepted. Lee then raised 300 cuttings which he sold at one guinea each. He introduced some 235 plants, including the orange *Buddleia globosa*.

The demand was modest until the arrival of the railways in the mid-19th century. Then increasingly rich middle classes made mass demands and the number of nurseries and the size of them exploded, creating a number of smaller nurseries which also grew and prospered. St Bridgets Nurseries, Exeter, was a pup of Veitches and eventually took over the original.

The Veitch family, first John Veitch at Exeter in 1832 and then his offspring in Exeter and Chelsea to the fifth generation Anna who died in 1969, were phenomenal nurserymen. They sent more than 20 plant-hunters around the world, including William and Thomas Lobb as well as E. H. "Chinese" Wilson. In Victorian times they acted as an employment agency for many gardening posts. If gardeners wanted to move, Veitch's knew where the vacancies were and, if you moved on their recommendation, naturally business was directed to them.

Large nurseries were dependent on mail order and the railways for delivery. V. N. Gauntlett's Japanese Nurseries at Chiddingfold, Surrey, in the Thirties produced a 400-page catalogue, two pages of which listed over 600 members of the aristocracy, from King George V downwards, as patrons. They printed "Witley (Southern Railway) 3 miles" alongside the address and listed 64 different species and cultivars of clematis. Good garden centres today offer over 70, so the demand for variety continues.

Now is the age of the specialist, with camellias flown in from New Zealand and grafted wistaria from Japan. Even so, leading nurserymen – Blooms, the Notcutts, the Hilliers, the Williamsons – are still investing in the search for new, better and more attractive garden plants. They, like the old-time nurserymen before them, have to back their hunches by investing considerable sums of money in growing plants for a still-speculative market.

birth in 1976, amounted to more than 600 still being grown in British gardens, and another 400 no longer traceable.

Leaving aside his lilies (if one can leave aside *Lilium regale*), his anemones, primulas, and all his herbaceous plants, his score runs to 65 rhododendron species, 22 cotoneasters, 22 berberis, all the Kurume azaleas, 14 maples, 3 mountain ashes, 9 magnolias, spruces, numerous firs and viburnums, *Rosa moyesii*, the pink *Clematis montana* . . . Nurserymen now had plenty to work on. Every golden or purple or blue-grey form of a tree, every variegated plant, every weeping or upright or otherwise smartened-up version of anything we grow, owes its survival to nurserymen.

While there is an undiscovered species left someone will want to claim it. In 1905 rhododendron fanatics commissioned George Forrest to ransack the jungle north of Burma and east of Tibet which they suspected was the epicentre of this promiscuous genus. Forrest was employed for 28 years in this extremely dangerous country in which monks and brigands were one and the same. He clocked up 300 new rhododendron species, besides many primulas and other plants.

Reginald Farrer was an amateur when he joined with the experienced William Purdom to hunt for alpines *On the Eaves of the World*, as the title of one of his books describes Tibet. Rock-gardeners still regularly refer to Farrer's books, but so should anyone else who loves plants and good writing. His description of discovering the pale-purple weeping *Buddleia alternifolia* is famous. We have him to thank, too, for the winter-flowering *Viburnum fragrans*.

The Second World War and the communist revolution put a stop to collecting in China. Even during the war in not-very-remote eastern Szechwan, a splendid tree was discovered which had been thought extinct. *Metasequoia glyptostroboides* (more happily known by its Chinese name, the water larch) caused a sensation when its seeds arrived in Britain in 1948. We now have specimens approaching 80ft.

What else may the mysterious Middle Kingdom hold? In the last 10 years a new series of expeditions has begun. Roy Lancaster is the best-known of western collectors collaborating with the Chinese in combing their remoter ranges. Young Chinese plants of unknown promise are even now germinating in European nurseries.

But will we do them justice? The auguries, alas, are far from encouraging. The age of the great pioneering nursery seems to be over. Hilliers of Winchester was the last. Ten years ago the Hillier catalogue offered nearly 7000 woody plants – until the sad realisation that the gardener of today has lost the spirit of adventure. The vast majority want only plants that they can see in everyone else's gardens. The dismal spirit of the garden centre has descended on the land: nothing will sell (we are told) unless it is available in a container and in flower.

Tradescant, thou should'st be living at this hour.

The great advantage of crab apples like Malus "Red Sentinel" is the spread of interest through the year – attractive spring blossom, and brightly coloured fruit that hangs on well into the winter

CUT TO THE QUICK

No aspect of the garden has been more central to man's designs, or more accommodating to his interference, than the hedge

By Hugh Johnson

The notion of clipping trees and shrubs into unnatural forms or to conform to architectural ideas is one of the oldest in gardening. Our word topiary derives from the Latin *topiarius*, the word for gardener – which in turn is derived from the Greek for a confined place: almost a definition of a garden.

Pliny's description of his villa on the shore just south of Rome makes it clear that one of his particular pleasures was shrubs cut into animal forms. Quite independently, nothing is so characteristic of the gardens of Japan as the strictly-pruned tree or shrub; the life-size bonsai, as it were.

The Roman model was artificial and fanciful, the oriental one an exaggerated aping of natural forms. Both use the principle that most woody plants, regularly trimmed back, react by forming dense clusters of buds, which in time present a smooth and even surface.

Hedges are by far the most common form of topiary today. They often take the place of garden walls, which have become prohibitively expensive. To be effective as a barrier and space-divider, a hedge needs to be dense. How densely it will grow depends on the capacity of the plants used to form new buds and "break" from mature wood. In this regard yew is the supreme champion. You can cut an old yew right back to its stump and it will soon be a mass of green shoots again.

Many of the plants commonly used for hedging today, and most notably the cypress family, are middling to poor in their capacity to sprout from old wood. A cypress hedge will react well to repeated light trimming, but once it has grown too tall or wide there is no chance of a drastic reduction.

The secret of growing a good hedge is to choose a relatively slow-growing plant – yew is best – and give it as much encouragement and nourishment as possible. Regard a hedge as you would a row of vegetables which were going to remain indefinitely. This means a deep wide trench, generously filled with compost (but also with good drainage: it should never be allowed to become a puddle).

Like any other kind of sculpture, topiary can be representational, abstract or boldly informative

IV

The Quest For Colour

By Penelope Hobhouse

A garden is like no other work of art. It is never finished but always in transition, reflecting the restless nature of the gardener and his incurable preoccupation with improvement. Gardeners are not content simply to improve upon their own schemes; they must also improve upon nature. Plants that begin as small, insignificant species, culled from wild places all over the world, are altered by selective breeding until they are as different from their wild progenitors as peacocks from amoebae. Every century presents garden designers with a different flora with which to work: always there are more varieties, a wider range of colour and form. By understanding the chronology, you can lay bare the secrets of your border and read the plants like the pages of a history book.

English classic: a traditional deep herbaceous border, backed by a protective high wall, includes densely-planted drifts of popular border favourites, including wallflowers and forget-me-nots, with an edging of aubrietia and the ubiquitous lilac against the wall

The floral world. Our map shows the native origins of the wild species from which our most popular garden varieties derive. From Siberia to South America, Canada to Australia and the torrid heart of Africa, there is not a stretch of earth, mud or sand that has not yielded a grain of colour to the English garden

Above: for more than a century, the suburban ideal has remained little altered – smooth, well-groomed lawns with a mixture of perennial and annual plants, and shrubs

British native flora has a limited range compared with continental Europe. Glacial surges and recessions which ended 10,000 years ago left the country isolated from the mainland mass, over which plants could migrate northwards as the ice retreated.

Fortunately, flowers in the wild do not concern us as gardeners; a flowering plant's importance begins only when it can be evaluated for its decorative contribution to the garden. More fortunately still, to make up for the restricted range of native flora the British climate since the Ice Age has been peculiarly favourable for gardening. With a little help, many foreign plants thrive and multiply here to make the English flower garden the envy of the world. With no great extremes of temperature, the climate provides almost unique growing conditions – so good that many non-woody exotics actually perform better in this country than they do in their own habitats.

Cool English summers prolong flowering periods for all herbaceous plants (though lack of hot sun may prevent seed ripening – most commercial seed is produced in warmer countries). Rainfall occurs regularly during the year, and without summer droughts many foreign plants continue to produce both new foliage and flowers until the first frosts. In gardens where plants are grown for overall beauty, of course, flowers are not the only consideration. In Britain the leaves of many perennials and biennials remain green and attractive throughout the summer (some herbaceous perennials still look good during mild winters), further extending and enhancing the appearance of the garden.

Alpines introduced from high mountains, bulbs and annuals from hotter countries, bog plants from swamps, as well as perennials (mainly from the northern hemisphere), have all proved amazingly adaptable to English gardens. In the 20th century, English gardening as a style has become synonymous with beds and borders within which herbaceous plants (perennials, biennials, annuals and bulbs) from all corners of the world are arranged to make colourful pictorial compositions which perform for a long summer season. The origins of these plants, and their development and use as garden-worthy flowers, make one of the most fascinating strands in the history of the garden.

Even with limited flora there is still a surprising number of British natives which are sufficiently decorative or fragrant to be grown in gardens as original species or, more frequently, to have become ancestors of a race of garden plants. Among the latter are heartsease *(Viola tricolor)* from which the cultivated large-flowered pansy evolved in the 19th century, and the wild primrose *(Primula vulgaris)* which by the end of the 16th century was prized in several coloured forms and in strange double shapes known as "Hose in Hose" and "Jack in the Green". Today these "sports",

Far left: the joys of spring, Victorian style
Left: carnations and dahlias from the Sutton's catalogue, 1887

and some which owe breeding to a pinker form, *P. vulgaris* ssp. *sibthorpii*, introduced to England from the eastern Mediterranean in the early 17th century, are sought-after connoisseurs' plants.

The field poppy *(Papaver rhoeas)* is a hardy annual. By the end of the 19th century the Reverend William Wilks had selected various colour and double garden forms which became the Shirley Poppies, now available from seedsmen in shades of pink and red. Of the related *Meconopsis* genus, *M. cambrica*, the humble Welsh poppy with yellow or orange flowers is found in Britain and Europe – the only representative of its genus in the west. All the other *Meconopsis* grow in the Himalayan regions of Asia and were not discovered until the 19th century. Botanists now believe the Welsh poppy is a survivor of pre-glacial times; once an unbroken chain of *Meconopsis* species may have stretched all the way from Wales to the high mountains of Hupeh.

Jacob's ladder *(Polemonium caeruleum)* with either blue or white flowers, is still grown in garden beds. Bulbs such as the wild lenten lily, *Narcissus pseudonarcissus*, found in natural woodland, and the snakeshead lily, *Fritillaria meleagris*, which spreads in damp river meadows, are thought to be native. In the 14th century Friar Daniel maintained a private botanical garden at Stepney, where he distinguished between two related species of native cranesbill, *Geranium pratense* and *G. sanguineum*. By 1597 both a striped and a white version of the field geranium were known, and by the end of the 19th century the double-flowered forms in white,

Edge of Brightness

The herbaceous border, which was popularised at the turn of the century, has become the very essence of Englishness

By Penelope Hobhouse

William Robinson and Gertrude Jekyll are generally credited with the invention of the herbaceous border in the last quarter of the 19th century. In fact, their recommendations, freely expressed in contemporary journals and books, served to popularise a planting style which had been developing since Tudor times.

As well as making borders fashionable, both writers must be credited with improving their artistic merit. They saw the flowerbeds as pictorial compositions to be viewed from across the main lawn or to be discovered as planting schemes unfolded on a peripheral walk. Either way, stress was laid on creating garden pictures where shapes and colours in blending harmonies and planned contrasts gave desired effects.

Robinson was didactic, insisting that only hardy plants and no "specimen plants from the greenhouse" were included.

Jekyll was more catholic in taste, using any plants which would improve effects (she had been trained as an artist and used her developed colour sense to plan her borders) and extend the length of the flowering season. Her schemes were generally mixed in content: hardy *Anemone hupehensis* (newly introduced from Japan), delphiniums, lythrums and hemerocallis were grouped with drifts of tender cannas and dahlias, annual marigolds, lily bulbs (sometimes grown in pots to be sunk in the ground) and foliage plants with an emphasis on the silvers and greys which acted as a foil to pale tinted flower colours.

None of this was completely new; it merely gave the borders status. Already in 1828 William Cobbett described English gardens where "flowers are cultivated . . . in borders, where an infinite variety of them are mingled together . . . so that they may blend with one another in colour as well as stature."

Twenty years later great double borders of flowering perennials were included in a scheme for a new ornamental garden at Arley Hall in Cheshire; these borders, their essential style unaltered, still exist today.

In 1856 Shirley Hibberd confirmed that herbaceous plants were essential in any garden layout: "The bedding system is an embellishment . . . the herbaceous border is a necessary fundamental feature." Even if Arley Hall was exceptional in the 1840s in including borders in the main layout, it is clear that all grand gardens continued to grow hardy flowers in walled kitchen areas; they were specially for picking rather than arranged for admiration.

Robinson and Jekyll, and others of the Arts and Crafts movement, also looked back nostalgically to old-fashioned flowers which could still be found growing in idealised cottage gardens; these augmented the supply of improved "garden" varieties and the many newer introductions.

The true herbaceous border, where only hardy perennials were used, was designed to reach a peak in high summer. These schemes, even at the height of their Edwardian popularity, existed in gardens only where space permitted such seasonal indulgence. Most gardens, as today, made their borders work on a more all-year-round basis and border plants included mixed shrubs, bush roses, perennials, biennials, bulbs and some annuals artistically woven to give form as well as flower and foliage colours.

Paintings and photographs of gardens in the 1900s showed borders composed only of sturdy perennial clumps, others where glorious mixtures of summer-performing herbaceous plants were used to knit together a framework of taller woody specimens, many of which flowered early in the season but gave architectural interest all the year. This style of gardening was in fact a

Above: herbaceous borders at Bledlow, Bucks, dominated by spectacular peonies and delphiniums

sophisticated form of cottage gardening. With some variations in detail and execution it remains as a style in the Eighties.

During the Thirties, Percy Cane introduced a more naturalistic approach; instead of straight-edged borders always edging a lawn or pathway, he encouraged gardeners to design curving beds which disguised the strict rectangular framework even of a city garden.

More recently Alan Bloom of Bressingham in Norfolk has encouraged the creation of island beds where clumps of herbaceous plants can be viewed from both sides; early-flowering perennials can be hidden in the centre as other plants grow up, and those with shorter stems are used as edging. This sort of scheme, in open sunny situations, extends the seasonal interest of the old-fashioned herbaceous border without using other plant types.

The traditional herbaceous bed or border needs completely replanting every four or five years; plant groups are split up and the relative areas of planting are adjusted. This gives a chance for complete cultivation and enrichment of the soil. The mixed border which is found in most modest-sized gardens today contains a pattern of bulbs and woody plants as well as herbaceous ones; it needs finer annual adjustments and reshuffling as the permanent trees and shrubs increase in height and spread. These borders and beds of variable shapes and sizes, framed by an expanse of lawn or paving, are often the only planting feature in a garden. They are three-dimensional in scope rather than looking like a flat canvas.

lavender and deep violet were available for planting in hardy flower borders and for naturalising in wilder garden areas.

Daniel also brought into his garden the woodland bluebell, *Endymion non-scriptus*, and four native ferns. The foxglove *(Digitalis purpurea)*, common mullein *(Verbascum thapsus)*, teasel *(Dipsacus fullonum)*, and stinging nettle *(Urtica dioica)* are all native plants for the outer fringes of the garden, the latter especially valuable for butterflies.

The garden is as much prey to shifts in fashion as any other decorative form, yet some flowers have become established as unshakable favourites. Those shown above and overleaf are the 10 most popular annuals, biennials, perennials and bulbs currently selling in British garden centres

Clearly the Romans, besides growing vines, introduced many plants to Britain, but most of the smaller herbs disappeared during the Dark Ages. A few flowers survived and became naturalised; the periwinkle (both *Vinca major* and *V. minor*) which the Romans grew for wreaths and garlands, and the Christmas rose *(Helleborus niger)*. The Romans are also given the credit for introducing ground elder *(Aegopodium podagraria)*, which they ate as a salad. Although most English gardeners fear the spread of ground elder as a weed the less vigorous variegated form is becoming a popular foliage plant.

It is clear that the Venerable Bede, writing at the beginning of the eighth century, knew the Madonna lily *(Lilium candidum)*, emblem of the Virgin Mary. The white

6 *Pansy* *"Giant Fancy"* 7 *Candytuft* *"Dwarf Fairy Mixed"* 8 *Nemesia* *"Carnival"* 9 *Marigold* *"Crackerjack Mixed"* 10 *Night Scented Stock*

6 *Delphinium* *"Special Mixture"* 7 *Myosotis* *"Royal Blue"* 8 *Aubrietia* *"Large Flowered Hybrids"* 9 *Aquilegia* *"Selected Lone Spurred Hybrids"* 10 *Hollyhock* *"Double Mixed"*

petals symbolised the purity of her body, the golden anthers the glowing light of her soul. The Madonna lily was well known both to the Greeks, who imported it from Asia Minor, and to the Romans, who both ate the bulbs and used them medicinally as the basis for an ointment for corns. It grew throughout most of the Roman Empire, probably including Britain. By around 975, the Benedictional of St Ethelwold, illustrated at Winchester, shows Queen Ethelreda holding a single bloom.

The Madonna lily was grown with roses in many enclosed monastery gardens but today it is sterile in cultivation and the double forms known in the 16th century have disappeared. It is rare to find it massed under rustic pergolas as it so often was in Edwardian gardens.

Before AD 1000 there is little written evidence to show how plants from other countries were first grown in English gardens, and none to indicate a love of flowers for their beauty alone. It is obvious that certain herbs, as well as having fragrance (an important medieval consideration), Christian symbolism and medicinal and culinary qualities, are also highly ornamental, but man had to rise above the level of bare subsistence before he could think of growing for pleasure rather than for food or profit.

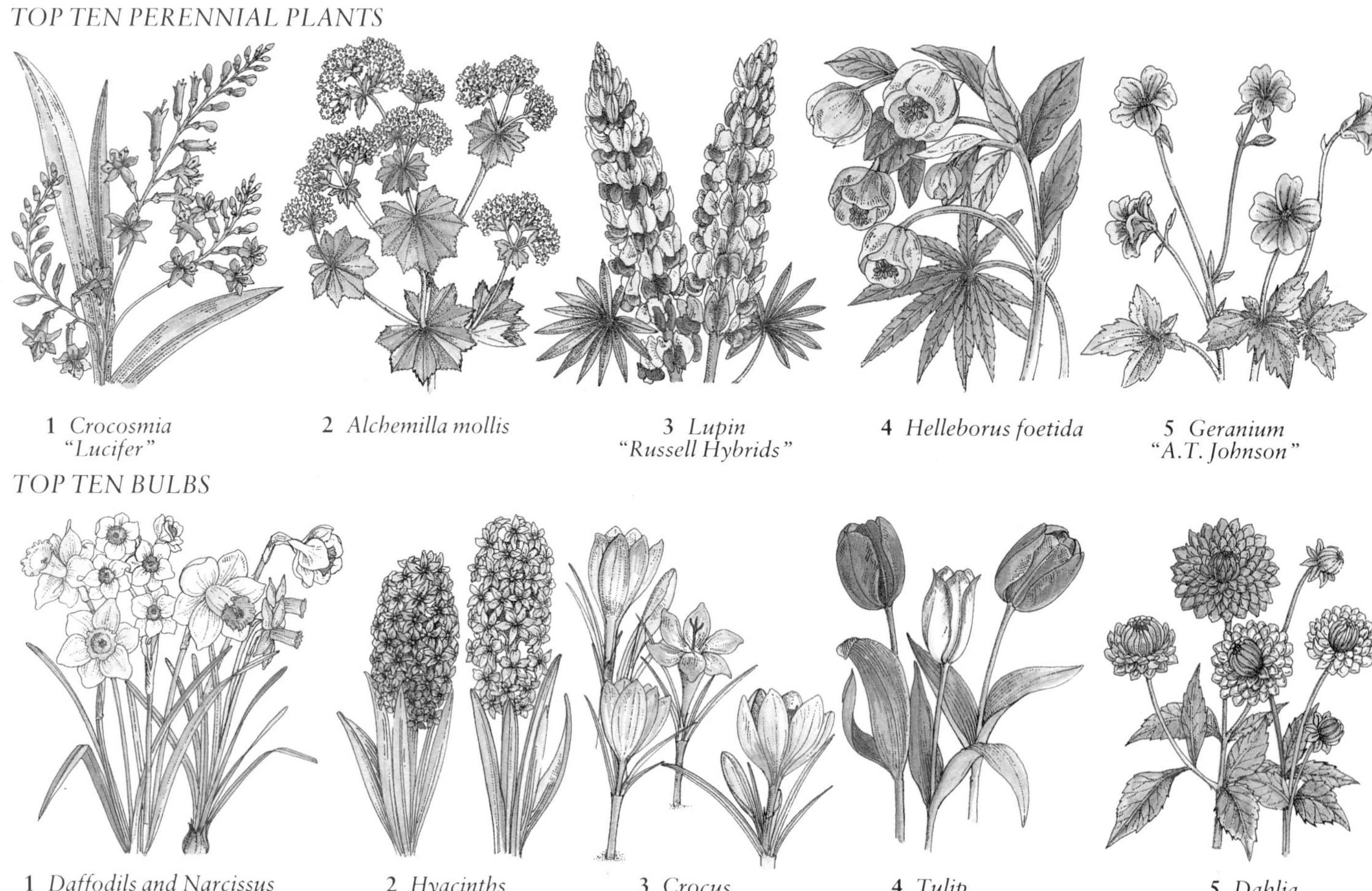

TOP TEN PERENNIAL PLANTS

1 *Crocosmia "Lucifer"* 2 *Alchemilla mollis* 3 *Lupin "Russell Hybrids"* 4 *Helleborus foetida* 5 *Geranium "A.T. Johnson"*

TOP TEN BULBS

1 *Daffodils and Narcissus* 2 *Hyacinths* 3 *Crocus* 4 *Tulip* 5 *Dahlia*

One of the earliest records of an aesthetic attitude to flowers is Walafrid Strabo's poem *Hortulus*, written in 840. Strabo was Benedictine Abbot at Reichenau, on Lake Constance, who obviously not only appreciated flowers but was a practical gardener used to working the soil and digging in manure. He attacked nettles armed with "mattock and rake". Strabo's experience was in Switzerland but we can surmise that there was contemporary contact with religious establishments in England during the Dark Ages (500–1000). From Charlemagne's *Capitulare de Villis*, a list of plants drawn up in about 800, it is possible to identify herbs which have attractive flowers rather than any purely utilitarian function. Among the 73 herbs mentioned were chicory, clary, fennel, flag iris, mallow, poppy, southernwood and tansy. All these *could* have been grown in England before 1000; if not, they will have been introduced by the Normans soon after 1066.

The Norman Conquest brought England into the mainstream of European civilisation. Traditionally the wallflower, ancestor of our spring "bedder", was introduced from Normandy with stone for building. Stock came from European cliffs, and soapwort, still used for cleaning valuable fabrics, arrived from southern Europe. The flag iris, the French royal symbol *fleurs-de-lys* (after 1339 incorporated

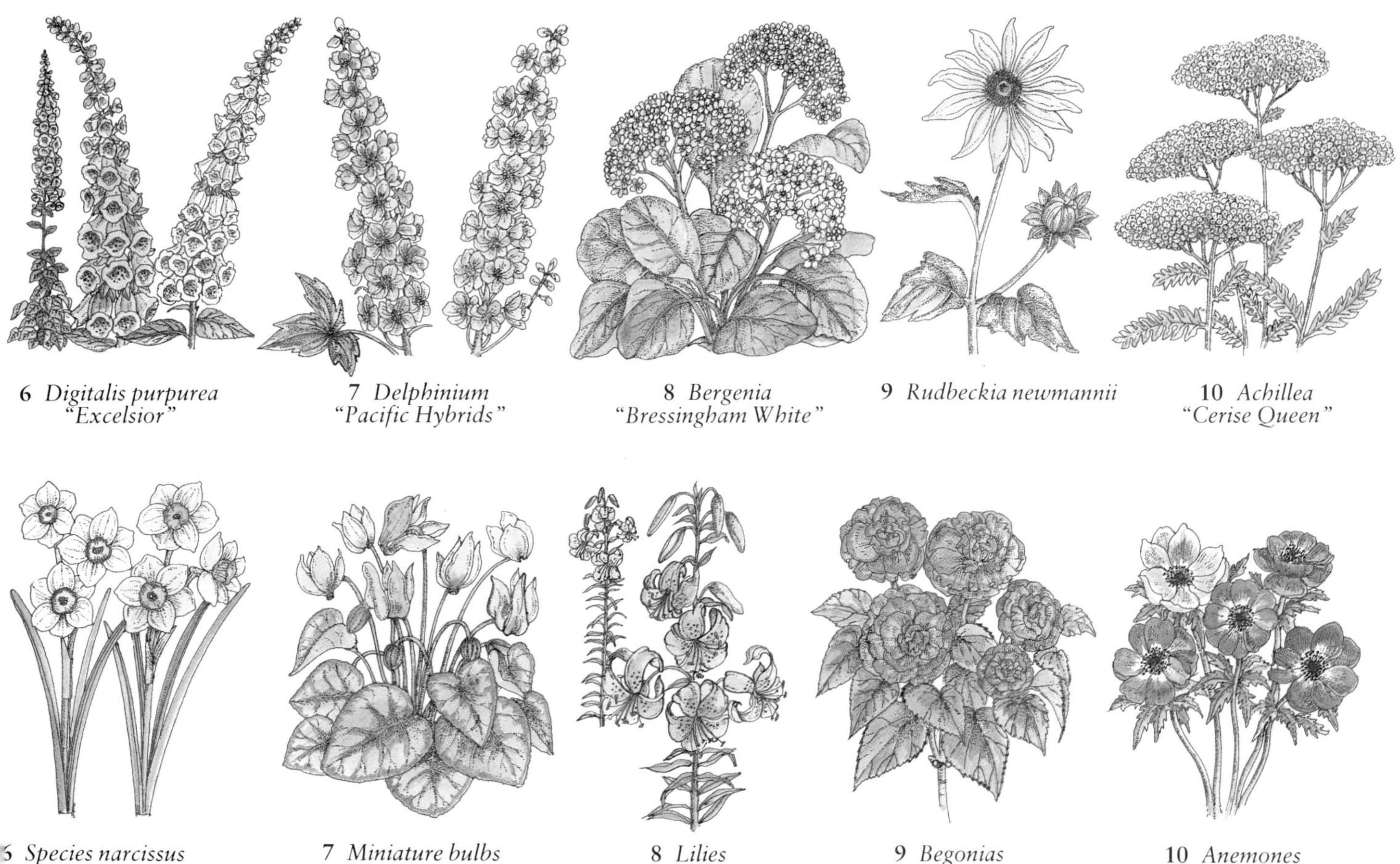

6 *Digitalis purpurea* "Excelsior"

7 *Delphinium* "Pacific Hybrids"

8 *Bergenia* "Bressingham White"

9 *Rudbeckia newmannii*

10 *Achillea* "Cerise Queen"

6 *Species narcissus*

7 *Miniature bulbs (miscellaneous) e.g. Cyclamen coum*

8 *Lilies*

9 *Begonias*

10 *Anemones*

in Edward III's Royal Arms), *Iris florentina* and *I. germanica* were all grown here, the last two coming from Italy but introduced to Europe from Syria in very ancient times, probably before 1500 BC.

From the 11th century on, there was a constant interchange of ideas with European classicists (usually in Latin or French), and with scholars in Moorish Spain (the latter translated Greek and Roman botanical texts such as Dioscorides and Pliny). In about 1200 Alexander Neckham made a list of plants grown in England – a list which remained a standard reference throughout the Middle Ages. It included the slightly tender *Acanthus mollis* and mandrake *(Mandragora officinarum)*, with bushes such as pomegranate, oranges and lemons which may have been grown as pot plants and given winter protection. Neckham's catalogue is a useful reminder that until 1300 the climate in Britain was warmer than it is today, providing at least an extra month of good growing weather.

The establishment of Benedictine monasteries throughout the British Isles led to the introduction of many more plants. As well as those from Europe, many of which already had long garden histories and were of uncertain origin, seeds and bulbs were brought back by pilgrims and crusaders. The illuminated manuscripts, poetry,

What's in a Name?

Although some gardeners find botanical names baffling, intimidating and unintelligible, the scientific naming of plants is basically simple

By Professor William T. Stearn

The system used resembles that of other objects similar enough to be usefully recognised as a group, a *genus*, but also needing to be distinguished as individual kinds, *species*. Thus within the genus "knife" we distinguish species such as "bread knife", "carving knife", "fish knife". This two-word method of naming species is called *binomial*.

Botanical names are generally of Latin form, though the words may come from other languages: *Lonicera japonica, Hydrangea macrophylla, Cattleya aclandiae*. They are regulated by an elaborate set of internationally agreed rules forming part of an *International Code of Botanical Nomenclature*. There is also an *International Code of Nomenclature for Cultivated Plants* for garden-raised variants such as those of lettuces, peas, potatoes, chrysanthemums, lilies. The codes aim to prevent confusing and arbitrary changes in the names of plants, although gardeners sometimes think they fail to do so. Contrary to common horticultural opinion, most botanists detest name-changes, even though such changes are in fact relatively few. They result from the adoption of the earliest correctly applied available name in accordance with the *International Code of Botanical Nomenclature*, or from revised classification based on study of the plants concerned. Some examples are given below.

International Use

The Latin form of botanical names are both historically and politically neutral. This together with their stability and precision, has led to their international use, while vernacular, "common or garden" names have only a local or national use. The marsh-marigold or king-cup *(Caltha palustris)*, with its large heart-shaped leaves and conspicuous bright yellow flowers, attracts attention wherever it grows and has a wealth of local names – at least 33 in Britain, 45 in France, 27 in The Netherlands, 50 in Scandinavia, 120 in Germany, Austria and Switzerland. But none is suitable for international use. Internationally known *Caltha palustris* has remained constant and unchallenged since its adoption in 1753, the starting point of modern botanical nomenclature, and was already in use in 1561.

A problem with vernacular names is not only the diversity of names for the same plant but also the use of the same vernacular name for different plants in different parts of the world. Nevertheless, scientific and standard vernacular names, often centuries-old, should be regarded as alternative and complementary rather than competitive. Columbine, daisy, ivy and dandelion are every bit as right for everyday use as *Aquilegia, Bellis, Hedera* and *Taraxacum*.

Origin of Names

Modern botanical names, somewhat erroneously called "Latin", are of very mixed origin indeed. Many plant names passed from Greece to Italy and became part of our scientific nomenclature: for instance, *Acacia, Acanthus, Aconitum, Adiantum, Amaranthus, Anemone, Asphodelus, Aster*... Roman names include *Acer, Alnus, Arbutus, Bellis, Beta, Convolvulus, Malva, Potentilla, Saxifraga*.

To such classical names modern botanists, confronted with a vast number of new plants from all over the world, have added a strange mixture of names taken from what the ancient Greeks and Romans would have considered barbarous languages: *Abelmoschus, Abutilon* and *Berberis* from Arabic; *Ailanthus* from Indonesian; *Aucuba, Fatsia, Kirengeshoma, Nandina, Sasa* and *Skimmia* from Japanese. Much more numerous are names commemorating persons: *Bergenia, Boronia, Camellia, Cattleya, Clivia, Dahlia, Dalea, Davidia, Forsythia, Freesia, Fuchsia, Gaillardia, Gardenia, Kalmia, Kochia, Kniphofia, Magnolia, Monarda, Robinia, Saintpaulia, Sansevieria, Stapelia, Stokesia, Tolmiea, Warscewiczella* (commemorating a Polish plant-collector and best pronounced Varshev-i-chel-la) and *Zinnia*, in honour of English, Dutch, French, German, Italian, Polish, Scottish, Spanish and Swedish botanists, gardeners and plant-collectors. So cosmopolitan in origin are the "Latin names" of plants!

Early Sources of Names

Ancient Greek and Roman plant-lore is recorded in much-copied manuscripts which refer to a vast number of works now lost. Obviously they listed plants and plant-products valued as sources of food, medicaments and timber. But an interest in plants from a philosophical and scientific, as distinct from a utilitarian, standpoint is first evident, and extensively so, in the work of Theophrastus. Born about 371 BC on the island of Lesbos, he spent most of his life in Athens (where he died about 287 BC) as a teacher of students and as an associate, later successor, of Aristotle. Aristotle was primarily interested in animals, Theophrastus in plants. His work had no stimulating scientific influence, being in Greek, until the 16th century. Far more important was a work on medicinal plants and drugs compiled in the first century AD by another Greek, Dioscorides, who may have been a much-travelled doctor in one of Nero's armies. So much used and esteemed and consequently copied over and over again and translated into Arabic and Latin, Dioscorides' work and others based upon it ensured the survival through the Middle Ages of many familiar plant names: *Achillea, Althaea, Alyssum, Androsace, Antirrhinum, Colchicum, Cyclamen, Cytisus, Delphinium, Echium, Epimedium, Foeniculum, Geranium, Helleborus, Hyacinthus, Hypericum, Lithospermum, Myrrhis, Nerium, Origanum, Paeonia, Pancratium, Phlomis, Platanus*.

In the 16th century, when printing made widely available many works of antiquity, people began to question received knowledge and to look closely at the plants around them. This spirit of enquiry began in Italy but spread into Germany and elsewhere including England. Finding innumerable plants that had no Latin names, they had to invent names for them. The German herbalist Leonhart Fuchs coined the names *Campanula* (little bell) and *Digitalis* in 1542. The Swiss scholar Conrad Gessner found in the Alps the globeflower which local people called "Trollblume", leading to the generic name *Trollius*. Meanwhile diplomats sent to Constantinople became acquainted with a wealth of new plants found in western Asia and the Balkan Peninsula, like the garden tulip *(Tulipa gesneriana)*, the white horse-chestnut *(Aesculus hippocastanum)* and the lilac *(Syringa vulgaris)* as well as many plants with tubers or bulbs.

Their introduction into European gardens from about 1560 to 1620 made those years possibly the most exciting period in the history of European gardening. Until seedlings reached flowering size the white horse-chestnut was known for many years only from its prickly fruits containing large brown seeds, our "conkers", from which the Turks made a medicine for horses: hence a herbalist, Mattioli, coined the name *Hippocastanum (Gk hippos*, horse; *Castanea*, sweet chestnut). The word "lilac" derives from Sanskrit *nila*, "dark blue", by way of Arabic *laylak*; but *Syringa (Gk syrinx*, pipe), now the scientific generic name of the lilacs, was formerly used also for the mock-orange *(Philadelphus)*. Under the heading "*Syringa*, the Pipetree" the herbalist John Parkinson in 1629 distinguished two special kinds – the "blew Pipetree" or common lilac, *Syringa vulgaris*, and the "single white Pipetree", the strongly scented mock-orange, *Philadelphus coronarius*. The only character they had in common was their pithy branches which could be hollowed into pipes.

Carl Linnaeus

During the 17th and 18th centuries, the overseas expansion of the British, Dutch and French resulted in an enormous number of new plants from around the world becoming known in Europe and many of them introduced into gardens. They needed names. Passion flowers, for example, now put together in the genus *Passiflora*, were listed under *Clematis indica, Granadilla, Flos passionis* and *Passiflora* down to 1753, with *Passiflora caerulea* being named

Where science meets the gods: Thornton's painting, from "New Illustrations of the Sexual System of Linnaeus", shows Aesculapius, Ceres, Flora and Cupid honouring the bust of Linnaeus

both *Flos passionis major pentaphyllus* and *Passiflora folius palmatis quinquepartitis* etc.

Then in 1753 a Swedish naturalist of extraordinary ability, method and industry, Carl Linnaeus, published a very remarkable two-volume book in Latin called *Species Plantarum,* which classified and named all the then known plant species of the world, about 5900; to each of these species he consistently gave a two-word name, such as *Passiflora caerulea, P. cuprea, P. rubra, P. incarnata,* for everday use.
Besides shortening or rejecting previously used generic names, e.g. *Rheum* for *Rhabarbarum, Erythrina* for *Corallodendron,* he thus revolutionised the naming of plants.

Many of Linnaeus's contemporaries did not share his opinion of his own importance and much disliked his drastic alteration of names, although the convenience of his system ultimately led to its world-wide adoption. Linnaeus's *Species Plantarum* is now taken as the starting point of modern botanical naming; names published before then have no standing. The letter "L" after a scientific name indicates that it was published by Linnaeus, e.g *Pisum sativum* L., *Homo sapiens* L.

Classification and Naming

The classification of plants into groups and their naming are closely linked. Linnaeus arranged them according to his so-called "sexual system" based on the number of their reproductive parts. *Pentandria,* for example, described as having "five husbands in the same marriage" and *Polygamia necessaria* "when the married females are barren and the concubines fertile", a state of affairs in the marigold *(Calendula)*! His critics called this a "lewd method", too licentious to be taught to studious youth; it was nevertheless appreciated in Hanoverian England. Although now long superseded, it provided a useful stopgap system.

Nowadays plants are classified into major groups called *Families* (earlier *Natural Orders*), with smaller groups within them called *Genera,* which includes one to many individual kinds called *species,* which may in turn be divided into *subspecies, varieties* and *cultivars.* They are defined by the features they have in common. For example, the edible garden pea *(Pisum sativum)* and the sweet pea *(Lathyrus odoratus)* have in common a flower of distinctive shape, with a large erect back petal (the *standard*), two smaller side petals (the *wings*) and two forward-pointing linked petals (the *keel*) covering the stamens, and the fruit a pod. The same characteristics occur in *Laburnum, Ulex* (gorse), *Lupinus* (lupin), *Robinia* (false-acacia), *Vicia* (vetch, broad bean), *Phaseolus* (scarlet runner, etc.). Accordingly these are put together into a large family, the *Leguminosae* or *Fabaceae,* consisting of about 12,000 species, to which most botanists add two major groups with different flowers but similar pods (sometimes called *Mimosaceae* and *Caesalpiniaceae*) consisting together of about 5000 species. The names of most families end in *– aceae*: *Liliaceae, Paeoniaceae, Primulaceae*; time-honoured exceptions are *Leguminosae, Umbelliferae, Compositae, Palmae* and *Gramineae.*

Pisum and *Lathyrus* are *genera* within the family *Leguminosae.* Though much alike they are kept apart on account of small differences in the stamens and style. Within each genus there may be several species *(Lathyrus grandiflorus, L. japonicus).* The name of the genus is always written with a capital letter, the word indicating the individual species, the *specific epithet,* with a small letter. Within the species, one may distinguish *varieties. Pisum sativum* has several main varieties, sometimes called *convarieties* or *cultivar groups,* known only in cultivation: *sativum,* the common garden pea, with seeds sweeter than in other varieties; *arvense,* the field pea, with more mealy seeds; *macrocarpon,* the sugar pea or mangetout.

The interest of gardeners lies naturally in garden-raised *cultivars* which have non-Latin "fancy" names such as *Pisum sativum* "Feltham Advance", "Gladstone", "Kelvedon Wonder", "Little Marvel", "Onward". The *International*

paintings and tapestries of the Middle Ages are important evidence for the garden historian. But even in the 14th century – when herbalists such as Henry Daniel gave more scientific plant descriptions, Geoffrey Chaucer wrote with poetic enthusiasm of flowers which embellished gardens, and Master John Gardener, probably a head gardener to Edward III, listed plants in a more practical gardening context – it is difficult to identify flowers with absolute certainty. Early painters and writers undoubtedly used artistic licence.

Depictions of the medieval "flowery mead", in which small flowering plants were spaced in short turf inside a trellised enclosure, were usually only a detail in a larger picture. Violets, daisies (probably the ox-eye) and periwinkle, grown as ornamentals in grass and on turf benches, are the flowers most usually shown. Taller plants such as columbines, lilies and roses, flag irises and peonies were shown in raised flowerbeds around the edge. By the 13th century not only did monasteries trade as nurserymen, providing seeds and plants, but commercial seed centres existed in both London and Oxford. By the middle of the century a London nursery could supply trees, flowers and turf for a new garden.

By the second half of the 13th century, royal gardens and those of important noblemen had "herbers" or pleasure grounds where flowers were for delight. Queen Eleanor of Provence (wife of Henry III) and her daughter-in-law Queen Eleanor of Castile (wife of Edward I) showed an interest in gardens. Eleanor even brought gardeners from Aragon and was credited with introducing the hollyhock *(Althaea rosea)* from the Holy Land via Spain.

A recent reconstruction of a garden inside the walls of Winchester Castle is based on a description of 1272. The modern planting includes only flowers which could have been grown by the two queens; many are natives, or are known to have been introduced earlier. Among them are flowers for spring: columbine, primroses and cowslip *(Primula veris)*, daffodil *(Narcissus pseudonarcissus)*, pansy and sweet violet *(Viola odorata)*, sweet rocket *(Hesperis matronalis)*, periwinkle and wall flower (by now the symbol of faithfulness in adversity or undying love). For early summer there are irises and peonies. Later in the season come bellflowers *(Campanula spp.)*, borage *(Borago officinalis)*, camomile *(Anthemis nobilis)*, cornflower *(Centaurea cyanus)*, feverfew *(Chrysanthemum parthenium)*, hollyhock, lavender, Madonna lily, mullein, opium poppy *(Papaver somniferum)*, soapwort and tansy *(Chrysanthemum vulgare)*. Later still, *Helleborus niger*, grown in a sheltered spot, will open for Christmas.

The gillyflower *(Dianthus caryophyllus)*, progenitor of the florists' carnations and pinks in the 17th and 18th centuries, as well as of modern garden "pinks", is first mentioned in Chaucer's translation of the *Roman de la Rose* in the early 14th

Herbaceous perennials – lady's mantle, sweet william, achillea, lysimachia, lupin – are classic ingredients of the well-stocked border

century, though principally as a spice. Daniel records the perfumed single pink growing in Queen Philippa's "herber" in the middle of the same century, and brought it to his own garden in Stepney. Queen Philippa also introduced rosemary in 1340 and was known for growing unusual plants. By the end of the 15th century there was a carnation cult, and special flowerpots or frames were devised to support the long stems and heavy double-headed flowers.

The earliest herbals were written by physicians who, as apothecaries, grew in their gardens the plants they needed for their medicines. The sciences of botany and medicine were inseparable. After the invention of printing in the 15th century, the herbals codified all known plants, though for useful qualities only. There were some strange theories. The Doctrine of Signatures, for example, held that the form and colour of plants indicated the diseases they would cure (thus the spotted leaves of *Pulmonaria* would cure the lungs, and hence lungwort as a common name); and

Astrological Botany stressed the influence of planets and stars on each herb. None of the herbals can have been much help to gardeners, but they do guide the historian.

The Grete Herbal, published by Treveris in 1526, was the first one to be illustrated, and remains a useful reference for the plant historian. William Turner's *A New Herball* (mid-16th century) included original plant descriptions and records of British natives, made from personal observation. John Gerard's famous *Herball* of 1597 provides a handy reference for plants available to the contemporary gardener. Gerard includes recent introductions from both North and South America.

The herbal was revised and improved by Thomas Johnson in 1633. Already many of the plants mentioned are garden cultivars rather than species. Some, such as the flag irises, peonies, day-lilies, daffodils and impatiens grown in 17th-century gardens, have unknown or incomplete histories. Impatiens *(Impatiens balsamifera)*, from India, had been cultivated in China since the seventh century and the opium poppy, from Asia, had been grown for at least 2000 years.

The florilegia of the early 17th century are a particular delight for flower gardeners. Decorative cultivated plants are crisply illustrated with copperplate etchings or engravings of a rare standard of excellence. Tulips, lilies, irises, peonies and narcissi, ranunculus from Asia (these were also to become a cult), sunflowers from America, tobacco plants and marvel of Peru *(Mirabilis jalapa)* were all illustrated to show their potential garden value.

The French marigold *(Tagetes patula)* and the African *Tagetes erecta*, both from Mexico, were 16th-century introductions. By 1610 John Tradescant was already helping Robert Cecil plant his new garden at Hatfield, and travelling in Europe to

It takes hours of work in the glasshouse to prepare a display of annuals grown from seed – one of the reasons why it is the keen amateur, rather than the parks professional, who now keeps alive the tradition of bedding out

find new flowers and fruit trees to put in it. Many of the newer plants were later wrongly presumed to be his or his son's introductions. In many instances the Tradescants were the first to try out plants which were already well documented, and by the 1630s their garden could be visited and plants assessed while growing.

Herbals considered flowers only for their practical usefulness, but Crispin van de Passe in his *Hortus Floridus* of 1614, and Parkinson in his *Paradisus Terrestris* of 1629, described their ornamental value. *Hortus Floridus* contained plates for the buyer himself to colour in. Arranged according to the seasons it made a useful garden catalogue to help in the choice of flowers to grow in contemporary knot garden patterns at great houses such as Theobalds (where John Gerard was gardener to Lord Burghley) and Wimbledon, and at the royal palaces at Nonsuch and Hampton Court. The open knots, "fitted for the groweth of choyse flowers", will have been planted with some of the newer introductions. Tudor and Jacobean knots were delineated with germander, hyssop, savory, thyme, thrift and santolina, and above all the new Dutch box *(Buxus sempervirens* "Suffruticosa"*)*. The flowerbeds within the patterns were planted with daffodils, fritillaries (including the crown imperial *Fritillaria imperialis*), Martagon lilies, hyacinths, crocuses, irises, tulips, anemones, auriculas and the simpler primroses or cowslips. Parkinson particularly recommends the gillyflower for summer effects, the cyclamen for autumn and hepaticas for early spring. He also suggests leucojums, muscari and bellflowers; more interestingly he mentions recent introductions brought in by the Virginia Company or the Spanish. These include spiderwort *(Tradescantia virginiana)*, sunflowers and marvel of Peru. He goes on to give instructions for growing "outlandish flowers" including bulbs to "give such grace to the garden, that the place will seem like a piece of tapestry of many glorious colours".

During the 17th and 18th centuries, systematic botany and knowledge of plant anatomy developed rapidly, and new plants were introduced at an ever-increasing rate. Sir Thomas Hanmer, the friend of John Evelyn and John Rea, wrote his garden notes during the Commonwealth, though his manuscript was not published until 1933. The *Garden Book* describes the cultivation of many flowers introduced in the previous 50 years, and much of the advice is practical. Rea's book, *Flora, Ceres and Pomona* (1665), intended originally as a revision and "updating" of Parkinson's *Paradisus*, is valuable to historian and horticulturalist alike. When he died, his own collection of flowering plants, including many auriculas, went to his son-in-law Samuel Gilbert, author of *The Florist's Vade Mecum* (1683).

A nursery price-list found among Sir Thomas Hanmer's papers included gillyflowers for 1s 6d a root, 11 anemone roots for 8s, and 6 kinds of auricula, with a double costing as much as 4s.

Alpine plants always seem happiest when, as here, they are planted among rocks and gravel

ROCKERY NOOK

Alpine plants have climbed to reach a pinnacle of popularity with British gardeners

By Stefan Buczacki

There was no particular moment in horticultural history when gardeners awoke to an appreciation of the exquisite beauty of the many and varied plants that have come to be known as alpines. Of course they do not all come from the Alps – similar growing conditions can also occur at sea-level in the far north, as well as at high altitude on the equator.

Many species whose natural homes are in rocky, high altitude areas (including, of course, those of the Scottish Highlands), had been collected and transplanted to gardens but the inherent problems in their cultivation were soon realised. They are plants of exacting habitats. They often experience widely differing extremes of temperature, both diurnally, between the scorching mid-day sun and the penetrating wind and frost of the night, and also seasonally, the mountain peaks often being baked in the height of summer but buried beneath snow for months on end in winter. Rainfall is very high, but the air is in constant movement and what little soil exists is very well drained. In the herbaceous border or formal bed, therefore, very few saxifrages, gentians or their alpine companions will survive.

The increase in foreign travel and the gradual attraction of the Alps and other mountainous areas to visitors and mountaineers in the early years of the 19th century prompted a great interest in the possibility of cultivating alpine plants. It became apparent that gardeners would have to find a way of duplicating their native conditions.

Various crude attempts at building mountain-tops in British gardens ensued, and one of the earliest seems to have been created in a quarry at Fonthill, Wiltshire, around 1820. Others followed, often attempting to build on a small scale entire mountains or even mountain ranges.

The Alps around Chamonix were recreated at Hoole House in Cheshire, and planted with a range of alpine plants in the 1830s. But rather typically, the whole was set in a garden of formal beds and later, miniature Swiss chalets were added too. Other rock gardens included alabaster snow on the peaks and even afforded to visitors the opportunity to view the scene through telescopes.

By the end of the last century serious alpine plant gardening gradually took over, to a large degree under the inspired guidance of the Yorkshireman, Reginald Farrer. He was dismissive of the rock gardens of the time: "The chaotic hideousness of the result is to be remembered with shudders ever after." Rock gardens came to be built as replicas of small, alpine habitats rather than entire mountains and by building them of stone appropriate to the region in which the gardens were sited, by carefully setting the rock in its natural bedding planes and by not placing the whole in an incongruous surround, success slowly followed.

Even so, the more difficult alpine plants were and still are grown in unheated, well-ventilated greenhouses where they are protected from the clinging damp of the British winter. Rock gardening on a grand outdoor scale has waned in recent years, largely because of the small size of most modern gardens and the astonishing cost of obtaining and transporting rock. Today, alpine gardening has never been more popular, but the plants are generally grown in small, raised "table" beds or in troughs or other containers of real or simulated stone.

Right: alyssum, Cytissus x praecox, aubrietia and saxifrages are all rock-garden favourites

When ground-space is at a premium, the ingenious gardener raises his horizons with hanging baskets and pots

Leonard Meager, in *The English Gardener* (1670), arranged his plants in separate categories: "Herbs for setting knots" and "Florist's Flowers", for example, as well as fruit trees and vegetables. By 1677 William Lucas's nursery listed 75 flower seeds and about 40 bulbs and rhizomes. The named flower "rootes" show how intensive selection had multiplied the numbers of plants available over the preceding 100 years. Alas, not all are known today. New garden layouts in the post-Restoration period called for large numbers of flowering plants to fill the knots and French parterres. The effect can be seen today in gardens such as Moseley Old Hall in Staffordshire and Westbury Court in Gloucestershire, where the beds are restricted to flowers known at that time.

Early in the 18th century, many new flowering plants reached this country from the eastern states of America. Henry Compton, Bishop of London, at Fulham Palace experimented with seeds sent by the Reverend John Banister, one of his ministers in Virginia. The shooting star, *Dodecatheon meadia*, first flowered at Fulham in 1709 and *Aster novae-angliae*, the forerunner of garden michaelmas daisies, in 1710. Not long before he died in 1713, he received a first batch of seeds from Mark Catesby, famous later for his *Natural History of Carolina, Florida and the Bahamas* (1747), who had just arrived in America. Catesby collected *Gillenia trifoliata*, two species of *Liatris* and the decorative garden lily *L. superbum*.

Peter Collinson, a Quaker, visited Fulham as a child to see the rare plants and later, through seeds sent by John Bartram and others, grew many new flowers in his garden at Mill Hill. These included late-flowering *Aster ericoides*, the white form of *Actaea alba, Cimicifuga racemosa* and *Geranium maculatum*. In 1734 John Custis of Williamsburg sent the superlative but difficult blue-flowered cowslip, *Mertensia virginiana*. Collinson and Bartram reached a financial agreement of five guineas a box of seeds, and Collinson distributed these to many other keen gardeners, including Philip Miller at the Chelsea Physic Garden.

Phlox, including the stoloniferous *Phlox divaricata*, *P. subulata*, *P. maculata* with cylindrical flowerheads, and *P. paniculata*, from which most of our named varieties descend, all arrived in the first half of the 18th century. It was hardy perennials like these that transformed the possibilities of the English flowerbed.

In 1722, in *The City Gardener*, Thomas Fairchild, a London florist and nurseryman, suggested flowers for growing in city squares, courtyards and balconies. He was the first person to make a scientific hybrid, crossing a carnation with a sweet william to produce *Dianthus caryophyllus* × *barbatus*, known as a "Fairchild's mule". Furber's *Twelve Months of Flowers* (1730–2), an illustrated nursery catalogue with engravings from flower paintings by the Flemish Casteels, lists 25 American plants as well as all the usual florists' flowers. Seeds of the sweet pea came from Sicily in 1699; it was included in the June painting for Furber's series and was the ancestor of all our modern cultivars.

Mary Somerset, Duchess of Beaufort, had two gardens, Badminton in Gloucestershire and one in Chelsea adjoining the Physic Garden. In both she grew exotics and commissioned botanical artists such as the Dutch Kyckius and his English pupil Frankcom to paint them during the first years of the 18th century. Well-preserved at Badminton, these illustrations are a useful source for dating introductions, many of which came from the Cape of Good Hope. The ivy-leaved geranium, *Pelargonium peltatum*, the Guernsey lily, *Nerine sarniensis*, and the magnificent foliage plant *Melianthus major*, were all grown by the duchess.

A small garden is no handicap to large ambition, particularly if the gardener specialises in a limited number of plants. Among the favoured species in this case are delphiniums, begonias and marigolds

Peter Collinson, like Sir Joseph Banks later in the century, was in touch with the leading botanists of the day; through them he obtained rare seeds from Russia and China as well as North America. Carl Linnaeus came to Collinson's garden at Mill Hill, and Collinson helped to promote his new *Systema Naturae* which revolutionised the study of botany. By 1768, in the eighth edition of his famous *Gardener's Dictionary* (first published 1731), Philip Miller adopted the Linnaean system and added descriptions of many new plants from America and elsewhere – though not from Australasia, whence Captain Cook and Sir Joseph Banks had not yet returned. Miller, in charge of the Chelsea Physic Garden from 1722 to 1770, and William Sherard, who endowed the Oxford Botanical Gardens, were influential in growing new plant introductions.

Hortus Elthamensis, by Dillenius (1732), catalogued the plants in Sherard's brother's garden at Eltham, described by a contemporary as "one of the richest

SEEDS OF MADNESS

The passion for tulips in the 17th century was so extreme that aficionados were prepared to offer the equivalent of £1500 for a pair of bulbs

By Penelope Hobhouse

The extraordinary folly of the tulip trade speculation in Holland, which reached its height in 1634–37, had little to do with a love of flowers. It was a form of gambling in "futures", in which self-coloured bulbs with their potential to "break" (now known to be caused by a virus infection spread by aphids) and produce a new form with bizarre striped variegation, were auctioned to the highest bidders. Eventually purchasers were unable to pay and dealers incurred enormous losses.

A happy legacy of the disastrous "tulipomania" is the wealth of 17th-century florilegia with fine-coloured and copperplate engravings showing some of the most striking flower variations.

There are two stories of the introduction of the tulip from Turkey to Europe. One theory gives credit to Portuguese travellers; from Portugal bulbs went to Flanders in the 1530s. The other, more generally accepted, is that Ghislain de Busbecq, ambassador from the Austrian Holy Roman Empire to the Sultan Süleyman the Magnificent in Constantinople from 1554–62, procured seed and bulbs. These first flowered in Augsburg and were described by the Zurich botanist Conrad Gessner in 1561.

Gessner had his first glimpse of a tulip in the garden of "the ingenius and learned Councillor Herwart . . . growing with a single, large reddish flower, like a red lily, with a pleasant smell, soothing and delicate, which soon leaves it". Most importantly, Busbecq also gave seed to the Flemish botanist Charles de L'Ecluse (Carolus Clusius) in 1573; and it was he who introduced tulips to England before 1582.

Clusius went on to deal extensively in yellow, red, white and purple as well as double forms and he was first to observe the tulip "phenomenon"; a single-coloured tulip will occasionally "break" into striped variegated forms with curled or fringed petals. But, while the Turks continued to favour elegant lyre-shaped flowerheads with pointed petals (the Ottoman Empire adopted the tulip as a symbol), Europeans liked a heavier oval shape with recurved petals; it was the latter type which were used as "breeders".

Clusius, professor of botany in Leyden by 1593, asked so high a price for his bulbs that "no-one could procure them even for money . . . the best and most of his plants were stolen by night . . . and those who had stolen the tulips lost no time in increasing them from seed." By the early 1600s tulips were all the rage in Paris and the seemingly absurd trade in bulbs began.

A miller exchanged his mill for one bulb of "Mère Brune" and a young Frenchman accepted a rare tulip appropriately named "Mariage de ma Fille" instead of the conventional dowry from his bride's father. Another exchanged a brewery, valued at 30,000 francs for "Tulipe brasserie", and ladies in Paris sewed tulip flowers, from bulbs worth 4000 florins each, on their dresses instead of costly jewels. By 1623 in Holland one of the most famous tulips, "Semper Augustus", with red and white petals, was sold for "thousands of florins" plus a carriage and pair, an owner refusing an offer of 3000 florins (£1500 today) for two bulbs.

At the height of the *Tulpenwoede,* or mania, dealers and tulip "fanciers" would strike a bargain: when planting time came in the autumn, if the market price had fallen the dealer paid the fancier the difference; if it had risen, the tulip-fancier paid the dealer. No bulbs actually changed hands.

Self-coloured cultivated tulips were known as "breeders"; from time to time these would "break" into the desirable variegated forms. These could be increased by offsets which would probably have a variegated flower. Seed, which took seven years or more to flower, could also be used. The highest prices paid by speculators were bizarre and often in kind. For one "Viceroy" bulb the goods exchanged included two loads of wheat, four loads of rye, four fat oxen, eight fat pigs, twelve fat sheep, two hogsheads of wine, four barrels of eight-florin beer, two barrels of butter, 1000lb of cheese, a complete bed, a suit of clothes and a silver beaker. The whole value was 2500 florins.

A group of Haarlem florists, hearing that a cobbler at The Hague had grown a black tulip, haggled to purchase it for 1500 florins. Once it was in their possession they threw it on the ground and trampled it underfoot. They explained to the astonished cobbler that they, too, had bred a black tulip and wanted no competition in the market, adding they would have willingly given him 10,000 florins for it if he had proved a more persistent bargainer. The cobbler was inconsolable, took to his bed and soon died of disappointment.

In England a more commonsense approach prevailed. Parkinson in his *Paradisus* (1629) praises tulips "above and beyond" all other flowers "both for their stately aspect, and for the admirable varieties of colours, that daily doe arise in them," planting so that "one colour answering a setting of another, that the place where they stand may resemble a piece of curious needlework, or piece of painting". Thomas Johnson, editor of Gerard's *Herbal* in 1633, assured the reader that tulips were the "lilies of the field" of the New Testament, and the Tradescants grew 50 different varieties in their Lambeth garden.

In the 1650s Sir Thomas Hanmer, close friend of John Evelyn and John Rea, writes of the tulip in his *Garden Book* as "the Queen of Bulbous plants" and gives instructions for tulip cultivation in raised beds 4ft wide, and with soil mounded in the centre "that all the flowers may bee seene the better". He describes ranks of named tulips growing in four little bordered beds at Bettisfield, his own garden in the Welsh Marches; he recommends growing them alone or with anemones on the outside edge. Blue and white Delft pyramid vases with a series of tubular spouts were especially made for tulips at the end of the 17th century. A fine pair can be seen at Dyrham Park near Bath.

Striped tulips remained fashionable until the Napoleonic Wars. After that, instead of being mainly grown by Florists' Societies for perfection of individual flower, tulips were massed in flowerbeds and single-colour petals became more fashionable. Later, for commerce, the Dutch developed short-stemmed Flamandes while the French favoured longer-stemmed Bizarres.

Experiments in breeding were designed to produce our modern groups of cultivated tulips planned to cover a long spring-flowering season. Among these, parrot and fringed have most resemblance to 17th-century virus-produced "broken" tulips. Rembrandts, with stripes and splashes of colour, are no longer available commercially because of a danger of the virus spreading to other bulbs. By the 1890s hybridists in England favoured the late-flowering cottage-type tulips, which are still a recognised type although they are too mixed in breeding to be an official category.

Small species introductions from central Asia have provided parent plants for other modern tulips; *T. fosteriana* (in particular the creamy-white "Purissima"), *T. greigii, T. kaufmanniana* and *T. praestans* are all recognised hybrid groups from which, given suitable culture, bulbs will last for many seasons. The lily-flowered tulip, a hybrid from 1914, has several fine garden-worthy forms. "White Triumphator" is tall and elegant; one of the best with a strong sweet scent is "Mrs Moon" with lemon-yellow petals on shorter 12in. stems.

The yellow *T. sylvestris* is a European (and English) native found in woodlands and known by the end of the 16th century; it is now rare and protected in the wild. *T. clusiana* from Persia (later it was found to be a native of the Mediterranean basin) was in flower for Clusius in April 1607; it is mentioned by Parkinson (1629) as growing in English gardens but he found it neither hardy nor able to set seed in the damp climate.

Tulips to sell your soul for: Dr Thornton's "Temple of Flora", of 1811. Clockwise from top: Louis XIV, Duchess of Devonshire, General Washington, Earl Spencer, La Majestieuse, Gloria Mundi, La Triomphe Royale

Best of the Bunch

"There is your garden mallows, double hollyhocks, snapdragons, toadflax, foxgloves, thistles, scabious, mullein, fennel flower, bindweed, lark-heel, Canterbury bells, thorn apples, apples of love, garden lupins, scarlet beans, snails, caterpillars, oak of Jerusalem and Cappadocia, trifles adored by country women in their gardens, but of no esteem to a florist who is taken up with things of most value," wrote the Reverend Samuel Gilbert in 1683

By Mary Keen

By the time of the Restoration, the traditional cottage garden mixture had started to lose its universal appeal. Many cottagers and artisans now began to concentrate on the value of individual flowers, which meant growing them in a limited number of varieties and cultivating them to a state of perfection. In the age of metaphysical conceits, the flowers of quite ordinary men were as rarified and artificial as poetry. Today hybridisers seem concerned with extending flowering seasons or inventing dwarf strains of perfectly good plants. Our ancestors were more interested in the quest for the perfect flower. By the 18th century the quest had narrowed to only eight varieties – anemone, auricula, carnation, hyacinth, pink, polyanthus, ranunculus and tulip. The intense cultivation and showmanship associated with these few species came to be known as Floristry.

The craze may have been accelerated by the arrival of the Huguenot weavers, who are thought to have introduced the auricula at the end of the 16th century. Strongholds of the art of floristry, and of the auricula in particular, were around the weavers' towns where the Huguenot refugees settled. These plants were scarcely ever grown by the aristocracy or the gentry, possibly because they needed constant attention. Gardeners at great houses were too busy growing fruit or tending trees to bother with such small-scale horticulture. By the end of the 18th century the botanists of the day, who were discovering new plants from North America and the Cape, looked down on the trifling preoccupations of the Florists.

Trifling in the sense of small it certainly was, but these people were gardening on a tiny scale, where space and not time was at a premium. Their concentration on the particular was like the art of the miniature: their hobby became an obsession. People would spend two weeks' wages on a new form, or walk 50 miles to see another. Elaborate rules and rituals accompanied their displays; they even built theatres to stage their plants, sometimes painting scenery to hang behind the pots. (At Calke Abbey in Derbyshire an example of an auricula theatre exists in an alcove in the kitchen garden.) The attraction of Floristry in close-knit communities was so strong that it remained popular until the end of the 19th century, when the artificiality of striped or variegated flowers suddenly fell from favour, and naturalism was all the rage. By that time the Florists had had a very long innings, but almost three centuries of specialisation has left us with very few of their flowers. Most of the plants they grew were too highly bred to survive without the dedication of their creators.

Florists' favourites: carnations from Dr Thornton's "Temple of Flora", 1803

The art of bringing flowers to a perfect state of bloom by artificial means was well suited to the weavers and lacemakers who worked at home. They concentrated on flowers which needed no heat but benefited from some protection. If it rained they could leave their looms and have a pot under cover before the "farina" on the leaves of the auricula could be disturbed. Great attention was paid to the merits of different manures. Some growers even fed their plants with raw meat, while others preferred to put their trust in goose or sheep dung.

gardens that England ever possessed". These garden lists, together with botanical treatises and books on garden design which proliferated in the 18th century, give a valuable insight into the development of British horticultural methods.

Many plants were first tried out in nurseries, whose owners were skilled in propagation. The generally held view that flowers were banished from the English 18th-century garden during the second half of the century becomes untenable as more is known of designers other than Capability Brown, though the flowers recommended for use in published garden plans reveal no widespread use of the new exotics. Spence used pinks, carnations and "little flowers" to edge walks; violets and cowslips were scattered in meadow grass. At Woodburn Farm, Philip Southcote decorated the fronts of his shrub beds with well-established favourites such as hollyhocks, lilies, peonies, sweet williams, sunflowers and crown imperials as well as golden rod, *Solidago* and asters (probably newly introduced from America through Bartram).

At Paisley, the weavers specialised in pinks. Sacheverell Sitwell suggested that their bright colours must have been one of the few consolations for living in that dour Presbyterian town, where drinking and dancing were banned. In Cheshire and Lancashire polyanthus in gold- and silver-laced forms were prized. In Derbyshire, tulips appealed – although these were slightly less popular until the 19th century because bulbs were so expensive.

For all of these flowers and the several other Florist's varieties, competitions were held. In the early days the prize was likely to be a copper kettle, but by the 19th century it was more often plate, to the value of a quarter of the entrance fee. Thomas Hogg of Paddington wrote the definitive work for the Florist in 1832. He describes preparing a carnation for show with tweezers and bodkins, "to assist the petals in falling to their places". (Mr Nunn, a barber of the same date, used to shear off any irregularities in the flowers with a practised hand.)

"Pluck out," writes Mr Hogg, "all pouncy and superfluous dull leaves, and those that will not lie, whirl with our bodkin into the crown of the flower." No wonder the artificiality of such methods repelled the botanists and naturalists.

If the Florists concentrated on growing flowers for close inspection, there were others who took a more general view of the pursuit of excellence. In the 17th and 18th centuries, learned societies of gentlemen gathered for lectures on philosophy or gardening, where plants were also featured. Tea or coffee, tankards of ale, 12 clean pipes, an ounce of tobacco, a chamber pot and both Greek and Latin lexicons were provided at these meetings. Something less rarefied was arranged in 1827, when the first horticultural fête was held at Chiswick, with refreshments and a brass band. This proved so popular with the aristocracy that more shows had to be held in the summer months, under canvas. By 1866, Prince Albert was interested enough to act as patron to an even bigger show, at Kensington Gardens.

This led to a series of spectacular fêtes at the Embankment Gardens of the Inner Temple, with huge horticultural displays, refreshments and military music. By 1912 the Templars had had enough of the disruption, and the show moved to the grounds of the Royal Hospital at Chelsea. All the exhibits were arranged to look like flower-beds; there was a heated marquee where you could buy 100 orchids for £5, and Mr Cutbush's cut bushes walked off with the topiary prize. There were tools and sundries, like leather boots for the pony that pulled the lawnmower, and everyone had a thoroughly enjoyable day.

This example inspired the Royal Horticultural Society, to follow suit. In 1913 the first Chelsea Flower Show was staged under its auspices. This was a resounding success and continued as such until 1917 when it was cancelled out of patriotism. When the war was over, the shows resumed at Chelsea with a week's delay for the General Strike and a break for the Second World War. Afterwards, Lord Aberconway remarked even in the midst of rationing and stringent national economy that, "Whatever else we do without, we should not go without a Chelsea Flower Show next year."

Gradually the show became less of an event for the aristocracy and more of an outing for the mass of amateurs. Nurseries did the bulk of their trade at Chelsea until the introduction of garden centres from America meant that it lost its marketing edge. More crowds than ever have been attracted to the spectacle in recent years, so that in 1988 for the first time, entrance to the show was rationed and tickets allocated in advance. In the great marquee at Chelsea in the last half of the 20th century, the scientists and Florists finally meet. Stands of auriculas or small collections of Florist's tulips can be seen next to exotic and alien species plants. In an age where gardens are shrinking as leisure expands, it may be that Floristry is due for a revival.

A group of auriculas, also from Thornton's "Temple of Flora"

Paintings by Thomas Robins show Richard Bateman's garden at Old Windsor in about 1740; colourful circular flowerbeds resemble those designed by William Mason in the (recently restored) walled garden at Nuneham in the 1770s, and those surrounding Gray's monument at Stoke Park in the 1790s. Mason's flowers included hollyhocks, lupin, lungwort, marvel of Peru, pink-flowered achilleas and the sweet-scented mignonette, recently introduced from Egypt, as well as roses.

Within some of his large layouts, Humphrey Repton designed garden areas for American plants, and by the 1800s he and his sons were advising that flowerbeds, edged with low basketwork trellis, should be scattered in the grass.

By the close of the 18th century the trickle of plant introductions had become a flood. Hardy American flowers continued to arrive, and Francis Masson, the first official collector for Kew (sent by Sir Joseph Banks), brought back flowers from South Africa which needed hot dry summers. He also searched for plants in the Canaries, Azores, Spain and Portugal. In the Cape of Good Hope Masson found sun-loving bulbs such as crinums, gladioli, ixias, nerines and, of course, agapanthus, though these had been known in England since 1692.

He also discovered tender perennials such as crocosmias and kniphofias, which with ericas, succulents, cacti and proteas proved sufficiently drought-resistant when packed in dry sand to survive the journey home. Few were hardy in English gardens but many of the bulbs could be treated as annuals and dried off when dormant. Gazanias, arctotis and osteospermums became popular for Victorian bedding schemes. Today the garden hybrid *Crinum × powelli*, summer hyacinth *(Galtonia candicans)* and the graceful angels' fishing rods *(Dierama pulcherrimum)* are among the South African flowers which will survive most English winters.

The popularity of the many new annuals from both South America and South Africa was greatly enhanced by the new glass and hot-bed technology of the 19th century. Victorian bedding-out schemes remain popular today, and many of the same plants are still used. Tender plants such as cosmos, dahlias, zinnias and *Lobelia fulgens* came from Mexico before 1800. Blue-flowered *Lobelia erinus* (already brought to England from South Africa in 1752) was of immense importance in garden schemes by the middle of the 19th century. South American alonsoas and petunias (close relatives of the tobacco plant) came from Brazil in 1823; calceolarias, verbenas and *Salvia splendens*, the garish scarlet bedding sage still seen in municipal layouts, were all available by the mid-1800s. As early as 1829 *The Gardener's Magazine* describes a circular bed of salvia, underplanted with mignonette.

By the middle of the 19th century, flowerbeds were designed as floral ribbons or in concentric bands of colour. Yellow calceolarias, scarlet or blue salvias, tender pelargoniums (by the 1840s the first dwarf zonal geranium "Tom Thumb" became generally available), petunias and lobelia were grown annually from cuttings or seed. In 1834 David Douglas died after searching for new plants on the western coast of North America. From California he had sent back seed of new annuals – clarkias in multi-coloured tints; golden-yellow *Eschscholzia californica*; red and yellow daisy-flowered gaillardias; the self-seeding poached-egg flower *Limnanthes douglasii*, which was used at first in formal bedding schemes but was quickly adopted by cottage gardeners; and *Phacelia tanacetifolia*, with blue bell-like flowers. Douglas also introduced tender penstemons from the American north-west which, with their many garden hybrids, remain valuable border plants with a long flowering period.

Victorian head gardeners such as Fleming at Trentham and Beaton at Shrubland Park took advantage of the new introductions to develop their own highly contrasting colour schemes, which they popularised in horticultural journals. Tender bedders and annuals could not be put out until after the last frost – probably in

The triumphant mixture of fruit, vegetables and flowers is in the great rural tradition of the 19th century

early June. Writers such as Shirley Hibberd encouraged the massing of tulips and hyacinths for spring effects, with biennial wallflowers and forget-me-nots which could survive the cold of winter; the bulbs were lifted each year after flowering.

Nurserymen and hybridisers responded to the fashionable demand for highly-bred tulips with specific flower characteristics and reliable times of flowering. Daffodil breeding received a similar impetus; by the 19th century it was difficult to differentiate between species and garden varieties. By now, daffodil-hunters were searching for true species such as *Narcissus cyclamineus* and *N. triandrus* on the slopes of the Pyrenees. Sometimes they were found still growing in old gardens but needed firm botanical identification. Today there are more than 1800 narcissi cultivars to choose from.

By the 1860s, semi-tropical foliage plants were sometimes used in place of the floral displays. At Battersea Park, tender bananas *(Musa ensete)* from Abyssinia, *Begonia rex* from Assam, *Wigandia caracasana* from Mexico, and black-leaved perillas *(Perilla frutescens)* from the Far East made the garden famous during the 1870s. The castor-oil plant, *Ricinus communis*, from tropical Africa, known since the 16th century, was also used.

Alternative "styles" included low-growing carpet-bedding in which exotic foliage plants such as purple and golden-leaved alternanthera and *Iresine herbstii*,

A Barmaid on a Stalk

Plant-breeders have taken the dahlia bravely into new realms of blowsiness, where no flower has gone before

By Peter Seabrook

Botanists travelling with the conquistadores in the 16th century first noted the wild dahlia species. It grew 30ft or more high, straggling up among the trees in Mexico. For centuries the Aztec Indians had used the stems to make water pipes, with little thought for the single, daisy-type flower. A sweet extract from the root had also been prescribed for medicinal use.

But it was another 200 years before the first seeds and tubers were grown successfully in Spain. Although named as *D. pinnata, D. rosea* and *D. coccinea,* it seems likely that they were hybrids raised by Spanish settlers rather than true species. They were grown in the Royal Gardens of Madrid in 1789 by the curator, Abbé Cavanilles, and described in detail in his book, *Icones.* He was helped by a Swedish botanist and former pupil of Linnaeus called Andreas Dahl, and the apparently generous abbé kindly named his new-found plants Dahlia in honour of his able assistant.

Dahlias spread slowly across Europe in the early 19th century, when the French tried to sell the tubers as an alternative to potatoes. In London they were offered as Jerusalem artichokes, but people found them tasteless and relegated them to animal food.

Change was not long coming, however. Dahlias grow from seed to flowering in a single summer, and every seedling is different. By the 1830s, therefore, their potential flower power and remarkable ability to provide a wide variety of colour and shape was fully appreciated. Top of the popularity charts at this time was the double globe form, called Double Show (single colour) or Fancy (several colours) and now known as the Ball Group.

The tree dahlia, Dahlia imperialis, was discovered by the conquistadores in Mexico in the 16th century

There soon followed a rush of high fashion and high prices – 100–200 guineas a plant – as thousands of new cultivars were introduced. The arrival of spiky-petalled cactus dahlias in the latter half of the 19th century increased their popularity still further among the wealthy Victorians. Named *Dahlia Juarezii* after a Mexican president of that time, the first spiky-petalled flower was, by all accounts, raised in The Netherlands.

One serious problem remained. While many different colours and flower types had developed, the stems were still long and weak. It took the arrival of the semi-double, broader petalled and stiffer-stemmed peony type from across the Channel to make the necessary improvement.

Popularity fell away somewhat in the 1930s, although single, fairly dwarf Coltness types in red, yellow and mixed colours were grown for bedding. Then, in the Forties, Charles Unwin, working in his back garden rather than in the fields of his family firm, raised the Unwins Dwarf Double Bedding Dahlias. After the Second World War there was an insatiable demand for colour, and bunches of gaudy cut-flower cactus and decorative dahlias were sold by the million at factory gates and flower stalls. Dobbies of Edinburgh staged great displays of bloom at the Chelsea Flower Show, and orders were delivered by rail in a matter of days. At the same time, other dahlia specialists were building displays of their latest novelties at summer flower shows.

The abandonment of railway parcel delivery and the cost and length of parcel post sounded the death knell of the mail order trade. The switch then was to small, so-called pot tubers produced by the tens of millions by the Dutch, and still sold today, packed in polythene bags.

Membership of the National Dahlia Society is a handy barometer of popularity. It remained at just a few hundred from 1881 to 1950, soared to more than 7000 in the Sixties and now stands at 4000. Keen exhibitors still grow many different varieties in the 10 groups and five different flower sizes within each group. But today's trend is towards very free but small-flowering miniatures on compact plants to suit patio gardeners. This year for the first time sees an F1 hybrid double bedding dahlia, "Sunny Yellow", which, unlike any of its predecessors, comes true from seed.

From the infinitely subtle to the ultimately vulgar: five modern dahlia hybrids, shown actual size

Miniature Cactus
"Rokesly Mini"

Anemone
"Scarlet Comet"

Giant Decorative
"Hamari Gold"

Collerette
"La Cierva"

Medium Semi-Cactus
"Vuurvogel"

KEEPING STOCK

The future of our most important flower species is safeguarded by the keeping of national collections – many of them held by amateur enthusiasts in their back gardens

By Geoff Hamilton

The importance of the collection and conservation of plants has long been recognised in Britain. The first collections were gathered together in botanic gardens as long ago as 1621 when the Oxford Botanic Garden was founded.

The main function of botanic gardens was originally connected with medicine, hence their frequent association with universities such as at Oxford, Cambridge, Edinburgh and Liverpool. Another notable example is the Chelsea Physic Garden, founded in 1673. But botanic garden collections refer mainly to species – plants as they occur in the wild – and they do not generally include cultivars.

This has traditionally been left to enthusiasts who have collected plants for aesthetic reasons and without any real thought to conservation. There are many examples of huge collections built up in the 18th and 19th centuries when the vogue for plant-hunting in foreign parts was at its height. Alas, there are almost as many instances of the demise of these collections through loss of interest, because large gardens have been split up, or for economic reasons.

Custodian of the national narcissus collection is Martin Harwood. He has more than 1800 varieties in his garden at Chobham in Surrey

The first attempt at a true National Species Collection was made shortly after the Second World War when the Ministry of Agriculture made finance available for a number of botanic gardens to plant collections of some genera felt to be horticulturally important. Kew, Wisley and Cambridge were among the participants. The scheme never really got off the ground and was abandoned 10 years later.

In May 1977, the Royal Horticultural Society's journal *The Garden* was devoted mainly to the increasing concern for the conservation of threatened plants and gardens. It became clear from the subsequent correspondence that there were many organisations and individuals already working in the field of conservation, but there was no coordinated effort.

The conference on "The Practical Role of Gardens in the Conservation of Rare and Threatened Plants" was held in October 1978 and this resulted in the establishment of the National Council for the Conservation of Plants and Gardens (NCCPG) in 1979.

The aim of the scheme was to set up a series of collections consisting of all the representatives in cultivation of particular groups of plants. These would include both cultivars and species, though not necessarily in the same collection.

Despite the difficulties of such an ambitious project, the response was remarkable. In 1988 there are 400 collections of 315 different genera and part genera (some are duplicated), ranging from Abelia to Zelkova.

Among the holders of the national collections are botanic gardens, schools and colleges, local authorities, the National Trust, commercial

with translucent carmine stems and leaves (both introduced from South America in 1864), were massed in geometric schemes with fleshy-leaved South African crassulas and Mexican echeverias. By 1866 *Iresine herbstii* already patterned the flower beds in Hyde Park. Today few private gardens can afford such fine seasonal displays, though municipal Victorian-style bedding schemes keep up the demand. In many towns, elaborate floral clocks laid out in flowers or foliage still record the passing of the hours.

Many of the South African and South American plants, with Banks's introductions from Australia (among which are very few good non-woody garden plants), needed special conditions often beyond the means of ordinary gardeners. But hardy plants which would survive English winters without hothouse protection had also continued to arrive from the northern hemisphere. A list of hardy plants grown in England before 1799, published recently by The Cranborne Manor Garden Centre, offers a good idea of the variety available. It is based on William Aiton's *Hortus Kewensis*, which in 1789 listed a total of 5535 plants in cultivation at Kew, including 1400 bulbs, tubers, corms and herbaceous perennials which were nurseries and private individuals. The lilac collection, for example, is held by the Brighton Parks and Gardens Department, the clematis collection by nurseryman Raymond Evison in Guernsey, the autumn crocus (*Colchicum*) and the snowdrops (*Galanthus*) are at the RHS gardens at Wisley, and michaelmas daisies are held by private gardeners, the Misses Allen and Huish, near Bristol. The Lychnis collection is maintained by the Hinchley Wood First and Middle School at Esher in Surrey – an enterprise which in 1987 won them the youth section of the European Conservation Awards.

Owners of collections are asked to keep an agreed number of specimens and to improve the collection where possible. The collections should be accessible to the public where possible, and propagation material should be made available, for which the owner may charge.

There are three main functions of the national collections. The first is to conserve garden plants threatened with extinction. Second, the collections should be accessible for research purposes – not just scientific but artistic, horticultural and historic, too. Third, the collected plants could be important as a source of propagation material. The advent of laboratory methods of increasing plants through tissue culture has made this all the more possible.

Until recently, for example, the deep maroon, chocolate-scented *Cosmos atrosanguineus* was so scarce it could be classified as rare. It is a tricky plant to propagate by normal methods, so any re-introduction would have been slow. But it has been found to respond to micropropagation and is now readily available in garden centres.

The task of collecting all known garden plants is immense. Though the NCCPG enters into agreements to transfer collections if owners have to give them up, some are likely to fall by the wayside. So the aim for the future is not only to make collections of *all* genera that are cultivated in gardens, but to form three duplicate collections – one in private hands, one held by a public institution and one by a scientific body.

Isabel Allen (left) and Joy Huish, who keep the national collection of michaelmas daisies in their garden near Bristol

hardy in English gardens. Catmint, scabious and the autumn-flowering gentian had come from the Caucasus in the early 1800s; the perennial evening primrose, *Oenothera missouriensis*, arrived from Missouri in 1811. By 1831 the Reverend H. T. Ellacombe was able to include all these recent discoveries among the 600 bulbous and herbaceous plants in his vicarage garden at Bitton in Gloucestershire.

Sixty years later his son, the better-known Canon Ellacombe, added a new range of hardy plants from the Far East. And by the end of the century many new hybrids, particularly of asters and delphiniums, had extended the range of hardy perennials for use in the herbaceous borders made popular by Gertrude Jekyll.

It seemed as if there were not a corner of the world which might not contribute its mite of colour to the English garden. By the middle of the 19th century the interiors of China and Japan had been opened up to plant explorers, and collecting in earnest had begun in northern India and the foothills of the Himalayas. This new material was a survival in the wild from pre-glacial times, demonstrating the ice-cap's less southerly advance in the Far East. The range of native European and North American flora, originally linked throughout the northern hemisphere, by comparison

Making a Packet

The seed trade provides the lifeblood of the amateur's garden, and is one of history's greatest growth industries

By Arthur Hellyer

Seeds have always been the most convenient way of transporting and distributing plants, especially over long distances. They also provide a natural means of introducing genetic variations, some of which can be useful to farmers and gardeners, and they are far less likely than cuttings, divisions or other vegetative methods of increase to pass on acquired diseases.

By the 12th century, farmers well understood they would get better crops if they used seed-corn grown on different land rather than continuously saving their own – a development which probably led to the later involvement of corn chandlers and provision merchants in a more general seed trade. Certainly by the 13th century, seeds of numerous plants were being purchased freely. In 1275 one William Gardiner was paid for fruit trees, bulbs and seeds, and so could be regarded as a very early nurseryman and seedsman. In 1395, the accounts of Winchester College include a pound of onion seed – enough to sow a quarter of an acre.

In medieval times, new or improved varieties of plants were distributed from the monasteries, both as plants and as seeds, with instructions about their cultivation. After the dissolution of the monasteries, much of this work passed to the landed gentry, who by this time were able to build themselves comfortable houses, surrounded with good gardens cultivated by trained gardeners. Seeds and plants began to be distributed even more freely, and the emerging middle classes, as well as the peasants, started to reap the benefit.

Nevertheless, the first known seed list did not appear until 1677, from William Lucas, who described himself as a milliner with a shop at Strand Bridge, London, at the sign of the Naked Boy. It was remarkably comprehensive, containing 74 flower varieties and, even more surprisingly, seeds of 30 shrubs and trees. Among them were pyracantha, myrtle, cork oak, *Hibiscus syriacus* and two kinds of laburnum. The entire list is reproduced in John Harvey's excellent *Early Gardening Catalogues,* published by Phillimore in 1972.

Despite all this enterprise and activity, John Harvey believes there was no really *popular* demand for new introductions until after 1775, and that another three-quarters of a century passed before the coming of the railways encouraged a rapidly expanding middle class to demand enough plants to justify mass production. Thereafter, the story moves on rapidly and dramatically.

First, a large number of fiercely competing firms came into being. Sutton and Sons established themselves in Reading, James Carter and Son in London, Samuel Dobie and Son at Chester, Thompson and Morgan at Ipswich, Bees at Liverpool, Dickson, Brown and Tait at Altrincham, Dobbie and Co. at Edinburgh, J. L. Clucas at Ormskirk, Unwins at Histon, W. H. Simpson and Sons at Birmingham, Ryders at St Albans, and many more. Large wholesale firms also emerged, both to supply some of the retail seedsmen and to sell seeds direct to shops.

At first, all the seed was sold by weight or measure. It was stored in drawers or bags, and weighed on delicate scales similar to those used by chemists. Alternatively, if the seeds were large, they were ladled out by the pint, or fraction of a pint, in wooden seed-measures resembling thimbles on sticks, in a range of 20 different sizes. Big firms found it worthwhile to employ travelling salesmen who not only visited the retail shops but also the larger gardens, where they met the head gardeners and discussed their seed orders for the year. At this stage it became a highly personalised trade, with the result that an endless proliferation of names was applied to varieties practically indistinguishable from each other, and in many cases actually identical.

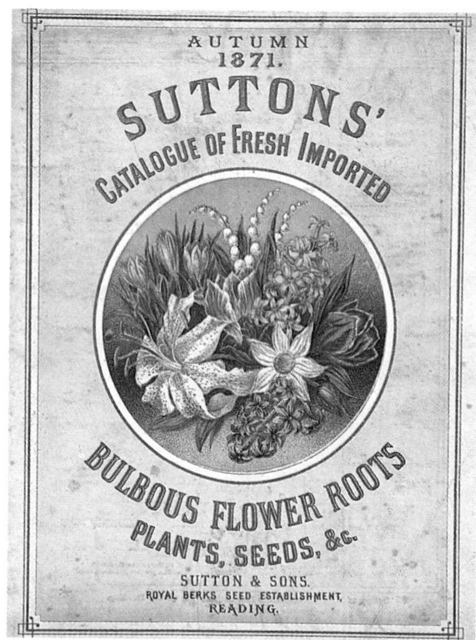

Major seed firms were well established by the latter half of the 19th century

The idea of pre-packeting seeds, so that they could be sold in any shop that cared to display them, gave another great boost to the trade, though for many years it was only the cheaper varieties that were sold like this. The first penny pictorial packets were sold by Bees, through Woolworths, in 1925. Gradually the practice spread, however, and in the early Sixties the introduction of hermetically sealed foil packets, ensuring the longest possible life for the seeds, changed the whole picture. Packeting became the rule for most flower and vegetable seeds, and eventually even grass seed followed the same way.

Until then the story had been one of expansion and diversification, with almost all the national firms introducing their own specialities. These were often bred in their own nurseries, though increasingly they were "bulked up" overseas in places like Italy, Czechoslovakia and western North America with climates more favourable than ours for cultivating and ripening seed crops.

By early this century, French, Dutch, German and American seedsmen were all engaged in successful plant-breeding programmes. Names rapidly multiplied and there was a great deal of duplication or near-duplication of varieties. It quickly became clear that there would have to be some rationalisation, and it came about partly because of the creation of the EEC and partly because of the much more difficult trading conditions after the Fifties.

Seed firms began to amalgamate, and many famous names disappeared. New regulations for vegetables made it illegal to market identical or nearly identical varieties under different names. Much of the breeding thereafter passed from the retail seed firms to the wholesalers, and also to specialist breeders who pursued their objectives with the aid of trained scientists.

At first, much of this breeding work was done in America, particularly in California and Colorado, but soon the Japanese were joining in with great success – and then came Costa Rica, a country whose advantages include cheap labour, and climatic zones ideal for many of the most popular flowering plants. Eighty per cent of the world's annual flower seed now comes from Costa Rica – distributed in bulk by air, and graded and packeted by the individual seed firms who buy and sell it on.

All these developments were accelerated by one crucial discovery – that first generation hybrids (F1 varieties in the seed catalogues) produce a far better standard of uniformity than non-hybrid varieties. By this means it also became clear that some popular perennial plants, including geraniums (strictly pelargoniums), previously increased only by means of cuttings, could be produced just as reliably and far more cheaply from seed. A third bonus was that the hybrid varieties gave the raiser complete exclusivity, since there was no need for the inbred parents from which they were produced ever to leave the seed farm. No rival could get at them and seed raised from the hybrids would produce only useless mongrels.

The latest move is for some of the big American seed producers to return part of their breeding programmes to Europe, and particularly to Britain, to take advantage of the different climatic conditions here. In the end, the best way to ensure success is to breed and test new varieties in the same environment in which they will be grown.

had been much reduced as the ice-cap spread. Most of the eastern plants were hardy and vigorous in the English climate, and many Asiatic flowers "naturalised" in their new environment – a potential fully exploited in William Robinson's exhortation to "wild" gardening published in 1870. Robinson encouraged gardeners to plant both exotics and natives in natural drifts, where they would thrive and spread.

Not all the new introductions were species. Many, including the day-lilies, hostas and peonies, had been cultivated in Chinese and Japanese gardens for centuries and, being tolerant of most soils, have since proved ideal subjects for hybridising. Breeders have also multiplied the range of Asiatic primulas and lilies. In general, these require acid conditions.

Between 1880 and the Second World War, plant exploration in the Far East yielded more and more good plants. Perennial rodgersias, ligularias, lilies and meconopsis were for woodland and waterside; *Gentiana sino-ornata* and yet more primula species proved to be lime-haters; sun-loving *Ceratostigma willmottiana* thrived in open borders. It is hard now to imagine a garden without them.

A meconopsis, *M. simplicifolia*, had flowered in England as early as 1848 – the first of the Himalayan poppies to be discovered, forging a generic link with the Welsh poppy, *Meconopsis cambrica*, on the other side of the world. Joseph Hooker, later director of Kew in succession to his father, collected an Asian meconopsis, *M. napaulensis*, with purplish flowers in 1852; later, variants with pink or yellow petals were found. But not all are grown for their blooms. Some such as the monocarpic *M. regia* from Nepal (1931) have grey-green or golden silky foliage rosettes which brighten a winter landscape.

Most exciting of all was probably the French missionary Abbé Delavay's blue meconopsis, *M. betonicifolia*, which he recorded in the Yunnan in 1886. It was sent home as a dried specimen in 1913 by Colonel Bailey, but finally rediscovered by Frank Kingdon Ward in south Tibet and introduced to England in 1926. Kingdon Ward memorably described his first sighting: "Suddenly I looked up and there, like a blue panel dropped from heaven – a stream of blue poppies dazzling as sapphires in the pale light."

Thanks to the diligence of Kingdon Ward and the other plant hunters, and to the skill of the home gardeners, there is now no need to travel to the foothills of the Himalayas to share such experiences.

Plant exploration still continues in the second half of the 20th century, though necessarily with rather less freedom. Today, in order to protect natural environments and dwindling stocks of native flora, the taking of wild plants has to be strictly supervised. Most countries allow only seed collecting, and many have had to restrict even that.

V

THE GREENHOUSE EFFECT

By Brian Jackman

In making the English garden, frost and cold winds are old and familiar foes. Temperate our climate may be, but growing tender plants calls for a degree of control over the environment. Protected gardening began the day someone realised a plant would grow better in the lee of a south-facing rock. Later came the discovery that warmth was essential to the wellbeing of growing plants, and last of all came an understanding of the need for light – an understanding which gave rise both to the spectacular glasshouses of Victorian England and today's continuing vogue for conservatories and back-garden greenhouses.

Joseph Paxton's "conservative wall" – an elegant series of stepped glasshouses at Chatsworth, built originally for camellias

Most visitors to Tresco in the Isles of Scilly come by boat from the neighbouring island of St Mary's. Clambering ashore at the lonely quay of Carn Near, it is hard to imagine anything but gorse and grass growing on this windswept Atlantic island. Yet within half a mile at Tresco Abbey Gardens is a collection of plants without equal in Britain.

Here, 28 miles off the toe-end of Cornwall, the air is distilled over 2000 miles of ocean and the climate is quite out of synchrony with the mainland. Summers are benign. Frost is unknown. Only the wind is hostile; but wherever there is shelter – a granite wall, a close-clipped escallonia hedge, a windbreak of holm oaks to shut out the gales – flowers bloom months ahead of their English counterparts and tender plants from warmer climes thrive in the open. Anywhere else in the country they would quickly perish.

In 1834 an autocratic eccentric called Augustus Smith acquired the leasehold of the Scillies and the title of lord proprietor. Within the year, "Emperor" Smith was indulging his passion for botany by establishing a garden of exotics in the grounds of Tresco Abbey. During his reign the local flower trade began, almost by accident, when he sent a hatbox of narcissi to Covent Garden.

Today Tresco Abbey Gardens is an extraordinary place. Outside, the sea wind beats against an impenetrable wall of Monterey pines but, inside, the drowsy warmth, the brilliant light and dazzling Greek blue of the distant ocean are pure Mediterranean. Bees drone among azure spires of echiums. Succulent aeoniums

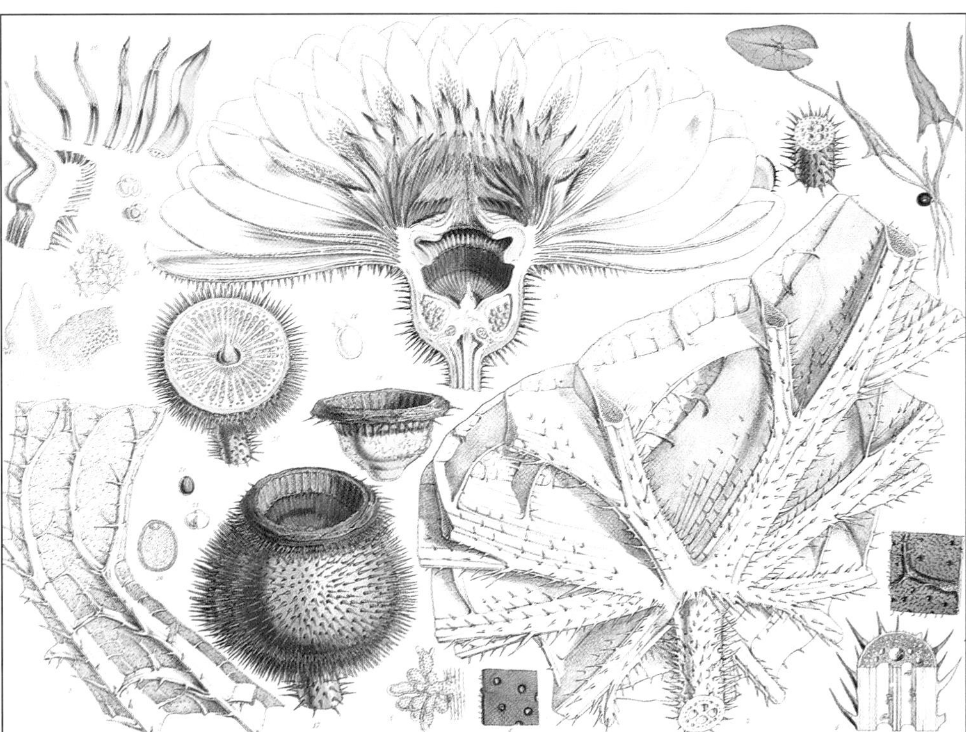

The giant Amazonian water lily (Victoria amazonica) has been raised annually from seed at Kew since 1850. The leaves (centre) can grow up to 6ft across, yet it took improved microscopy to enable 19th-century botanists to describe the plant's anatomy (above). The hand-coloured lithographs are by Walter Hood Fitch (1817–92)

from the Canaries bask against walls of sun-warmed granite overwhelmed by cascades of pink mesembryanthemums. There are proteas from the Cape, agaves from Mexico. Tree ferns from New Zealand grow cheek by jowl with spiky turquoise puyas from Chile. Only the blackbirds tell you this is an offshore fragment of England, a supreme example of a protected garden in which walls, windbreaks and shelter belts have been employed with inspired effect to create a haven for tender plants. Yet even Tresco is not immune from the cruel extremes of our fickle climate.

In January 1987, Scillonians awoke to the unaccustomed sight of their islands buried under six inches of snow. The combination of frost, snow and bitterly cold gales unravelled the work of more than 150 years and killed off many of Tresco's most beautiful and unusual plants. Happily, replacement is now well under way.

The entire history of gardening could be summed up as man manipulating nature, cosseting and refining selected species at the expense of others, eliminating pests and disease and, above all – especially in Britain – creating a protected environment with its own microclimate in which favoured plants can flourish unaffected by unkind excesses of wind and weather.

Native plants need no such help. Evolution long ago weeded out those unable to live through our northern European winters. The survivors spring up, flower, fruit and shed their leaves or withdraw again into the ground with the first hard frosts of autumn. So the earliest idea of a garden as an enclosed space called for nothing more than a hedge of thorns, a wattle fence or palisade sometimes reinforced with a ditch

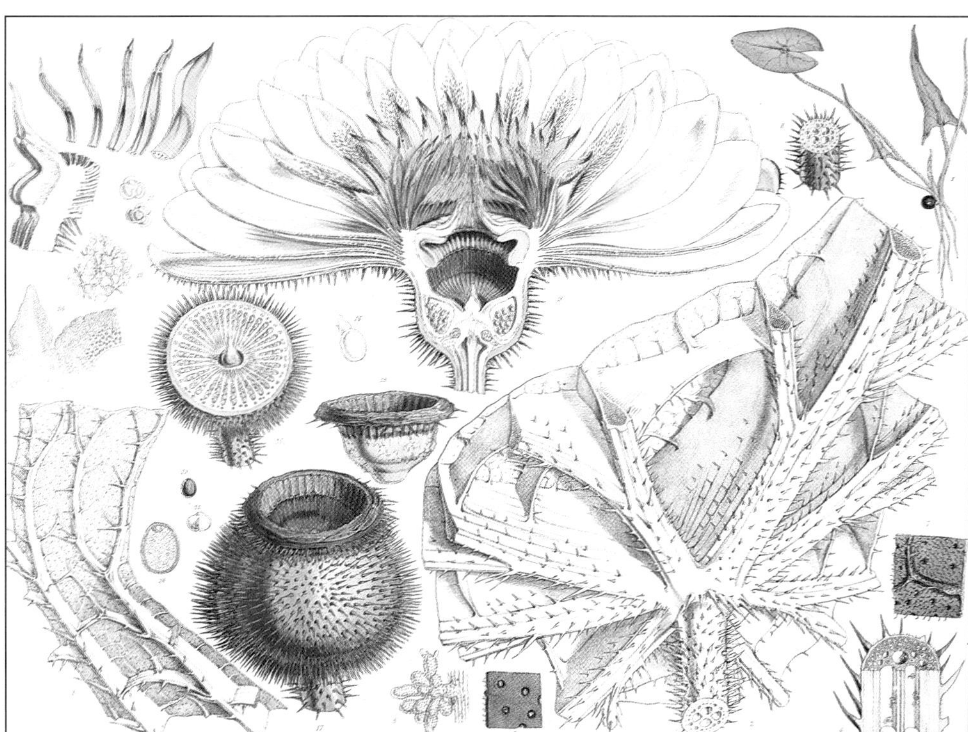

The giant Amazonian water lily (Victoria amazonica) has been raised annually from seed at Kew since 1850. The leaves (centre) can grow up to 6ft across, yet it took improved microscopy to enable 19th-century botanists to describe the plant's anatomy (above). The hand-coloured lithographs are by Walter Hood Fitch (1817–92)

from the Canaries bask against walls of sun-warmed granite overwhelmed by cascades of pink mesembryanthemums. There are proteas from the Cape, agaves from Mexico. Tree ferns from New Zealand grow cheek by jowl with spiky turquoise puyas from Chile. Only the blackbirds tell you this is an offshore fragment of England, a supreme example of a protected garden in which walls, windbreaks and shelter belts have been employed with inspired effect to create a haven for tender plants. Yet even Tresco is not immune from the cruel extremes of our fickle climate.

In January 1987, Scillonians awoke to the unaccustomed sight of their islands buried under six inches of snow. The combination of frost, snow and bitterly cold gales unravelled the work of more than 150 years and killed off many of Tresco's most beautiful and unusual plants. Happily, replacement is now well under way.

The entire history of gardening could be summed up as man manipulating nature, cosseting and refining selected species at the expense of others, eliminating pests and disease and, above all – especially in Britain – creating a protected environment with its own microclimate in which favoured plants can flourish unaffected by unkind excesses of wind and weather.

Native plants need no such help. Evolution long ago weeded out those unable to live through our northern European winters. The survivors spring up, flower, fruit and shed their leaves or withdraw again into the ground with the first hard frosts of autumn. So the earliest idea of a garden as an enclosed space called for nothing more than a hedge of thorns, a wattle fence or palisade sometimes reinforced with a ditch or moat; not so much for protection against the weather as a barrier to keep out marauding animals, both wild and domestic.

By the Middle Ages the concept of the enclosed garden was well established: even the Garden of Eden was often depicted with a wattle fence – although wealthier landowners were already building walls as a more durable deterrent against intruders.

But long before then the introduction of new plants, first by the Romans and later by the Normans, posed problems when trying to establish less hardy species. In AD 280, when the Emperor Probus issued an edict to encourage the cultivation of grapes in various parts of the Roman Empire including Britain, one of the first considerations must have been to find suitably sheltered and south-facing sites.

Around the time of the Norman Conquest, *Domesday Book* boasted 38 vineyards in places as far apart as Dorset and East Anglia, and the grapes of Gloucestershire produced a wine as good as any to be found in France. Townsfolk and country people still tended their garden plots of leeks, onions, beans and garlic; but change was everywhere. As monasteries grew wealthier, the monks followed the example of their brethren on the Continent. Outside the monastery walls, apple orchards blossomed as the Norman taste for cider was added to the Anglo-Saxon thirst for ale. Inside, cloistered gardens were created and new plants introduced to the herbarium – among them carnations, pinks and wallflowers. By the middle of the 12th century even the grim fortress of the Tower of London had a small walled

An unlikely venue for the banana economy, these fine, upstanding fruits luxuriate in a glasshouse in a private garden in Norfolk

garden; and at Woodstock Henry II created a secret garden called Rosamund's Bower, in which he made love to Rosamund Clifford, his mistress.

Here was a true innovation straight out of the Age of Chivalry: a garden for romance and dalliance as opposed to the strictly practical herbarium or kitchen garden. The idea of gardens to please the senses was taking shape. In the early 15th century James I of Scotland, imprisoned at Windsor Castle, could write of the garden below his window with its secluded arbours and alleys sheltered by hawthorn hedges and "the sharpe greene sweet Juniper".

A century later the medieval world had passed away, leaving its embattled walled gardens to the Tudors. By now English gardeners knew the value of a lofty south-facing wall, absorbing the sun's warmth by day and giving it back slowly at night. For men like Lovell of Richmond, Henry VIII's gardener, whose duty was to provide "damsons, grapes, filberts, peaches, apples and other fruits, and flowers" for the king's table, the protected garden was now essential.

At Sheen and Nonsuch and other royal palaces, roses basked against sun-warmed Tudor brickwork alongside ripening figs, pears and medlars. Almonds and quinces were now commonplace and even pomegranates and apricots were in cultivation. The age of discovery had aroused a passion for exotic plants and, at Beddington in Surrey, Sir Francis Carew was proudly showing off the first orange trees to be grown in England. (In winter they were covered with wooden "tabernacles" and kept warm by stoves – hence the early name "stove" to mean a greenhouse.)

The Jacobeans maintained the tradition of high walls against which they grew sun-loving figs, peaches, nectarines and other fruits. The new gardens at Hatfield House had a vineyard planted with 30,000 vines – a gift from France – and John Tradescant the elder, the great Jacobean plant collector, sent rare roses, cherry trees and mulberries from Holland.

At Woburn in the late 17th century, oranges, lemons, myrtles and aloes stood in pots on the terrace below the state rooms in summer. In September they were moved into an orangery in which a stove kept the winter frosts at bay. Increasingly, as collectors such as the Tradescants, father and son, returned with tender plants from places as far apart as Russia and America, the great gardens of the day boasted a winter-house in which oranges and other prized "exoticks" were protected.

Of all plants, the orange revolutionised protected gardening in England. Said to have been introduced to the west from southern China by Marco Polo, these sought-after trees were a prized status symbol throughout the 17th and 18th centuries. Samuel Pepys in an amusing confession describes how in June 1666, fascinated by the sight of Lord Brooke's oranges at Hackney, he "pulled off a little one by stealth and ate it".

Overleaf: a modern application of an ancient technique: the garden at Sissinghurst Castle in Kent, laid out this century by Harold Nicolson and Vita Sackville-West, uses thick hedges to screen plants from wind and form warm micro-climates in their lee

GLASS WARFARE

Nicotine, arsenic and predatory wasps are among the weapons with which gardeners over the years have attempted to stem the assaults of glasshouse pests

By Graham Rose

The gardener John Rose presents an English-grown pineapple to his master, Charles II, which was probably infested with minute bugs, flies and spiders. Detail from an unattributed painting (English School), 1670

What we can't see on the pineapple which the gardener John Rose was presenting to his master Charles II in the much reproduced 17th-century painting are the mealy bugs, scale insects, white fly or red spiders which it probably concealed about its scales and leaves.

Although they would be too small to attract the artist's attention, they probably infested what is thought to have been the earliest pineapple grown in England from a mother plant brought back from the tropics.

No-one is sure whether these pests were introduced with the pineapple. But certainly they are the major insect problem for glasshouse growers. Together with caterpillars like those of the tomato, angle shades, silver Y and tortrix moths, aphids, leaf miners and hoppers and onion thrips, they are the most damaging among a small collection of pests which chew the roots and foliage or suck the sap of our indoor plants. All these pests are capable of causing damage, even death.

Many fewer species of pests afflict our indoor plants than maraud our gardens. But that number has increased slowly over the centuries as more and more tropical and subtropical plant imports have brought their specific problems with them. Over the past 50 years the rate of invasion has accelerated as air transport has increased the complexity of the trade.

Franklinia occidentalis – the western flower thrips – for example, first became important on the west coast of the USA, moved into German glasshouses and recently reached Britain along with plants from Holland. *Bemisia tabacci* – the cotton whitefly – a devastating pest elsewhere, is another recent arrival from Holland, imported with a batch of poinsettias.

For no clear reason, other pests like *Otiorhynchus sulcatus* – the vine weevil, which have been with us for generations, have become a greatly increased menace to both indoor and garden plants during the last decade. Some researchers suggest that this pest has become much worse since DDT was withdrawn.

Leaf curl of peaches and apricots, powdery mildew of grapes, early blight of tomatoes, sclerotinia on lettuce and celery, and damping off and grey mould of many plants have been the major disease scourges of indoor plants during the past century. But latterly it was hoped that strict plant quarantine regulations had prevented further disease imports. Sadly that optimism proved ill-founded when a new tomato disease – a powdery mildew of the erysiphe family – was identified recently.

Hand-picking the caterpillars, water-jetting the aphids, fumigating by heating sulphur or cutting off and burning disease-affected parts of plants were the only remedies available to the early orangery and conservatory growers. The effectiveness of their armoury increased greatly as, during the last century, dangerous sprays like nicotine sulphate and arsenic preparations became available, and sulphur and copper-based fungicides were developed.

Without realising that their plants were suffering from a build-up of pests and diseases in the soil, the earliest indoor gardeners knew that some plants grown in the same soil for a long time suffered from what they described as "sickness", and they dug out and replaced the soil to counter the problem. This practice became obsolete after it was shown during the 19th century that soil could be sterilised by heat. Large ovens were built for the purpose, but were superseded when large-scale high-pressure steam boilers were introduced to force steam through the soil from outlets in buried pipes. That practice continued until it became uneconomic during the oil crisis in the Seventies, when fumigation with volatile chemicals like methyl bromide or DD began to be used for this work.

From the turn of the century glasshouse growers used the succession of insecticides and fungicides developed for the control of pests and diseases of outdoor plants. And as far as the pests were concerned, while many of these products were very effective for a time the two main pests – white fly and red spider – always seemed to develop resistance to them. Only recently have growers begun to readopt the method of biological control, which was used with success to suppress white fly in the mid-Thirties.

In 1926 scientists at the Cheshunt research station in Hertfordshire identified a tiny wasp called *Encasia formosa* which was parasitic on white fly; by 1935 it was being reared in millions at insectaries and sold for release in infested greenhouses. It was understandably forgotten when highly effective synthetic insecticides like DDT and the organophosphorous compounds became available during and just after the Second World War. However, in the late Fifties white fly was beginning to show resistance to them and the parasite began to be used again.

A piece of sharp observation in Germany in 1960 led to the identification of a predatory mite, *Phytoseilus persimilis,* which would attack and kill red spider, the other major glasshouse pest. That predator, too, is now available to growers.

Since 1973 a bacterium – *Baccillus thuringiensis* – has been available which, when used as a spray, will infect and kill caterpillars including those of tomato moth. Its wider adoption, plus that of many other biological control organisms which are now being developed, is the more likely because biological control is proving to be more cost-effective than applying pesticides. The newer quick knock-down, short persistence pyrethroid sprays or the old but dangerous-to-apply nicotine sprays will still kill white fly but they have to be applied up to 20 times per season, whereas the parasite need be introduced only once. Chrysanthemum growers, in fact, calculate that the parasite is 18 per cent cheaper.

These observations have greatly encouraged researchers at the Institute of Horticulture's Glasshouse Crops Research Station at Littlehampton in Sussex, where they are working on strains of bacteria which will infect both caterpillars and beetle larvae, and a fungus which will kill aphids. They are also investigating the role of what have been called biological exocets – certain eelworms which will seek out soil-active caterpillars, fly and beetle larvae, penetrate them through the anus or even by burrowing through the cuticle and introduce a bacterium which will kill and consume them. The eelworms benefit from this symbiotic relationship because they feed on the biomass, which increases greatly as the bacteria multiply in the victims' corpse. The Littlehampton researchers think that glasshouse growers in future will practise integrated pest control, using biological agents against their major pests and a few very specific insecticides – such as pirimcarb which only kills aphids – to cope with their other problems.

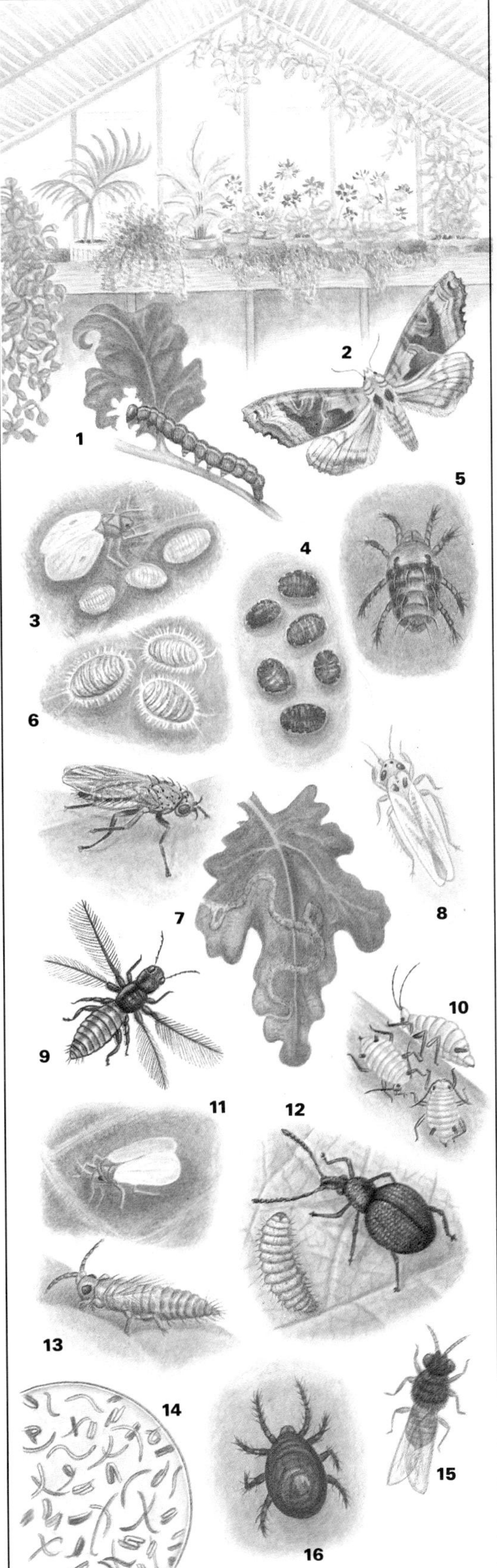

PESTS, PARASITES AND PREDATOR

PESTS
1 *Caterpillar (just under ½ size) with*
2 *angle shades moth (⅘ size).*
3 *White fly with scale (× 10) and*
4 *Scale insects (× 2½).*
5 *Two-spotted mite (red spider mite) (×29).*
6 *Mealy bugs (×2½).*
7 *Chrysanthemum leaf miner (×8) and leaf damage.*
8 *Leaf hopper (×5¾).*
9 *Onion thrips (×14).*
10 *Green aphid (×5).*
11 *Cotton white fly (×10).*
12 *Vine weevil with larva (×2).*
13 *Western flower thrips (×14).*

PARASITES
14 *Eelworms (×400) infiltrate larvae with killer bacteria, then eat them*
15 *Encasia formosa (×20), wasp parasite on white fly.*

PREDATOR
16 *Phytoseilus persimilis (×29) kills red spider and other pests.*

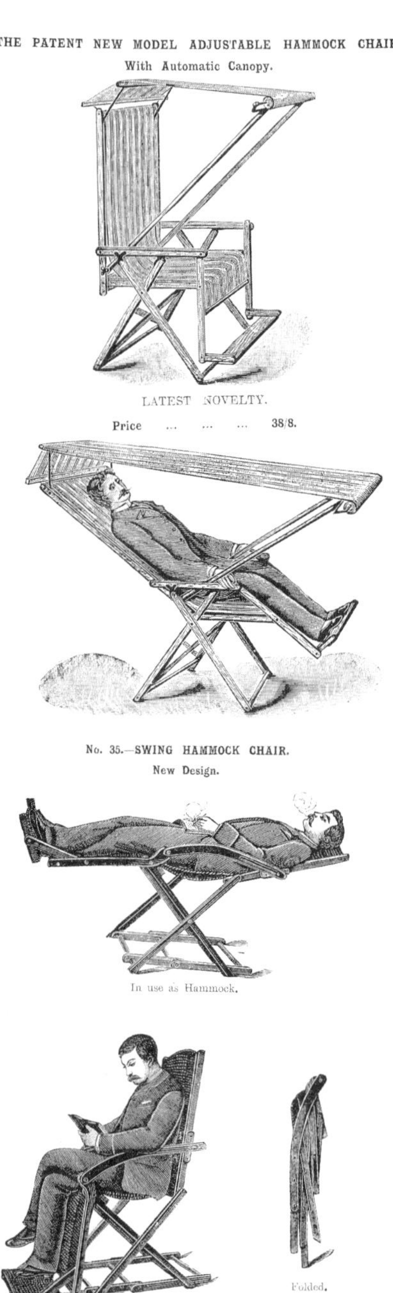

Not all the Victorians' creative energy was devoted to plants. Gardeners too needed protected environments

The winter-house was a lofty building with large, south-facing doors and windows which could be opened on mild days. In hard weather they could be covered with mats, and on very cold nights the stove would be lit.

By the 17th century a new term – greenhouse – had been coined to describe such buildings; so-called because they were designed to protect tender "greens" (citrus, pomegranates, myrtles, bay and other evergreens). One of the finest early greenhouses was Nicholas Hawksmoor's at Kensington Palace, designed for Queen Anne in 1705, with its rotundas, Corinthian columns and niches in which oranges and statues could be placed.

In the same century another new word – conservatory – entered the dictionary of gardening. Used for the first time by John Evelyn in 1664, it was originally a synonym for an orangery or greenhouse – a building where plants were conserved in winter; but a century later the greenhouse was to become a place for growing and propagating tender plants, while the conservatory was designed to show them off.

Most of the distinguished architects of the 18th century – Wren, Wyatt, Vanbrugh at Blenheim – were designing greenhouses or orangeries, bringing a new sense of dignity to the garden landscape with their classical glazed temples. The Georgian orangery with its arched windows may have been influencd by the earlier practice of glazing the formerly open arcades and loggias of the Jacobeans. In summer the windows could be opened or even removed altogether, and the unglazed north wall often contained flues through which hot air could circulate from braziers or charcoal stoves. Other narrower glasshouses were built specially for grapes and figs, and the famous Black Hamburg vine planted at Hampton Court by Capability Brown still produces up to 600 bunches of grapes every summer.

Right up until the end of the century, orangeries and conservatories relied upon the archaic system of stoves and flues. Sometimes potted plants stood in a pit of fermenting tan-bark for additional warmth, and it was not until the 1830s that hot-water boilers provided a cleaner and more efficient source of controlled heat. Installed in cavernous boiler-houses, they were stoked with coke which sent hot water flowing around the glasshouse through a network of gurgling pipes.

Another feature which lingered on until the late 18th century was the stone or tiled roof. The importance of light as opposed to heat was only slowly understood, and the Industrial Revolution provided a timely aid in the development of cast iron as a material in glazed roofs. Nash's conservatory at Barnsley Park, Gloucestershire, was one of the earliest examples. Later came visions of curvilinear glass roofs and elegant ironwork that echoed the great vault of the sky; in 1816 that dream became possible with the invention of curved iron glazing bars, patented by the Scotsman J. C. Loudon.

Tree ferns under glass at the Glasgow Botanic Gardens

Early glazed models had small panes but improving technology brought cheaper sheet glass, and in 1845 the prohibitive "glass tax" was lifted, allowing the light of heaven to flood in on anyone rich enough to afford a greenhouse. Now the wealthy could build glasshouses for special collections: dry houses for succulents; humid ones for ferns and orchids.

The advance in structural engineering and the availability of cheaper glass brought about a return to the idea of detached conservatories such as Charles Fowler's domed masterpiece at Syon. Completed in 1830, it was big enough to hold mature forest trees – a far cry from orangeries with their modest tubs.

The previous year, a chance discovery by Nathaniel Bagshaw Ward, a London doctor, was to become invaluable to plant collectors. Ward found that plants would thrive happily in completely closed glass containers. Light and moisture were all they needed – moisture which they transpired and which then condensed to be returned to the soil in an endless cycle. Before this discovery, many plants collected abroad perished on the sea voyage home. Now, thanks to the Wardian case, they could be sent safely from the farthest corners of the world.

Wardian cases were popular in Victorian times for keeping decorative displays of plants indoors; all kinds of shapes and styles were evolved, from simple bell jars to miniature versions of the Crystal Palace. Ward's own decorative fern case displayed a miniature arch from Tintern Abbey. They were ideal for the ferns Victorians loved

COOL TEMPERATE
Min temp 8°C(46°F).
Ambient humidity

MOIST TEMPERATE
Min temp 10°C(50°F).
Relative humidity 85%

DRY TROPICS
Min temp 13°C(55°F).
Ambient humidity

SOME LIKE IT COOL

Technology exists to enable you to create artificially any plant environment in the world, from cool desert to tropical rain forest

By Graham Rose

It takes very little effort or ingenuity to recreate the cool temperate climate of, say, the Canary Islands. All you have to do is ensure the temperature in your conservatory or greenhouse never falls below a modest 8°C (46°F). There is no need to adjust the atmosphere – ambient humidity will do.

In these conditions you can comfortably sustain most of the houseplants commonly grown in Britain.

For *moist* temperate zones, however, you have to raise the humidity as well as the temperature. In the past, gardeners coped with this by copiously wetting the glasshouse floor or, in extreme cases, by keeping a kettle of water on the boil. These days, the old rustic techniques have been replaced by sophisticated spray-misting devices which are activated by electronic detector switches. Most amateurs can afford the equipment for small-scale glasshouses, though a moist atmosphere is not something that would greatly enhance the pleasure of relaxing in a conservatory.

Heat, however, is a costlier problem. While many amateurs can afford to insulate their glasshouses and heat them to an average

SEASONALLY DRY TROPICS
Min temp 15°C(59°F).
Ambient humidity

TROPICS
Min temp 15°C(59°F).
Relative humidity 75%

WARM TROPICS
Min temp 18°C(64°F).
Relative humidity 85%

minimum of 45°F on winter nights, very few would be prepared to meet the greatly increased cost of raising the average minimum to 55°F, which is the temperature you would need to maintain a dry tropical zone.

The six major climatic zones described here are similar to those maintained within the Princess of Wales Conservatory at the Royal Botanic Gardens, Kew. The illustration shows a selection of glasshouse plants which flourish in the appropriate conditions.

Cool Temperate
Rather like Britain in the summer months but with less temperature fluctuation; the type of climate found in the Canary Islands and in many areas of the subtropics through to New Zealand. It is easily reproduced in the greenhouse. Evergreen oak and bay forests shelter under-storeys of shrubs like gardenias and herbaceous plants like giant echiums and cinerarias.
1 *Cobaea scandens*. **2** *Mimosa*. **3** Oleander. **4** Browallia. **5** Codiaeum. **6** Cineraria. **7** *Primula obconica*. **8** *Exacum affine*. **9** Brunfelsia.

Moist Temperate
Generally warm, and with plenty of rain, these are the conditions typically found in the mountainous areas of North Island, New Zealand. It is in these regions that great trees like the big red-flowered metrosideros and the kauri nut shelter ferns and tree ferns below their generous canopies. In the picture: **10** Tillandsia. **11** Odontoglossum. **12** Ficus. **13** Aeschyanthus. **14** Schefflera. **15** Cymbidium. **16** Adiantum. **17** Miltonia. **18** Chelianthes. **19** Nephrolepsis.

Dry Tropics
With warm days and cool nights which sometimes fall below freezing point and a distinct summer and winter season, these conditions prevail in Mexico and the high plains of East Africa. Acacia thorns, cacti, tree-sized aloes and sage-brush stud grass which grows abundantly after rain and then withers quickly in the bright sun. In the picture: **20** Nepenthes. **21** Cereus. **22** Sarracenia. **23** Aloe vera. **24** Drossera. **25** Mammillaria. **26** Dionaea (Venus fly-trap).

Seasonally Dry Tropics
These are regions where heavy tropical rain alternates with very dry periods. Parts of Venezuela or inland districts in West Africa share these characteristics, supporting big trees like baobabs and oil palms, with tree cacti like pereskias, silver-foliaged air plants like the tillandsias hovering over hippeastrums. In the picture: **27** *Acacia tortilis*. **28** *Adansonia digitata*.

Tropics
These are the conditions found at high altitude, such as the Usambara Mountains in Tanzania, the highlands of New Guinea and parts of Central America, where there is some difference between seasons, and the nights are often cooler than the days; where mahogany trees overhang wild plantains and passion flowers rampage. In the picture: **29** Aphelandra. **30** Saintpaulia (African violet). **31** Begonia rex.

Warm Tropics
These conditions are typical of low altitudes in equatorial regions where the temperature hardly varies between day or night and seasons are not apparent. Great trees like dipterocarp dominate rain forests where marantas like arrowroot, airplants like the bromeliads, phalaenopsis orchids and ferns thrive. Maintaining the high temperature in the winter and the high humidity throughout the summer make reproducing these conditions costly and onerous for amateurs, though they are consistently achieved by orchid growers who specialise in families like the phaelenopsis or the paphiopedilums. In the picture: **32** Angiopteris. **33** Phalaenopsis. **34** *Pteris cretica*. **35** Paphiopedilum.

Bright-flowered cacti are favourite greenhouse subjects. Above: Mammillaria bombycina. Top centre and far right: two species of Echinocereus, originally from North America. Below centre: Mammillaria zeilmanniana

as well as other tropical plants requiring humid conditions. So began the vogue for "fern cases". Today the most popular version is the bottle garden in which small, slow-growing house plants inhabit a carboy or some similar container.

When Queen Victoria came to the throne in 1837 gardening had never been held in such high esteem. It was the heyday of growing under glass. The huge hothouses and squads of gardeners employed by the well-to-do encouraged the fashion for "bedding-out", in which parterre beds were filled with a succession of flowering plants – begonias, fuchsias, scarlet geraniums – massed in their thousands to form colourful patterns. One's social standing could be measured by the extent of the bedding-out list: 10,000 plants for a squire, 20,000 for a baronet, 30,000 for an earl and 50,000 for a duke. It is said that Queen Victoria woke up at Cliveden one morning to find the entire great parterre had been re-bedded overnight. Today the fashion lingers mainly as floral clocks in municipal parks.

The genius of the age was Joseph Paxton, a farmer's son from Bedfordshire. By the time he was 23 he had become head gardener to the sixth Duke of Devonshire at

Chatsworth, Derbyshire, where, within a few years, he built the finest conservatory in England. Known as the Great Stove, it was nearly 300ft long and so spacious that Queen Victoria and Prince Albert drove through it in a carriage and pair.

Unfortunately, heating costs were equally enormous – coal was brought by the truck-load through a special tunnel constructed under the pleasure garden. In the end it proved too costly to maintain and in 1920 the Great Stove was demolished, although Paxton's "conservative wall" – a separate, elegant procession of glass-houses climbing towards the stables – has survived.

In 1850 Paxton sprang to prominence when he coaxed the giant Amazon water-lily to flower for the first time in cultivation. This splendid plant, with its foot-wide flowers and floating leaves big enough to support a child, had been discovered in 1838. It was named *Victoria regia* in honour of the Queen, and kept in a warm-water tank in an ornate iron glasshouse which became known as a Victoria house.

The following year Paxton created his world-famous Crystal Palace for the Great Exhibition in London's Hyde Park. The palace covered an area four times the size of

St Peter's in Rome with iron and glass. In 1852–4 it was re-erected at Sydenham, where it was destroyed by fire in 1936.

The Crystal Palace started the fashion for winter gardens in England. Created by great estate owners as huge covered gardens in which they could promenade dryshod in winter and enjoy displays of colourful and exotic plants, they soon spread to municipal parks and seafronts. Winter gardens differed from the tropical houses of botanical gardens by being less intensively planted, allowing ample seating space and wide pathways. Some were even designed to stage lectures and concerts. Sadly, the ravages of two world wars, changing tastes and different priorities for municipal expenditure have led to the demolition of most English winter gardens. The expense of repairing and heating them was simply too great, and their story in the 20th century has been one of dereliction and decline.

Torquay sold its winter garden to Great Yarmouth, where it was resurrected as a skating rink with a solid roof. Others fared rather better. Rhyl preserved much of the original character of its winter garden when converting it into a butterfly jungle in 1986. Aberdeen, Leeds and Buxton never allowed their Victorian legacies to deteriorate, and Glasgow's winter garden has been completely refurbished after a successful battle by local conservationists. Another splendid survivor stands in the grounds of Avery Hill Park at Eltham, and is owned by the London Borough of Greenwich. During the Second World War it was badly damaged by a flying bomb, but it was lovingly restored by 1962 and its 90ft dome – covering 10,000 sq ft – was again extensively repaired in the 1970s.

Throughout Queen Victoria's reign, glass-making continued to improve. Panes became clearer, letting in more light, and were now embedded in putty. Then iron began to fall out of fashion. The conservatory framed in elegant ironwork, its black-and-white-tiled floors and jungle of hothouse plants, was a romantic display which only the very rich could afford. Wood was cheaper and easier to replace. Gardeners found that ridge-and-furrow roofs could provide just as much light, and in the 1870s an English glasshouse-maker, W. H. Lascelles, discovered how to bend wood under steam pressure. Henceforth iron, if used, was purely ornamental.

Perhaps the finest survivor from that golden age of iron and glass cathedrals is the Palm House at Kew. This immense and ambitious building was the result of a complex and ultimately controversial collaboration between Richard Turner, a Dublin ironfounder and glasshouse-designer, and Decimus Burton, architect to the Royal Botanic Gardens, who had already worked with Joseph Paxton on the Chatsworth Great Stove.

The first iron rib was raised in October 1845, only eight months after the repeal of the "glass tax". When it was completed three years later, the Palm House stood 63ft

Early cloches (left) were designed to look like miniature glasshouses. Tough, thick glass bell-jars were a more straightforward attempt to make the form fit the function

SAVED BY THE BELL

From the bell-jar came the cloche – a small but ingenious protective device which, with the cold frame, has had a profound effect on the survival of outdoor plants

By Geoff Hamilton

There is evidence that early European civilisations grew tender plants in wicker baskets, which they moved from place to place to take advantage of the sun. In ancient China, plants were protected from frost by overwintering in pits covered with bamboo matting – a technique still practised today.

In Britain in 1577 it was recorded that thick mattresses of straw were laid on long rods to protect plants from frost; and in 1613 Gervase Markham described a large frame mounted on "little rounde wheels of wood and filled with choyse earth". This device was planted with tender plants and pushed under cover when frost threatened.

Simple hotbeds were widely used by the Romans. A trench was three-quarters filled with fresh dung and topped up with soil. The fermenting dung warmed the root zone – an effective technique, which modern research has shown reduces the need for air-warming by several degrees.

Over the years, two principal kinds of "mini-environment" have been of major significance around the world: the frame and the cloche.

The Frame

The Emperor Tiberius in the first century used cucumbers as a medicine, and to ensure a year-round supply he had them grown in frames over a dung-filled hot-bed. It is thought that the frames were glazed with mica or talc – almost certainly the first recorded use of frame culture.

Centuries later the frame appeared in this country – a delay due, no doubt, to their dependence on expensive glass. Though glass cloches were recorded in Europe in the 15th century, not until a century later were they cheap enough to be risked in England – and only in very grand establishments. Lord Burleigh had frames in his garden by 1561, when his enthusiasm for glass even led him to build an orangery.

By the 17th century, frame and hot-bed culture was a fine art. Instead of building the hot-bed in a pit, which excluded air and restricted fermentation, more and longer-lasting heat was generated in beds raised above ground. A wooden frame was built to retain the manure and, if the backboards were higher than those at the front, glazed lights could be placed across to make a heated frame. In this way early and tender crops could be grown. By the following century it was common for gentlemen to keep rows of frames for growing melons, cucumbers and even pineapples as well as vegetables.

The Victorians brought the culture of exotic fruits to its peak. Frames were now permanent structures of brick, often heated by hot water pipes. Even where the heat source was still manure, a system of grilles and sliding panels enabled the dung to be removed and replaced without disturbing the crop. These frames were covered with heavy English lights, which needed to be handled by two people. The Dutch lights of the 20th century were smaller and lighter.

Nowadays the cost of fuel means that most frames are used unheated, either for acclimatising hothouse-raised plants to cooler temperatures before planting out or for raising crops slightly earlier without heat. Again, for reasons of economy, wooden and brick-built frames are now rare, replaced by cheaper aluminium or plastic. Occasionally frames are heated by electric cables laid under the soil as an aid to propagation.

The Cloche

As the name implies, the cloche originated in France, probably in the 15th century. The bell-jar started life on the alchemist's bench and it's unclear how it transferred to the garden – perhaps as part of an early experiment. Certainly it became very popular in France at about this time but the first mention of it in Britain seems to be in 1629 in Parkinson's *Paradisus,* where he describes growing melons "under great hollow glasses like bell-heads".

It never really gained the same popularity here, probably because of the difficulty of ventilation. The only way was to prop up the leeward side with a stone. This worked fairly well until the wind changed direction when they had to be done again. The Victorians modified the design to make planting in rows more convenient, and produced the lantern cloche which was designed exactly like a miniature square greenhouse.

Because of their shape, round or square cloches had their limitations in the vegetable garden, so the continuous cloche was a logical development. In 1912, the first tent cloche was patented by Major L. H. Chase, to be followed quickly by the barn cloche to give added height. Within a few years, millions sprouted in market gardens and the idea was quickly taken up by amateur gardeners, too. The Chase cloche is still in production.

In the Fifties, rigid plastic cloches proliferated and, in the early Sixties, came the tunnel cloche. Sheet polythene stretched over wire hoops was economical for everyone.

Meanwhile, the Japanese and then the Swiss were experimenting with floating cloches, the crop supporting a light plastic film which was perforated for ventilation and watering. Following tests in the UK, 1984 saw the introduction of a light-spun polypropylene which would protect from a few degrees of frost. Finally, this year we have a similar material which will stretch slightly to avoid damage to tender plants beneath.

BETWEEN THESE FOUR WALLS

Walls give shelter and create a microclimate, offer a vertical surface for added interest and a warm backing for tender plants. The different aspects of these four walls suggest a variety of climbers, shrubs and border plants for these positions

West wall, east-facing
1 *Clematis armandii*
2 *Hedera colchica*
3 *Euphorbia wulfenii*
4 *Celastrus orbiculatus*
5 *Armeria maritima*
6 *Parthenocissus quinquefolia*
7 *Genista tinctoria*
8 *Saponaria ocymoides*
9 *Jasminum nudiflorum*
10 *Ribes sanguineum*
11 *Phlox douglasii*
12 *Filipendula ulmaria "Aurea"*
13 *Anemone nemorosa*
14 *Hedera helix*
15 *Astilbe*
16 *Veronica gentianoides*
17 *Desfontinea spinosa*
18 *Hosta*
19 *Arum italicum*
20 *Saxifraga (mossy)*
21 *Muehlenbeckia complexa*
22 *Ligularia*
23 *Primula vulgaris*
24 *Gentiana*
25 *Mimulus*
26 *Anemone japonica*
27 *Garrya elliptica*
28 *Euonymus fortunei*
29 *Digitalis*
30 *Aquilegia*
31 *Ajuga*
32 *Hepatica triloba*
33 *Astrantia*
34 *Cimicifuga*
35 *Choisya ternata*

South wall, north-facing
36 *Morello cherry*
37 *Drimys winteri*
38 *Euphorbia robbiae*
39 *Polystichum setiferum*
40 *Pulmonaria*
41 *Rubus tricolor*
42 *Kerria japonica*
43 *Camellia × williamsii*
44 *Parthenocissus tricuspidata*
45 *Lamium maculatum*
46 *Epimedium rubrum*
47 *Viola labradorica*
48 *Polygonatum giganteum*
49 *Akebia quinata*
50 *Clematis alpina*
51 *Helleborus niger*
52 *Mahonia japonica*
53 *Hydrangea petiolaris*
54 *Aucuba japonica*
55 *Celastrus orbiculatus*
56 *Pyracantha "Orange Glow"*
57 *Geranium phaeum*
58 *Bergenia*
59 *Geranium macrorrhizum*
60 *Omphalodes cappadocica*
61 *Pachysandra terminalis*
62 *Iris xiphium*
63 *Chaenomeles speciosa*
64 *Schizophragma hydrangeoides*
65 *Alchemilla mollis*

East wall, west-facing
66 *Daphne odora*
67 *Ceanoths "Burkwoodii"*
68 *Rose "Complicata"*
69 *Astrantia*
70 *Campanula (dwarf types)*
71 *Primula denticulata*
72 *Phlox subulata*
73 *Carex morrowii*
74 *Papaver orientale*
75 *Jasminum officinale*
76 *Lonicera "Aureoreticulata"*
77 *Filipendula*
78 *Chrysanthemum (border types)*
79 *Androsace*
80 *Ceratostygma plumbaginoides*
81 *Campanula (border types)*
82 *Liatris*
83 *Aristolochia macrophylla*
84 *Clematis montana*
85 *Fuchsia*
86 *Bellis*
87 *Ophiopogon*
88 *Pulsatilla vulgaris*
89 *Nerine bowdenii*
90 *Peach/nectarine*
91 *Itea ilicifolia*
92 *Kniphophia*
93 *Stokesia laevis*

North wall, south-facing
94 *Dianthus*
95 *Alyssum*
96 *Anemone fulgens*
97 *Oenethera missouriensis*
98 *Geranium "Buxton's Blue"*
99 *Iris sibirica*
100 *Caesalpina japonica*
101 *Dimorphotheca*
102 *Lavandula*
103 *Acanthus spinosus*
104 *Perovskia atriplicifolia*
105 *Dahlia*
106 *Gladiolus*
107 *Trachelospermum asiaticum*
108 *Fremontodendron "California Glory"*
109 *Abutilon vitifolium*
110 *Wisteria sinensis*
111 *Solanum crispum*
112 *Passiflora caerulea*
113 *Rosa banksiae*
114 *Actinidia kolomikta*
115 *Cytisus battandieri*
116 *Thymus*
117 *Potentilla (shrubby)*
118 *Agapanthus*
119 *Lobelia ("Crystal Palace" or similar)*

In centre
120 *Bay*

Passiflora caerulea

N
W
E
S

Opposite: Paphiopedilum orchids make a wonderful greenhouse display. These slipper orchids are hybrids from species found in south-east Asia. There are several varieties which flower in late autumn

high, 100ft wide and 362ft long, and was soon filled with Kew's rapidly expanding collection of tropical and sub-tropical plants.

However, Kew still needed a new building to house the proliferating warm-temperature collections. Once again Decimus Burton was the architect, but this time he used wood for glazing bars and green-tinted glass to temper the scorching effect of the sun. Burton's Temperate House was begun in 1860 but not completed until 1898–9. It housed tree ferns, palms, acacias, rhododendrons, camellias, bamboos, succulents from Mexico and a yellow tree peony from Yunnan. In 1940 the building suffered bomb damage and continued to deteriorate until its full restoration in 1982. Today its airy octagons and spiral staircases are as good as new, its decorative wrought-iron arches joined by 16km of new glazing bars and capping, and 72km of neoprene sealing-strip to provide a perfect environment for botanic treasures such as the giant Chilean palm – the world's largest greenhouse plant.

The latest addition to Kew's historic glasshouses – the Princess of Wales Conservatory – was opened by the Princess last July. Its striking modern ridge tent design divides inside into six major climatic zones, ranging from wet tropics and cloud forest to desert conditions in which Mexican agaves and the Namibian *Welwitschia mirabilis* can grow.

The other great glory of the Victorian age was the walled kitchen garden, which became an integral part of every large country house. Fruit trees and vegetables had long been set apart from the formal parterres in a walled plot of their own. Some of these walled gardens attained an enormous size. Those at Blenheim, laid out in 1705 by Vanbrugh and Henry Wise, were spread across 12 acres and sheltered by 14ft-high walls which may still be admired today.

The invention of hot walls, heated by charcoal stoves which breathed warm air through a series of flues, helped to protect tender flowers and fruit and foreshadowed hothouses. By Victorian times the construction of a walled garden had become more of an exact science based on precise measurements to find the meridian line – where and when the sun was hottest on a south-facing wall – in order to determine where peaches and nectarines might be grown. Even then, warmth would be wasted if cold winds entered the garden; so windbreaks of fast-growing trees – larch, spruce and Italian poplars – were often planted outside the north walls.

Inside, in addition to vegetable beds and gravel paths, fruit trees trained in traditional fans and espalier shapes against the walls, there were numerous sheds and glasshouses, each with its allotted function: vinery, peach house, potting shed, forcing house, and rows of cold-frames for growing lettuces or bringing on flowers such as lily of the valley or Parma violets for the lady of the house.

In vine houses, hot-water pipes forced early grapes, while later varieties were trained to climb up sloping rafters. Some glasshouses were filled with the musky sweet scent of melons basking in individual nets beneath the glazing. In others, green-gold sunlight picked out the stalactite shapes of ripening cucumbers, each suspended from the roof in a long glass tube to make sure it would grow straight. Until 1914 even pineapples, the "king of fruits", were grown in special pine "stoves", in brickwork pits of fermenting bark.

This was not an age for eating everything in its season, and it was the head gardener's duty to provide a regular supply of fresh fruit and vegetables throughout the winter months. Vegetables were forced – in deep hotbeds of dead leaves and horse dung; in sunless sheds; in warm glasshouses or under frames, bell jars and lantern cloches. Rhubarb and sea-kale were forced in terracotta pots; celery and endive were blanched by earthing up to exclude light; soft fruits such as raspberries and gooseberries could be potted up and brought on in the glasshouse; even peaches were forced by growing them in pots in a heated vinery.

Such gardens were naturally labour-intensive, the head gardener employed a large staff including men trained in the arts of pruning and other skills, and humble "crock boys" whose tasks included potting and watering, laboriously spraying for hours on end to maintain the correct humidity for crops grown under glass. There were beds to be manured with barrow-loads of dung or precious guano imported from Peru; walled fruit to be painstakingly trained and tied by the fruit journeyman with his ladder and leather bag of nails; and blossom to be protected from frost with straw screens or canvas mats which could be taken down during the day.

Once the stately homes of England could no longer afford the walled kitchen garden with nectarines and hothouses and armies of waistcoated gardeners, they receded into the past. Notable survivors include Calke Abbey, near Ashbourne, Derbyshire, where the National Trust is restoring the Victorian kitchen garden. The Trust is also bringing back to life the kitchen garden at Clumber Park in the Dukeries, Nottinghamshire. They would like to restore its vegetable plots and splendid greenhouses to full working order, but that would need at least £1 million.

The demise of the kitchen garden coincided with the decline of the conservatory. Early this century, taste reflected a swing away from the ornate and the ostentatious. In their place arose smaller, humbler, unheated greenhouses of the kind anyone might erect in their back garden. The Second World War, with its emphasis on increased self-sufficiency, encouraged their popularity, and gardening under glass has never been more widespread than it is today.

The typical "cool" or unheated greenhouse may not allow the growth of orchids and other exotic plants beloved by the Victorians; but it keeps out wind, snow and

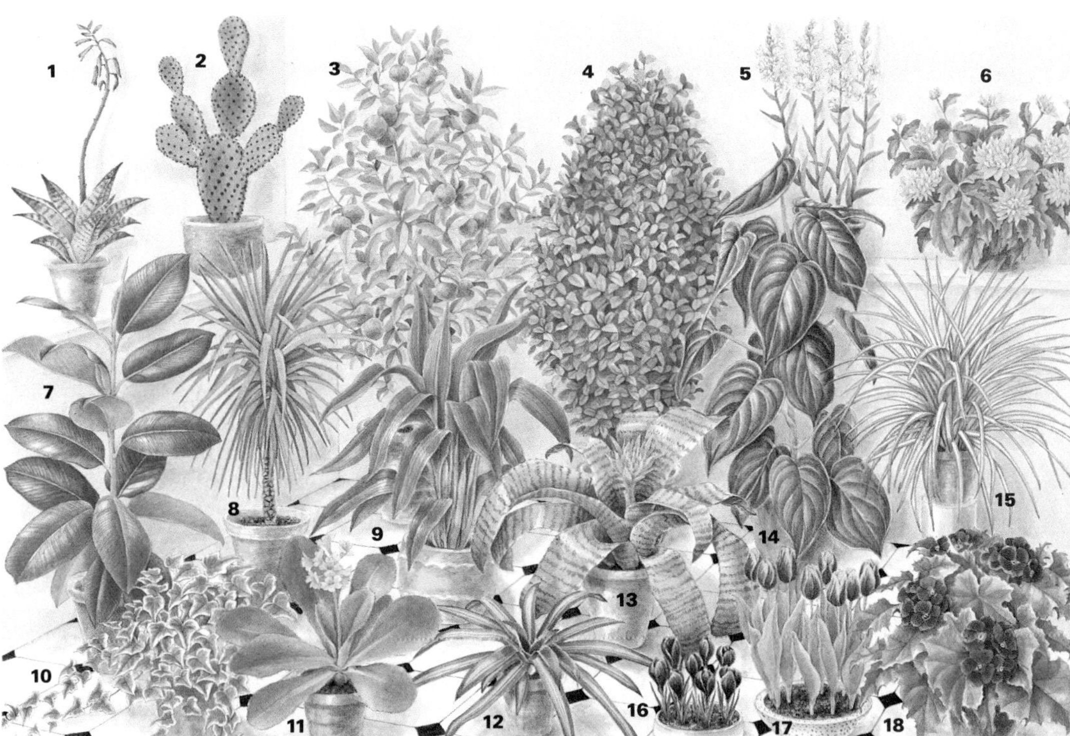

POTTED HISTORY
1 *Aloe variegata*
2 *Opuntia*
3 *Orange tree*
4 *Box*
5 *Tuberose – Polianthas tuberosa*
6 *Chrysanthemum*
7 *Indian rubber plant*
8 *Yucca*
9 *Aspidistra*
10 *Ivy*
11 *Primula auricula*
12 *Bromeliad – Neoregelia carolinae*
13 *Bromeliad – Aechmea rhodocyanea*
14 *Philodendron melanochryson*
15 *Spider plant*
16 *Crocus*
17 *Tulips*
18 *Begonia "Fireglow"*

In-House Training

The Romans probably began the practice of keeping plants in pots; the Victorians raised it to an art form

By Gareth Huw Davies

Some time deep in pre-history, a gardener realised that if he moved his flowerpots indoors at night, the plants would be spared from frost. Thus, we may suppose, was the popular houseplant invented.

Some of the earliest clues that plants may have been used for interior decoration were excavated from a Roman nursery in Pompeii. Ranks of painted flowerpots designed to stand in small enclosed courtyards were ancestors of the houseplant pots of today.

However, history has little to say about houseplants for another 1500 years – though hints do creep in as incidental features in paintings. A picture from the 1580s by Valkenborch makes a prominent display of several pots containing what look like aloe and prickly pear, newly received from the Americas. Such delicate plants may well have stood within the house.

In 1706 Louis Léger recommended the chimney campanula as a summer screen for the fireplace, flanked by pots of tuberose and scarlet lychnis. "Where there is not the convenience of a balcony, the chambers of a house may have their ornaments [houseplants] which may well last for a considerable time especially when fires are not in use," noted Thomas Fairchild in *The City Garden,* 1722.

Fairchild's sumptuous choice for fireplace or window was the potted, blossoming orange tree "with fruit upon it, intermixt with myrtles. It would remain until August and then be sent back to the garden to be taken care of."

By the late 1700s, mignonette was a favourite, environmentally beneficial window plant with a "perfume so powerful it is sufficient to protect the inhabitants from those effluvias which bring disorders in the air".

The chrysanthemum, introduced in 1764, gave an autumnal distinction to the cottage casement. Other plants commonly grown in windows included *Fuchsia globosa,* the Fair Helen geranium, crimson china roses and *Campanula pyramidalis.*

By the early 1800s came the backlash – the pot plant as health hazard. Detractors noted that at night plants "exhale carbonic acid gas, and inhale oxygen, making them, after twilight, undesirable neighbours in our living rooms".

The gardener R. Fish offered a simple remedy: "As gas is three times heavier than the common air, it will fall to the floor: injury might be avoided by seeing that the plants were lower than the seat or couch of the owner. I believe that healthy plants in rooms are decidedly beneficial and promotive alike of cheerfulness and health."

The passion for houseplants was shared right across the strictly-defined strata of 19th-century society. We find one writer observing that, "The more polished part of society admits the Ethiopian calla, a species of arum, into the most embellished saloons."

The Victorian house became a green and fecund place, with a growing emphasis on foliage from the 1850s onwards. One illustration shows a jungle of yuccas, New Zealand flax, palms, Indian rubber and ivy plants grouped in the drawing room. Vines were grown for the dinner table, the pot bases concealed in holes cut in mahogany tables and damask cloths.

The greatest threat to the Victorian houseplant, far worse than thrips, red spider and greenfly, was house gas. "The slightest escape is enough to cause leaves to droop and fall off prematurely," noted one book. The Wardian case provided a sealed solution: a self-supporting growing cycle in an enclosed glass case.

In the early years of the 20th century, the houseplant fell temporarily from fashion through much of Europe, while the heavy greenery of palms lingered in hotel lounges and ballrooms. After the Second World War the grower Thomas Rochford led a revival as the centrally-heated home and office became an increasingly welcoming habitat.

At first, Rochford and the other post-war growers were horticultural Henry Fords: everything they sold was green – mainly ivy and rubber plants. Gradually, however, colour complemented foliage as growers developed tougher, longer-lasting flowering plants. The Rochfords hybridised the once-delicate poinsettia, thereby extending the flowering life of the Christmas present at least until Easter.

Vriesea carinata – a bromeliad normally found growing in broken shade in tropical jungles. If it is to survive under glass, the temperature must never fall below 60 deg. F, or the humidity below 75 per cent

ice, extends the growing season and provides additional warmth as a result of the so-called "greenhouse effect" caused by sunlight penetrating the glass as short-wave radiation. Inside, it is reflected by the plants and soil to become long-wave radiation which cannot get out. Thus, having shut the greenhouse door, the gardener assumes the role of nature, controlling the plants' entire environment – warmth, light, soil and water. By juggling with these elemental requirements, there is almost no limit to what can be grown under glass.

The shape of the modern greenhouse varies enormously, from the traditional lean-to and free-standing span-roof styles (built nowadays with western red cedar or lightweight aluminium), to stylish glass octagons and greenhouses of geodesic design. Specialist buildings such as alpine houses are also available, and high technology in the shape of solar heating panels, double-glazing, fully automatic ventilation and irrigation systems, and heating controlled at the touch of a button, providing a protected year-round micro-climate well within the reach of the keen amateur gardener.

The boom in private greenhouses has been matched by commercial growers. The commercial glasshouse industry was established at Worthing in the 1880s but did not seriously expand until the inter-war years, when acres of tomatoes and cucumbers began to spring up under glass in North London's Lea Valley. Today, despite fierce competition from abroad, Britain has a glasshouse industry second to none, supplying a year-round chrysanthemum trade and catering for the ever-expanding houseplant market as well as continuing to grow major glasshouse vegetable crops.

The past two decades have seen an increasing use of plastics among commercial growers, with polythene "tunnels" replacing glass cloches and plastic mulch becoming widely used – sheets of black plastic spiked out on the ground to keep weeds out and moisture in, while allowing young plants to grow through it. However, plastics tend to be more costly and less efficient than glass in terms of light transmission. Also, although polycarbonate is guaranteed to last 10 years, polythene tunnels will last only for two or three years, while glass goes on for ever.

Another sign of the times is the huge increase in the popularity of container plants. For Britain's urban dwellers confined to flats and apartments, the need for greenery can now be satisfied by an extraordinary variety of houseplants. The modern trade is quite different from maidenhair ferns in porcelain jardinières burgeoning in Victorian drawing rooms. Now the local garden centre can supply African violets, begonias, pelargoniums, a *Ficus pumilia* with large glossy leaves, or a Swiss cheese plant, *Monstera deliciosa,* to enhance a living room. The traditional porous clay flower pot has given way to plastic, and nowadays indoor plants can even be made to grow without soil through the science of hydroponics, where gravel simply supports the plant structure and the container is topped up with a chemical cocktail of plant food and fertiliser.

In recent years the conservatory has returned as an extension of the house: an additional sun room for people as well as plants, with climbing vines and bougainvillaea, tubs and troughs of azaleas and fuchsias, hanging baskets and epiphytic bromeliads grown on a potted "plant tree".

But perhaps the most exciting development in this conservation-conscious decade has been the tropical butterfly garden: an indoor jungle, steamy and sunlit, filled with exotic shrubs and nectar-rich flowers, where visitors may walk among hundreds of brilliantly-coloured butterflies from the rainforests of Malaysia, the Philippines, India and Taiwan.

The first walk-through butterfly house in Europe was built in Guernsey by David Lowe; then Clive Farrell, a London property developer with a lifelong passion for butterflies, brought the idea to the mainland. In 1981 he opened the London Butterfly House at Syon Park, and he has since established other tropical houses at Weymouth, Edinburgh and Stratford-upon-Avon. Today Britain has more than 40 butterfly houses, attracting at least four million visitors a year with a turnover of some £5 million.

Butterfly gardening is encouraging a science of its own, calling for a knowledge of favoured hothouse butterfly food plants and their cultivation: *Lantana camara, Hoya carnosa* with its sweet, waxy pinkish-white flowers, and the African marigold, *Tagetes erecta.* It has also evolved a novel form of pest control. Since insecticides cannot be used, many butterfly houses keep a few miniature quails to snap up mites and spiders. Quails are essentially ground birds, and therefore present no threat to the butterflies. Eventually, by refining such techniques, it may become possible to reproduce and maintain entire eco-systems under glass, keeping alive at least a fragment of the tropical rainforest – the richest and most threatened of the world's wild plant kingdoms.

Medinilla magnifica – a spectacular denizen of the seasonally dry tropics. It requires a minimum temperature under glass of 55–60 deg. F.

VI

A Natural Romance

By John Brookes

Changes in the garden – the way we design, perceive and use it – are eloquent testimony to changes in the world at large. Once upon a time the function of the formal decorative garden was to create a human enclave – a civilised redoubt against the savagery and awfulness of the untamed natural world outside. Now it is precisely the opposite. The garden preserves a small, cherished echo of that long-lost natural world, and serves to insulate the gardener against the awfulness of man himself.

Water has been a key element in garden design throughout history. In this Oxfordshire woodland garden the architect Clough Williams-Ellis tamed a fast-flowing Cotswold stream by diverting it into pools

The concept of gardening, or the taming of nature, is as old as the concept of farming. As soon as man ceased to be nomadic, and built himself a shelter next to the land he tilled and surrounded it with a protective wall, it could be said that he had built himself a garden. This was not initially a decorative garden since at night it had to provide shelter for sheep, goats and pigs. Only gradually did the farmer consider growing plants for his own sustenance, by which time he had found alternative shelter for his stock. But the very fact that land around the home was fenced or walled marked its separation from the wild; man was starting, however incidentally, to condition the landscape in which he lived. This conditioning of what existed naturally has produced over the centuries specific garden forms, designed as extensions to the home. These developments have had little or nothing to do with the garden's horticultural content. For it was not until after the 18th century that a horticultural embarrassment of riches complicated the design concept and led eventually to the "gardened look" which we know today.

Opposite: the knot was one of the later developments of the medieval garden – a geometric pattern within one or more squares, made of clipped box hedging and herbs

The layout of those early gardens – known, though scarcely documented, from the Egyptian and throughout all the early middle-eastern civilisations – was, of course, conditioned by climate and water, or, crucially, the lack of it, for nothing would grow without regular irrigation. It was the grid-iron pattern of irrigational channels feeding the garden that was later reinterpreted to become the basic shape of the classic, formal layout – a shape which lasted until the end of the 17th century. The scale of the formal garden became more extensive over the centuries as man's attitudes to nature changed. He first subdued his response to the "awfulness" of nature, then conquered and understood it, until in the 18th century he presumed he could actually improve upon it.

As a reaction to this in the 19th century the garden became inward-looking again, for hundreds of new plants had been introduced from all over the world. Not until recently did these two aspects – nature and the formal tradition – recommence some sort of dialogue. It is therefore society's changing response to wildness which conditions the development of the garden plan, which in turn is interpreted according to prevailing artistic tastes. The form of the garden is part of contemporary cultural expression, touching all the social mores of the period.

The Formal Tradition

The Greeks, we believe, were not great gardeners, though they planted sacred groves around their temples. The Romans, on the other hand, were determined cultivators and brought to this country an established tradition which they applied to the grounds of their palaces. It was the Roman tradition, with an Islamic overlay from North Africa, which later reappeared as the early Renaissance garden in Italy.

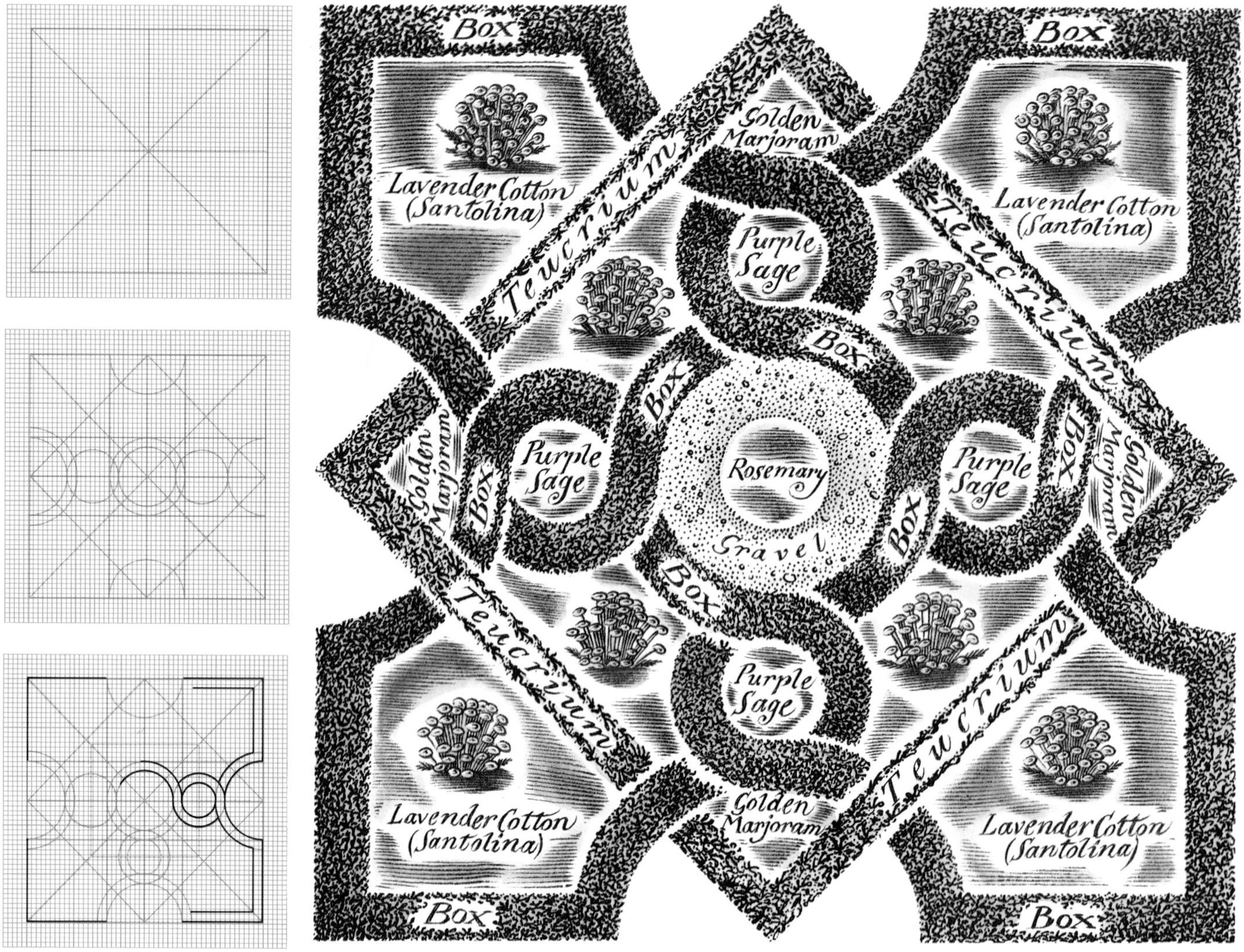

The drawings on graph paper show the three stages in the construction of the pattern for the knot. The scaled-up outline can be pegged out on the ground and planted as above. (Design by John Brookes.)

THE FORMAL KNOT

By John Brookes

It is easy to understand the fascination of a formal layout and the attraction of pure geometry when drawing up a knot.

The illustration shows the centrepiece of the Tudor House garden in Southampton, realised in teucrium, box and scented herbs. The outline is 24 ft sq., and the area is subdivided into four sections. On and from these axes the radii of all the circles generate to create an intriguing interlacing linear pattern.

Such a layout was probably pegged out with string and staves. Circles were scraped in the grass or earth surface using a peg as the fulcrum from which to describe an arc with string. The original planting would have been two sorts of herbs with contrasting foliage; smaller areas might contain purple sage, gold marjoram, lavender or rosemary.

This plan could be recreated with the main outline in box and the diamond in teucrium. Plant a rosemary in the centre in a circle of gravel with purple sage in the four adjoining circles. The four shields from the centre circle to the corners could be filled with grey-leaved santolina, and finally, golden marjoram could be planted in the corners of the diamond.

Right: the popular demand for colour has led public gardeners to use more flamboyant fillings inside the hedges of modern parterres. This mixture of tulips and primulas in Holland Park, London, is a good example

The practice of gardening was kept alive through the Dark Ages within monastic houses of learning. The garden emerged in Britain as an enclosed small space known as a "herber" (from *herbarium*), attached to a noble household. The pattern of the herber was not dissimilar from the traditional grid-iron – a cruciform shape with central pool, and raised beds punctuated by turf seats. Great emphasis was placed on perfume and the tactile pleasures of soft-leaved plants such as sage and myrtle. We know that red and white roses were grown, as were madonna lilies, flag iris, peony and honeysuckle.

Fruit trees, too, were extensively grown, and it was their need for extra space which perhaps triggered the outward expansion of the enclosed garden into the "pleasure garden", with plantings of apple, pear, cherry, medlar, plum, mulberry and quince trees.

One of the later developments of the medieval garden was the knot – a geometric pattern within a square, or series of squares, made of box and herbs clipped into shape. Royal knot gardens were decorated with carved wooden facsimiles of the King's (Henry VIII's) or Queen's (Elizabeth I's) beasts. The maze and the mount were also part of the late medieval layout.

At this stage in the development of the garden plan, the symmetrical orchard planting of the pleasure garden was replaced by an equally symmetrical scheme of limes, elms or horse-chestnuts, becoming in maturity the form of the avenue. Avenue planting has always been a mark of authority. In France, rides cut through surrounding forests extended the formal design deep into the countryside.

The French influence was introduced to this country through the writings of André Mollet in his *Le Jardin de Plaisir* of 1651. If the bird's-eye drawings of the Dutch illustrators Knyff and Kip are to be believed, avenues were planted traversing the English countryside hill and dale. The fashion was furthered by John Evelyn's writing in 1664. His *Sylva – or a Discourse on Forest Trees* encouraged planting to maintain the supply of timber for the Navy, and no doubt for further generations of timber-framed houses, too.

Trees for these vast plantings very often came from the nursery of London and Wise, which had begun in 1681 on the flat riverside land now occupied by the Victoria and Albert Museum in London's Cromwell Road. But even while the formal plantings were creeping across the countryside, other areas of ground were being designated as wilderness, in which a looser arrangement of plants was being grown. As early as 1692, Sir William Temple, a statesman and keen gardener, was describing the informality of the Chinese garden, known as the *Sharawadgi* – a new random approach which allowed for personal exploration of the state of wildness, albeit simulated.

In the 18th century, landscape designers "leaped the fence and saw all nature was a garden". Classic, formal plans were swept away and replaced with vast pastoral idylls

Nature and Romance

The next steps were the taming of that wildness and then the improvement of it – a process encouraged by writers on the romance of the pastoral. More practically the essayist Joseph Addison wrote: "Why may not a Whole Estate be thrown into a kind of garden by frequent plantations? . . . If the 'natural' embroidery of the meadows were helped and improved by some small additions of Art – a man might make a pretty Landscape of his own possessions." So, within a very short time, the fashion was to put away the grid-iron formality of a thousand years and to romanticise and "garden" nature.

The first landscape designer to make the transition was Charles Bridgeman, who died in 1738. He was followed by William Kent (1685–1748), who later emerged as an architect as well. Under the patronage of the third Earl of Burlington, Kent followed the fashionable Grand Tour and thus was well informed on developments in Renaissance Italy. He returned to foster the 18th-century Palladian revival, surrounding new buildings with a landscaped setting "in the modern taste" (Walpole), which was widely accepted as complementary.

Kent's designs had a disconnected quality, since he followed the school of thought that "all gardening is landscape painting". In Italy he had studied the work of the fashionable landscape painters Claude Lorrain, Poussin and Salvator Rosa, from whom he had imbibed a feeling for the Picturesque scene, which he translated into the English countryside. His landscapes were designed as a series of classic tableaux, like a gallery of separately framed paintings in an idealised "wilderness" of woodland, water and statuary, with varying degrees of light and shade free from all formality. They earned him the immortal praise of Horace Walpole: "He leaped the fence and saw all nature was a garden".

Kent was succeeded by Lancelot "Capability" Brown (1716–1783), who during his long working lifetime transformed the English, still largely medieval, landscape, removing many classic formal gardens to create idealised pastoral settings in the Picturesque manner. He welded together Kent's disconnected essays into what has been described as Britain's only truly indigenous art form – the landscape garden.

A typical Brown park would be approached through a lodged entrance, with the line of the drive leading the visitor's carriage on a circuitous route to the mansion, making the park seem as large as possible. On the way, you would get a snatched glimpse of the house rising from a lawn above a stretch of water, before plunging into woodland shade. Then you would get another view from the bridge over the lake; then back into greenery again before emerging at the approach to the forecourt. Within the house, you climbed a grand stairway to the reception room on the first floor *(piano nobile)*, from which you could look back out across the water (usually a river or stream dammed to form a lake). Around the lake, encircled by further green plantings in a gently rolling landscape, your eye would be caught by carefully placed architectural features – a temple, perhaps, or an obelisk – with occasional views into the countryside beyond.

Overleaf: designers of 20th-century parterres cannot afford to produce the subtle and intricate patterns of former ages, and have to content themselves with simple geometric designs filled out with solid blocks of only a limited number of contrasting plants. This example is at New Place, Stratford-upon-Avon

Brown grouped his mainly indigenous trees to screen the site boundaries, arranging them in clumps according to type. These often extended into the estate farmland, so that the park seemed to roll on for ever. The "offices" – stables, vegetable garden, even the flower border and staff houses – were well screened away from the main house. If the old tenant's house, or even the village, got in the way of the new development, then it would be re-sited, with only the church remaining to become yet another eye-catcher in the landscape. Where it was impossible to remove or hide

an unwanted structure, its architectural form would be carefully modified to make it more visually attractive.

Deer and cattle grazed the parkland to keep the grass down, but since one of the features of a Brownian landscape was for the house to sit uncluttered within a lawned space, there usually had to be some way to stop them coming right up to it. Bridgeman, Kent and Brown all used the ha-ha ditch. Only in the late 20th century are we seeing the culmination of what the 18th century could see only in its imagination. The full effect depends on the maturity of thousands of slow-growing hardwoods which Brown and others planted as saplings. The great 18th-century phenomenon was the patronage which allowed this revolution in garden thinking. Powerful though the literary and cultural influences were, it is doubtful whether they could have succeeded without concurrent social change.

The Enclosure Acts led to an improvement in agriculture; better transport and increasing economic expansion led to a period of great wealth and stimulus to development and improvement. Humphry Repton (1752–1818), who succeeded Brown, was trained in the principles of the 18th century, though he found himself serving clients in the 19th. In the preface to his *Fragments on Theory and Practice of Landscape Gardening*, in 1816, he commented on the decline of his profession which he said was attributable partly to high taxation, but more especially to a new type of owner – "solicitous to increase property rather than enjoy it", and anxious to "improve the value, rather than the beauty" of his newly-purchased estate. Prophetic words indeed.

Humphry Repton was disinclined to trust his clients' imagination, so provided "before" and "after" views to help them appreciate the impact of his designs on their parks. This is his vision for a water feature at Wentworth in Yorkshire

The 19th-Century Horticulturalists

The beginning of the 19th century was the beginning of a new industrial and scientific age. Great technological strides were being made in engineering, milling and mining, and with these advances came new affluence and the rise of a middle class

The Gardenesque style of the early 19th century reflected the affluence of a rising new urban middle class and was a showplace for the new technique of bedding out

living in smaller, more urban properties than their 18th-century predecessors. The precedent of the landscaped Picturesque park, with its classical allusion, ornament and sombre indigenous tree planting, held little significance for the new garden owner. He wanted a setting in which to show off all the newly-imported plant material, and the new colourful horticultural technique of bedding out. The writer J. C. Loudon proposed a loose form of design containing many of these new facets, which he called the Gardenesque.

But increasingly there was regret at the destruction of those earlier formal layouts and their replacement by the landscaped park, and new awareness of the formal layouts of continental gardens. So the mood once again was of transition, and a variety of garden styles emerged based on this symmetrical, historical precedent.

Repton himself had begun to scale down his designs adjacent to the house, and succeeding designers followed his example. The result was an inward-looking garden – but one which, for the first time, was furnished with flowering exotica: trees, shrubs and annuals, the more the merrier. By the 1840s there was a huge increase in the amount and variety of plant material available. Labour was still cheap, and after the abolition of the tax on glass in 1845 the greenhouse, too, was an essential part of the garden.

As this new gardening public had little horticultural precedent to turn to for advice, reference books and encyclopaedias poured from the presses, and specialist

Across the Water

By John Brookes

Water, already an attractive focal point in a garden, gains in importance if a bridge crosses it.

Bridges in gardens were a tradition in ancient China, and the Chinese particularly favoured a curved shape which joined with its reflection to make a perfect circle. Early Japanese gardeners often made bridges whose path contained a right-angle to prevent devils crossing.

Bridges started to appear in the 17th century and their design became more and more ornamental as gardens became simpler in the 1700s. Quite often chinoiserie motifs decorated the timber handrail. Grander bridges with classical ornament, even colonnaded superstructures, became a major feature – a sort of Palladian pavilion over the water. The one at Wilton House, Wiltshire, is most famous, with copies at Prior Park, Bath, at the bottom of a long vista, and at Stowe in Buckinghamshire. Another well-known 18th-century bridge is at Kenwood in Highgate. It seemingly marks the end of the lake; in reality it conceals a dam.

Many very refined bridges with metal balustrades were constructed for the first time in the last century; by contrast, the rustic timber bridge also made its appearance. Today, the Japanese influence has simplified the garden bridge and the interest lies in simplicity of form.

Above: the bridge at Wilton House in Wiltshire – a "Palladian pavilion over the water" – designed by the ninth Earl of Pembroke ("The Architect Earl") and Roger Morris, c.1737

Right: water and bog plants are a major feature in the garden at Coton Manor, Northamptonshire

The Grotto

To us a grotto might look like a dark, damp unappealing hole. How can it have been fashionable? But apparently just this awesomeness was their attraction: they aroused an almost primeval urge for the sanctuary of the cave, a romantic home for nymphs and ogres.

The concern for grottoes goes back to classical times; they were reintroduced into Italian Renaissance gardens where their coolness and shade must have been sought after. Jokes were played on unsuspecting pilgrims who ventured into their depths by dousing them with water, or barring the way with a waterfall, the devices controlled by valves and stop-taps.

In British 18th-century gardens, grottoes were either mossy and dark or with an inner surface covered with shells, mirror glass, quartz or flint. Dripping water seemed to be a fairly common feature, making them the ideal habitat for ferns. Among the greenery a reclining Nymph of the Grot held sway – as at Stourhead in Wiltshire, where natural stones and stalactites completed the scene.

The Victorians reinterpreted the concept as the backing to a conservatory or a north-facing fernery – "fringed pool, ferned grot, the veriest school of peace".

Rustic Appeal

Running concurrently with the 18th-century idealisation, even "improvement" of nature, was an interest in Rusticity, which was an idealisation of peasant lifestyle.

The Victorians followed the lead of the Romantics in literature, where ruins – not of ancient temples but of broken-down hovels – and old tree stumps were advocated as features. The gardener and writer J. C. Loudon said of this rustic style that it is "what is commonly found accompanying the rudest description of labourers' cottages in the country".

This rustic style was in addition to the high artificiality of much of the rest of the garden, although the two styles would combine in the use of stump curbs or edgings to beds, on which mosses and liverworts were encouraged to grow. The interest in rusticity and natural forms was taken up in the late 19th and early 20th centuries by the Arts and Crafts movement.

The heightened interest in new plants during the 19th century is reflected in this William Morris "Lily and pomegranate" wallpaper design dating from 1886

horticultural societies sprang up like mushrooms. J. C. Loudon was the author of much of this information, and established the first periodical dealing exclusively with the practicalities of gardening – *The Gardeners Magazine*.

While the 19th century fostered a prosperous new merchant middle class, it also established an industrial working one, unlike the previous yeomanry that had been tied to the land. Many first- and second-generation industrial workers, poorly housed in new industrial townships, looked back to their rural origins and, in the cottage tradition, tried to sustain a vegetable garden either in their mean backyards or on allotment gardens nearby. It was these "hardies" who formed the core of many of the specialist societies, and who established the tradition of the down-to-earth gardener, emulated later by the "gentry" in their country-house surrounds.

Throughout the century, the walled vegetable garden with its glasshouses, stove houses, bothy and fruit cage, were very much part of the Victorian garden look. The concept of the garden by now was fragmented into different forms serving each social class. And there was a new dimension: the social conscience of the prosperous industrialist, who felt an obligation to provide some form of recreational facility to alleviate the often appalling conditions in which his workers lived. The result was the emergence of the public park and the early beginnings of the garden city.

The Great Gardeners

The garden layout of the high-Victorian public park was extremely artificial. The style, still maintained by some of our older parks departments, involved dot plants and brashly colourful bedding-out schemes mixed with subtropicals. By the end of the century there was growing unease not only at the unreality of it all, but also at the high maintenance costs.

On top of this came a growing economic depression which affected both agriculture and the properties it sustained. Many country estates, if not broken up, were sold to industrial *nouveaux riches*, who injected new life into them and strove to replicate the lifestyle of the traditional country gent.

So the pendulum started to swing back towards a new vision of the countryside. This time, however, it was directed towards plants and planting rather than the pastoral landscape. William Robinson (1838–1935) was of Irish origin but moved to London in 1861 to take charge of the herbaceous section of the Royal Botanic Garden in Regent's Park. He increased his knowledge on visits to the Continent, during which he must have seen the swathes of wild flowers in the Alpine meadows. In 1870 he produced his book *Alpine Flowers for Gardens*, and soon afterwards *The Wild Garden*. His writings drew public attention to the beauty both of wild flowers and the random planting of hardy perennials "placed . . . under conditions where

Gertrude Jekyll (right in the picture) took her ideas from the simple, cottage gardens she saw in the countryside around her home near Godalming, Surrey

they will thrive without further care". This was an alternative to bedding out, and as such represented a major switch in gardening style. Robinson's *The English Flower Garden*, of 1899, is still a classic in its field.

Robinson's advocacy of the perennial used in a random way was furthered by the writings of his friend and associate Gertrude Jekyll (1843–1932), who succeeded him briefly in the editorship of the *Garden* magazine in 1899. Miss Jekyll was very much a product of her time. She came from a comfortable background and was always interested in what we now recognise as the Arts and Crafts movement. More specifically, her interest was the country way of life which she still saw going on around her Surrey home – the yeoman cottager, his lifestyle and, more specifically, his unsophisticated cottage garden, which had not succumbed to Victorian fashion.

This habit of looking back is common in times of economic stress. But at that time it was also a reaction against the industrialisation and mechanisation of most of the 19th-century. Even in the 18th century, much had been written and illustrated of the idyllic life of the peasant, and all those 19th century factory workers must have wondered what they had let themselves in for.

By the end of the century, however, the mood was definitely one of retrenchment – solid buildings in Tudor style, good oak and the red-nosed hearty squire. Even within my own lifetime I am aware of the tail end of this mood, represented by those dreadful sentimental watercolours of thatched cottages and bluebell woods. Miss Jekyll, while steeped in this tradition, was curiously progressive for her time. As a painter, she studied under the English Impressionist Hercules Brabazon, from whom she learnt valuable lessons in colour and its relationship with light. These lessons informed some of her earliest writings on practical planting design. By mid-life her increasing myopia no longer allowed her to paint and she diverted her attention to the garden next to her parents' house at Munstead.

For her own home at Munstead Wood she commissioned in 1899 the aspiring young architect Edwin Lutyens, with whom, until the end of her life in 1932, she worked in close partnership to create the archetypal turn-of-the-century small country house and garden. Both had a deep understanding of the use of traditional materials. Lutyens planned the layout of the garden as a formal-classic extension of the house, locking it into a series of planes and levels to create an impression of outdoor "rooms". Miss Jekyll's planting schemes employed a high proportion of herbaceous material and non-exotic trees and shrubs. It was the balance and textured qualities of her planting, its scale and colour graduation overlaying Lutyens's strict architectural layout, that made the combination of their work so superb. Miss Jekyll used the experience to produce a number of books on gardening techniques, culminating in her definitive *Colour in the Flower Garden* of 1908.

Also working at about the same time as the Jekyll/Lutyens partnership were Harold Peto (1854–1933), who created many of the Riviera gardens in the English neo-classical manner, and Thomas Mawson (1861–1933). Mawson's beautifully-crafted designs have fine terraces linking the house and garden, with a transitional flight of steps leading to the lawns and shrubberies with views beyond. He was the first President of the Institute of Landscape Architects, elected in 1929.

Fuelled by a growing army of plant collectors, hybridisers and nurserymen, and ably supported by the Royal Horticultural Society, a passion for gardening grew among all classes of English society. Though it had been formed as early as 1804, the RHS really came into its own at around the time of the first Chelsea Flower Show in 1913.

Reacting against the 19th-century obsession with introducing as much colour as possible into flower gardens, more sophisticated 20th-century designers opted for monochromatic schemes like this white garden initially laid out by Vita Sackville-West at Sissinghurst in Kent

Chelsea is still the only regular public platform for contemporary garden designs, though the RHS does not include design within its official mandate. Its primary responsibilities are the introduction, trial and showing of plants for the garden, plus related publications and educational facilities at its headquarters at Wisley in Surrey. In the early part of the century, the RHS's obsession for acid-loving species of rhododendron, combined with Miss Jekyll's example at Munstead and the popularity of the then newly hybridised Japanese cherries, earned the Thirties garden the not entirely complimentary designation of the "Surrey Look".

One of the results of this strong horticultural emphasis was a dichotomy of interest, separating horticulture from garden design. There is still a confusion, I believe, in current thought, and a misunderstanding of the concept of gardening. As we have seen, the garden is a place primarily for *people*. It is a setting for the house, and increasingly a place for relaxation, both active and passive, for the people who live in it. The role of the plants is to furnish the space to create a styled setting for its various functions. But the emphasis on horticulture, exacerbated by the often misleading influence of huge vested interests in the retail market, has brought about a situation in which the tail seems to be wagging the dog. It is to the detriment of many of the plants which were cultivated privately not so long ago, and has resulted almost in the demise of any designed form of layout to contain them.

Many of the "amateur" garden owners at the turn of the century created magnificent layouts and were experts in their own particular fields of horticultural interest. Gardens like Hidcote Manor in Gloucestershire and Sissinghurst in Kent are very much of this tradition – classic, formal layouts of green "rooms" with intricate tapestries of planting within them. It was the introduction of smaller gardens, combined with the shortage of labour following the First World War, that began to loosen up this hedge style. The two main designers working between the wars were Percy Cane (1881–1976) and Russell Page (1908–1985). Cane believed that "there should not be rival claims of formal and landscape styles", and he used a combination of both, with his often fluid garden forms of sweeping beds emerging from the character of the site itself.

Russell Page, famous for his book *The Education of a Gardener* (1962), worked rather more in the tradition of Miss Jekyll, combining a painterly eye with horticultural technique.

Increasingly, the smaller garden, urban and/or suburban, became the norm. Its layout was a scaled-down version of the Surrey look, with the vegetable garden and small greenhouse hidden behind a rotting, rose-covered rustic trellis.

A New Look

As early as 1898, the Czech architect Adolphe Loos published his first attack on what he considered the sham *fin de siècle* architecture and decoration of the period. This feeling of discord with the *ancien régime* provoked the sister arts of painting, sculpture and music to combine over the next 30 years in what became known as the Modernist Movement.

Buildings in England were largely unaffected, though the Scottish architect Charles Rennie Mackintosh gained an international reputation with the design of his Glasgow School of Art (1897–1898), whose uncompromising rationality was combined with a highly original interpretation of Scottish vernacular architecture. He increased his reputation with designs for furniture and fittings which broke away from the then current Art Nouveau movement, whose sinuous and interlacing lines were derived from natural forms. This tradition had developed through avant-garde painters such as Burne-Jones and Rossetti, and in the organic patterning of William Morris and his Arts and Crafts movement of the 1880s and 1890s.

Hard option: the modernist movement of the Thirties introduced concrete to the garden

Mackintosh's work had considerable influence in Austria and Germany, where from 1919 the Bauhaus movement founded by Walter Gropius was furthering a public acceptance of modern architecture. Teaching at the Bauhaus brought about a revolution in art education, allying it to the economics of the factory. In 1925 the architect Mies van der Rohe took control of the Bauhaus School, crystallising many of its theories.

This international and modernist approach was at odds with the Nazi nationalist outlook, and both its principles and its principals moved to the US. (Hitler, incidentally, was quite an accomplished draughtsman, according to his architect Speer, but together they sought to establish an imperial neo-classic form of building, remarkably similar to some current building styles. Hitler was not interested in the landscape or the garden.)

The small number of modernist designers in England formed the influential Tecton group in 1931 and were extraordinarily successful. (They were the pioneers of reinforced concrete structural techniques.) Among their earliest pre-war commissions were the penguin pool at London Zoo and Highpoint flats in Highgate.

While these buildings, with a range of domestic houses, expressed an uncompromising confidence in their structure and form, very few of them reached into their landscape. Rather, they sat "rising above the long grass in a meadow" in the manner of Le Corbusier's famous house at Poissy in France. An exception was a house at Halland, East Sussex, built in 1938, in which the architect Serge Chermayeff and landscape architect Christopher Tunnard achieved a masterly integration using an early Henry Moore sculpture.

In 1939, Tunnard moved to teach in the US, but not before he had published his manifesto, *Gardens in the Modern Landscape*, in 1938. Tunnard was supported by Frank Clark who, until he died in 1971, taught landscape architecture at first Reading and then Edinburgh University. His theory was that the new post-war landscape should be based upon function and utility. It should be asymmetrical when appropriate, allowing sunlight and views screened or framed with opportunities for activity and relaxation, and there should be an avoidance of axial planning and monumental construction. Clark was a founder member of the Institute of Landscape Architects (and, incidentally, of the Garden History Society), along with Geoffrey Jellicoe, Brenda Colvin and Sylvia Crowe.

The development of this new design concept – such as it was – in England was truncated by the Second World War. Not until the commencement of post-war rebuilding in the Fifties was the dialogue on architectural and landscape form reopened. The Festival of Britain in 1951 promoted contemporary landscape work unlike anything which had been seen here before. Landscape design, as opposed to garden design, was now a necessity, for there was new-town development and a growing social awareness of the effects of industry and communication on the landscape. Brenda Colvin's *Land and Landscape* had been published in 1947, and Geoffrey Jellicoe had pioneered the idea of long-term reclamation schemes for quarry operations at the Hope cement works in Derbyshire.

This post-war concern was, literally, a very long way from garden idealism, since the theatre of garden design had decamped to the United States in the late Thirties. Many of the social criteria portrayed on the ubiquitous silver screen had their roots in the garden setting of Hollywood. The Californian style built on the Mexican patio concept was a direct descendant of the Moorish interpretation of the courtyards of southern Spain.

The interpretation of the patio as an outside stage for affluent entertaining, swimming and general socialising, was a new phenomenon demanding active participation. The modernist movement in architecture was variously interpreted according to its location in the US, but in the garden the work of the late Thomas Church crystallised a new look, well illustrated in his *Gardens are the People*, published in 1955. His country-garden layouts were often of abstract shapes moulded into an existing landscape, exhibiting the classic simplicity of an 18th-century park. He also designed town gardens on the west coast. Both these aspects went hand in hand with a growing concern for wider landscapes and prestige industrial layouts.

Back in Europe, as a new affluence arose after huge post-war programmes of renewal, there was new popularity for the concept of the town house. With it came an awareness of the small garden as a viable extension of the often rather limited living space. The American precedent was reinterpreted. With a sideways glance at the extraordinary fluid landscapes of the Brazilian designer Roberto Burle Marx, who worked with native plants, a new form of small-scale outside "room" began to emerge – often urban but just as suitable for a summer terrace within a larger layout. For many of the larger pre-war gardens were now showing the sickness of neglect. The houses to which they were attached were no longer practicable and, lacking hired labour, their owners sought to rationalise and reorientate their layouts.

Garden designs in principle were looser, though commercial efforts still tended to be Surrey updates, interpreted through the eye of another new factor – the local garden centre. For the British public had not, and still has not, understood the concept of abstraction and asymmetry in terms of garden design. It seemed locked into an interminable image of the traditional cottage garden on the one hand, and the formality of gracious garden living on the other. The perennial border had given way to the mixed one; ground-covers were mentioned a lot; heather gardens were *de rigueur* with island beds of mixed conifers; and *Cupressocyparis leylandii* had reared its ugly head along with the eucalyptus grove. There seemed to be very little dialogue concerning their aspirations between designers and horticulturalists.

Sylvia Crowe, now Dame, sought a middle way in her *Garden Design* book of 1958, and Geoffrey Jellicoe, now knighted, sought also to infuse symbolism into the art of landscape through his *Studies in Landscape Design, 1959–1970*.

On the Continent, garden design *had* moved along with horticulture. Their marriage was perfectly illustrated at biennial horticultural expositions throughout Germany, Holland and Switzerland. A pale copy now exists in the apparent mania for garden festivals in this country. To date, their example has done little to further garden design or to give their visitors anything much more than a nice day out.

The Environmentalists

From the Sixties there has been increasing concern for the environment – vernacular architecture, ecology and conservation. It is not surprising, therefore, that the garden starts to look outward again, or at least establish its own identity within its location and site. The landscape profession, which to a large extent had alienated itself from garden design throughout the Sixties and Seventies, has begun to be concerned with smaller layouts again, and to adapt the ecological approach into its present

Still digging for victory. In the austerity of post-war Britain, the garden became a hard-working, linear extension of the internal living space

way of thinking. Hand in hand with this goes a revival in romanticism and yet another look at the cottage garden. There has been an enormous resurgence of interest in the perennial, not entirely unconnected with the re-publication of much of Miss Jekyll's writing. But there have been other influences, too. On the Continent, a wilder approach to landscape gardening has been practised for some time – due in part to a more severe climate (native plants survive much better), but there has also been a greater concern for "natural living" and a more holistic approach overall. This is not entirely to do with environment. A concern with health and diet has also had its effect, expressed through a revival of the herb garden. In the US, too, this

Meadow Gardening

By John Brookes

The meadow garden is a comparatively new technique which parallels our concern for ecology and conservation and – erroneously – many people's desire for low maintenance.

A successful and continuous wild flower meadow is extremely difficult to achieve in a short time; for meadows are really habitats that have been created over the years by the felling of trees and land clearance. The (man-made) meadow was traditionally grazed, and is now often mown, so that the species which grow there in full sun are mostly perennials, the annuals being represented only by such plants as can reproduce by seeds before the first mow. In old pasture-land the predominant species were those that could tolerate and survive cropping and trampling by cattle.

The wildflower meadow look can now be achieved in one of three ways, the easiest of which is to just not mow the grass. However, most people are not into scything and have to cut according to the setting of their mower blades. But, by mowing some areas once a month instead of once a week, wild flowers will start to generate and survive to the height of the cut grass.

With more intermittent cutting, say three times a year, better crops of wild flowers can be established. Rather than waiting for a natural regeneration of wild flowers in longer grass, you may accelerate the process by planting out wild flowers through the grass. They should be watered and sustained until established, when they will seed and spread.

Quite the most radical way to start a meadow is to kill everything over the desired area and seed both grass and wildflowers together in one mix. This way, fine grasses in the correct mix will not stifle the flowers seeds – which native grasses do when established. Just broadcasting wild flower seeds through established grass does not work.

Be sure to choose only wildflower seeds that are local to your area and can survive in your particular soil. Remember that you are upsetting an established ecological system which includes fauna as well as flora.

Above: a naturally regenerating wildflower display is not as easy to achieve as many gardeners suppose. Success depends on sympathetic planting and careful maintenance

Patios and Paths

One great difference in the gardens of the 20th century from those to which they are heir is their designation as outdoor rooms.

Earlier gardens were for passive enjoyment but their diminishing scale in recent times and our requirement of outdoor space, has intensified their usage. As an extension of the house, part of the garden needs to be hard-surfaced and the remainder serviced by paths.

A visit to any garden centre will show how much we rely, for instance, on precast concrete paving of different thicknesses, textures, colours, shapes and sizes.

The architectural work of Lutyens earlier this century, and his accompanying garden detail, has given brick paving a fillip, since stone paving is harder to come by now. Our preference for a soft natural look encourages mixing materials underfoot to provide an equally serviceable but less defined area. Sometimes gravel is chosen, either in combination with paving or as a semi-hard alternative to grass in small town plots. Both gravel – chippings or rounded pea shingle – and paving can be softened in appearance by the imaginative use of plants growing through them.

More leisure time, the influence of travel abroad and attention to health have made a terrace area (let's forget patio), almost obligatory in the warmest part of the garden.

Left: contrasting gravels contribute to a formal parterre at Moseley Old Hall, Wolverhampton. Right: three reasons why paths don't have to be plain concrete

approach has gained increasing popularity, along with a developing sense of more specific identity with local landscapes. People no longer live in the US, or in this State or that County: they now live in Something Valley. The conservation and management of the home environment has taken on an importance and degree of concern generally unparalleled in this country. I never cease to be impressed by the scope of American educational programmes in which design, horticultural and environmental concerns are all seen as inter-related parts of a wider whole.

British concerns for historic landscape and buildings seem to work more on a corporate than a personal level. The National Trust, for instance, continues to do remarkable restoration and preservation work. We have a Garden History Society too, which records the layouts of historic gardens, and a council for the conservation of endangered plant species – the National Council for the Conservation of Plants and Gardens. More progressively-ecological parks are being planned within inner cities, and it is arguable that their function is much more of a refreshment to the urban dweller than the serried ranks of multi-coloured wallflowers typical of the traditional park.

Reversing the social trend of as little as 25 years ago, and following the demise of the village shop and local transport, the elderly are now moving into the town while the young marrieds move to the country. It is difficult to be precise on how this is affecting the look of the garden. With a growing regard for environment, however, those with country properties are learning to introduce locally indigenous flora and fauna, and are discovering how to manage, rather than enclose, them by rejecting alien coniferous boundaries. Their concern is for a wilder look, using garden forms of native material, and bolder groupings, in scale with the surrounding countryside. They make more use of grasses, and of the wildflower meadow. It was very obvious in the aftermath of last autumn's storms that the native trees were often the ones that stood up best – the hollies, yew and oak.

The urban and suburban gardeners, too, are of a new breed. Weaned on the romantic appeal of Laura Ashley, they seek a softer look within their layouts. But it is a look held together by a strong basic pattern: there is even a return to a neo-classic form of layout. Gravel is being used as an infill ground medium. It doesn't need a weekly mow, and self-seeders can be encouraged to romp about in it to create the effect. Anything which cuts down on maintenance is now of interest. The lap pool, hot tub and Jacuzzi are coming through as desirable even in small areas, and the conservatory is there to cement the link between house and garden. The virtues of solar energy are, with luck, moving the Victorian look along a little. Influenced by developments in the US, builders are beginning to appreciate the value of a glazed area *within* the home, rather than one which is stuck on to it.

The modern, "environmental" garden is the polar opposite of its formal ancestors – a haven of "naturalness" with an open invitation to wildlife

Even the garden centres are changing. On the one hand their range of plant material is improving in quality, though the range offered is still often very thin. On the other hand, many of them are now looking more like pleasure parks than garden centres. The reverse of the coin is that there has been a resurgence of specialist growers – though they still have to find their markets through the garden centre.

Towards the end of the 20th century, through all the vicissitudes of social and economic change, the garden still remains for many people their own small paradise. Its form, function and plant content might change, but the concept of a private retreat remains constant. It is perhaps salutary, however, that the retreat is not now from the awfulness of nature, but rather from the awfulness of man himself.

Private worlds: the English garden is a place where not only flowers but fantasies grow, and ambition is the one thing that is never limited by the size of the plot

One Hundred Historic Gardens To Visit

Selected and written by Christopher Thacker

These gardens are chosen from the English Heritage register of listed Grade 1 historic gardens and parks. The County Registers are available by post from: HBMC Stores, Room 32, Building 1, Vision Way, Victoria Road, South Ruislip, Middlesex. Each volume costs £3.50 including postage and packing, apart from Greater London, which costs £4.50. Cheques should be made payable to "English Heritage".

Every attempt has been made to provide information about dates and times of opening, but these are liable to change at short notice. You are strongly recommended to check before setting out. Quite often, gardens open to the public are related to a house within the garden, which may or may not be open at the same time. Where possible, a telephone number for each house has been given, but in some other cases readers are directed towards regularly updated publications such as *Historic Houses, Castles and Gardens, Gardens of England and Wales* (the "Yellow Book"), the *National Trust Handbook* or the *Guide to English Heritage Properties*.

The wheelchair symbol implies "suitable for wheelchairs" but this may not apply to the house. Again, check before your visit. The entries that follow give some information about other facilities, including refreshments, and indicate where parking may be difficult. In other cases, the reader should assume that parking is adequate.

Abbotsbury Gardens

Though Abbotsbury Gardens were begun in the late 18th century (as the walled garden for the now-demolished Abbotsbury Castle), their signal importance as a setting for outstanding plantings of rare trees, shrubs and plants dates from the early and mid-19th century, when William Fox-Strangways, 4th Earl of Ilchester, and his successors pursued an energetic and adventurous policy of planting and garden development. By 1899, over 5000 different plants were listed as growing at Abbotsbury. Similar enthusiasm has been devoted to the gardens since the late 1960s, and their area was expanded to a total of 20 acres in the early 1980s.

The gardens lie in a sheltered hollow, further protected by large wind-breaks of evergreen oak. A stream flows through the gardens, feeding several small ponds.

The plant riches of Abbotsbury are many and glorious – old camellias and Chusan palms in the walled garden; superb *Stranvaesia nussia,* planted 1828, on the West Lawn (and named in honour of William Fox-Strangways – *Stranvaesia* being a Latinisation of his name). In the Valley Garden, westwards from the walled garden, are many rare mature trees – female ginkgo; Caucasian wing nut; Monterey pine; Monterey cypress; redwood; and many hydrangea and eucalyptus.

Since the 1980s date the conservatory, holding a national collection of *Salvia*; the peat and bothy gardens, for delicate Himalayan shrubs; a rose garden; and an area for Chinese plants.

Open mid-March–late October (peak season, spring). Telephone (030 587) 387. ♿. *Refreshments. Abbotsbury Gardens is in Dorset, off the B3157 Weymouth–Bridport road, 200 yards west of Abbotsbury village.*

Alnwick Castle

Round the 12th-century castle of Alnwick – developed and restored in the 18th century and then again, most notably, by Salvin in 1854–6 – one of the sublimer 18th-century landscapes survives in triumphant simplicity; some 500 acres within a larger estate.

The estate was landscaped for the 1st Duke of Northumberland by Capability Brown from the early 1760s until at least 1778 (related to his work for the Duke at Syon Park), and it is Brown's landscape which we admire today. Brown worked with the architects James Paine and Robert Adam, who were also principally involved in restoration of the Castle. Brown's plantations still shape the slopes of the valley through which the River Aln winds, crossed by Adam's bridge. To one side, the area of Hulne Park (related to the medieval Hulne Priory, founded *c.*1240) was enclosed and landscaped by Brown on an extravagant scale.

The paintings by Canaletto, *c.*1750, and Watts, 1783, show most clearly what changes Brown's "landscaping" produced.

Open April–end September, except Saturday, but open Bank Holiday Saturday. Telephone (0665) 602207 or 602196. Located in Alnwick, Northumberland, off the A1, and 30 miles north of Newcastle.

Althorp

The gardens and parkland of some 550 acres round the house go back at least until 1512, with several important stages in their development. In the 17th century, an imposing formal system was laid out. Traces of the long, straight avenues across the park remain, and it has been suggested that they were the work of a French designer influenced by Le Nôtre.

Much of the formal scheme was swept away in the 1780s, when Capability Brown was called in. In 1786 an ornamental dairy, reminiscent of Marie Antoinette's *laiterie* at the Petit Trianon, was built; it retains its original Wedgwood tiles.

In the early 19th century, the lake – the "Oval" – was created to the north-east of the house, with a wooden Doric temple at one end.

The arboretum at Althorp was begun in the 1820s, and its remarkable variety of species was given added lustre from 1863 onwards, as members of the Royal Family planted specimens.

In the mid-19th century formality returned to the gardens round the house, when W. M. Teulon designed the terraces with balustrades and geometrical bedding schemes, to the north and west of the house. Teulon also designed the pillars and ironwork of the forecourt, giving a remarkable setting to the house.

Open all year except Christmas Day. ♿. *Refreshments. 6 miles north-west of Northampton, on the A428.*

Alton Towers

These gardens in Staffordshire are extraordinary. Some 330 acres, varied, extravagant and eccentric, they were made from 1814 to 1835 for the 15th and 16th Earls of Shrewsbury, with the help of several architects and designers.

Alton Towers: 19th-century planting has clad the slopes of a previously bleak valley

While the great house (now a shell) was built mainly from 1837 onwards by Augustus Pugin, the gardens were laid out to the 15th Earl's own plan with R. Abraham, T. Allason, T. Fradgley and J. B. Papworth designing the numerous buildings and monuments he required. The site is a steep-sided valley below the mansion, down which flows the small River Churnet. This valley was once bleak and almost bare, but the lavish and varied planting of trees has clothed the slopes and all but conceals many of the buildings. The grounds also display fine conifers, a rock garden and a rose garden.

Abraham made the domed length of the conservatory, the Gothic prospect tower and the unforgettable pagoda with its cast-iron structure and a fountain jet at its pinnacle: it heralds the iron triumphs of the Victorian age.

Also at Alton Towers is a little Druidical stone circle; a "corkscrew" fountain; a Roman bridge; a Flag Tower; a version of the Choragic Monument to Lysicrates; a rotunda – and much more.

The parkland, on rising ground to the north, is now an amusement park.
Open daily, Easter–October. Telephone (0538) 702200. ♿. Refreshments. On the road from Alton to Farley, off the B5022.

ATHELHAMPTON

The many "areas" or "rooms" of the gardens at Athelhampton in Dorset were mostly laid out beside the 15th- and 16th-century house in the late 19th century, and have been splendidly restored and extended from the 1950s onwards.

The gardens, some 20 acres in varied formal styles, were laid out to the south-west, south and south-east of the house to the design of Francis Inigo Thomas in 1891, or shortly after. Thomas H. Mawson provided further plans around 1904, but it is the 1891 creation which survives. The Great Court, the first and largest of the formal areas, overlooked by the terrace and its pavilions, is square in plan, with a central pool and fountain, surrounded by twelve massive pyramidal yews. At a lower level, is the Corona, a circular walled garden, again with central pool and fountain. To the north-east is the Private Garden, a rectangular lawn with a long pool, flanked on two sides by borders and shrubs and overlooked at one end by the house, with its slight balustraded terrace.

Further areas eastwards include the White Garden, bounded by the River Piddle on the far side; the Cloister Garden and a long rectangular pool, made 1969–70; and the walled kitchen garden, symmetrically divided, with walks and clipped hedges of yew, beech and hornbeam. Lawns on the northern sides of Athelhampton lead down to the river, with a long terrace-walk.
Open Easter–early October, Wednesday, Thursday and Sunday, plus Good Friday and Bank Holiday Monday. Also open Mondays and Tuesdays in August. Telephone (030 584) 363. ♿. Refreshments. 5 miles north-east of Dorchester, and ½ mile east of Puddletown, on the A35.

AUDLEY END

The great house at Audley End was built between 1605 and 1614. It was exceptionally large, even as a "prodigy house", and today, after centuries of change (and reduction), the still-large central court survives as a splendid mansion.

In terms of park, landscape and garden this means a varied history! Walls to the south of the house recall a 17th-century walled garden, and a formal garden scheme was proposed in the 1720s. But when, in 1762, Capability Brown was called in by Sir John Griffin Griffin, the new "landscape" obliterated most of what had been before. In particular, the River Cam was widened to make a "lake" and crossed with a fine bridge by Robert Adam; his Temple of Victory completing the view on the slope of Ring Hill half a mile to the west. North along the Cam are the "Elysian Gardens" created by Richard Woods, with a cascade, and Adam's Palladian bridge (1782–3).

In the 19th century, formal gardens returned. William Sawrey Gilpin made a flower garden to the east of the house, further formalised in the later 1800s. This area is now being restored.
Open April–early October, daily. Closed Monday except Bank Holidays. Telephone (0799) 22399. ♿. Located in Essex, ¾ mile west of Saffron Walden, off the B1383.

THE BACKS

"The Backs" is the name given collectively in Cambridge to the 40-acre strip of landscaped grounds on both sides of the Cam, principally on the west between the river and Queen's Road, and stretching between St John's College to the north and Queens' College to the south.

Though the ground had been divided up since the late Middle Ages, it was not landscaped until the 18th and early 19th centuries. Different bridges, dating from the mid-17th century, give access from the colleges on the east to grounds and gardens on the west. Though Capability Brown produced a scheme in 1779 for general landscaping of The Backs, it was not accepted. (He did however work on the layout of the Wilderness or Fellows' Gardens at St John's in 1772.) The different colleges along the river – St John's, Trinity, Trinity Hall, Clare, King's and Queens' – have therefore each developed their grounds individually. While Clare's gardens extend on both sides of the river, offering spectacular herbaceous displays, the back of King's College extends as lawn and grazing land, allowing an uninterrupted view of the chapel. *Walks beside Queen's Road always open, walk and passages through and between the colleges generally open in daytime. Parking along Queen's Road.* ♿. *Located on the east side of Queen's Road, Cambridge.*

Batsford Arboretum

Batsford Arboretum occupies some 50 acres within a larger area of park and woodland, and was laid out from the 1890s onwards by A. B. Freeman-Mitford (later 1st Baron Redesdale). Having lived and travelled extensively in Japan and the Far East, he was both an expert in oriental species and an enthusiast for the "Wild Garden", which William Robinson advocated.

His arboretum therefore combined a wealth of oriental species (maples, flowering cherries, incense cedar, nutmeg), with oriental garden features (a Japanese rest house and bronze statues). Its sympathetic natural layout took advantage of both the "lie of the land" – a winding stream with rocky pools – and its views, and made the best use of the natural qualities of trees and shrubs. While his original collection of bamboos has been much depleted, the general scope of the arboretum has been widened since 1956, including a notable collection of oaks. *Open early April–end October. Telephone (0386) 700409. Garden centre. In Gloucestershire, 1½ miles north of Moreton-in-Marsh, on the A44.*

Belsay Hall

The 14th-century castle of Belsay was vacated in the 17th century in favour of a manor house nearby, and this in turn was replaced by a new house built in 1807–17 for Charles Monck, raised on a gigantic walled terrace, with views out over the landscape. Monck was responsible for the early 19th-century landscaping, much influenced by the style of Humphry Repton, and helped by the genuinely "natural" wildness of the terrain. Lawns with heather and shrubbery lead to the Quarry Garden, comparable in England only to the cliff grottoes of Hawkstone. Monck's valley (or gorge) garden passes below an immense rock bridge, among fine, mature shrubs and trees.

The gardens at Belsay, both formal and informal, are rich with their plantings – rhododendron and laburnum, backed by hedges of old yew – and enlivened by water features such as a lake, bridge and waterfall. *Open April–end September, daily, and Sunday afternoon. Telephone (066 181) 636.* ♿. *Refreshments. In Northumberland, 14 miles north-west of Newcastle, on the A696.*

Bicton

In 1957, the estate at Bicton in Devon was divided into three freeholdings. Bicton College of Agriculture is occasionally open to the public; the Bicton Park Trust Company, is frequently open.

The original estate was developed in the early 18th century, when the formal garden was laid out some 600 yards south-east of the house. This garden (*c.*1735), now called the Italian Garden (and the central area of Bicton Park Trust), has symmetrical grassed terraces descending to a formal pond with a fountain, and a designed vista on the far side leading to the obelisk. This design is often attributed to Le Nôtre.

At the head of the Italian Garden is the late 18th-century orangery – the Temple – flanked on the west side by the Palm House, *c.*1820. The latter is one of the earliest, and most interesting, surviving glasshouses in the world. East of the Italian Garden is the American Garden, begun in the 1840s with the Shell House.

In the 19th century, several areas in the estate were planted with collections of rare trees. In the western area of the estate, and south of Bicton House (now the College of Agriculture), the main arboretum was begun *c.*1830, and in 1842 the unique monkey puzzle avenue was laid out. *Open (a) Bicton College of Agriculture, three times a year in May, July and October, telephone (0395) 68353.* ♿. *(b) Bicton Park Trust, telephone (0395) 68465.* ♿. *Refreshments. 7 miles north-east of Exmouth, on the A376.*

Biddulph Grange

The 14 acres of gardens at Biddulph Grange were laid out between *c.*1842 and the late 1860s by James Bateman and his wife Maria, assisted from 1849 onwards by Edward Cooke. The gardens have several different and most carefully separated areas, and their eclectic, yet serious, design is quintessentially Victorian.

From the balustraded terrace in front of the house, we might be in an Italianate garden, with steps, urns and vistas. But out of sight behind shrubbery, trees and raised walls of rock and rubble are a rhododendron ground, a collection of monkey puzzles, a bowling green, quoit ground, "stumpery" and many other features.

Also at Biddulph are "China" and "Egypt" – the two most extraordinary Victorian garden features in Britain. "China" is a 4-acre Chinese garden, with a pavilion, bridge and plantings of bamboo and maple, all enclosed by the "Great Wall" with a lookout tower. "Egypt", guarded by pairs of sphinxes, looks like a tomb-entrance, flanked by huge pyramidal yew hedges. Its tunnel-opening leads not to Pharoah's tomb, however, but to a Cheshire cottage, looking over the pinetum. *Visiting by appointment. Telephone the National Trust (0782) 513149. Located at Biddulph, Staffordshire, near Stoke-on-Trent.*

Birkenhead Park

Birkenhead Park – some 125 acres – is a large, tangible and memorable landmark in the history of the "public garden". It is the first, and indeed one of the best, of the parks in England to be established at public expense.

It was designed by Joseph Paxton (who was shortly to design the Crystal Palace, erected in Hyde Park for the Great Exhibition of 1851), laid out in 1843–7, and opened to the public in 1847. In 1844 two lakes were excavated, one in each area of the park, and their spoil was used to make hillocks to vary the level of the ground.

Belts of trees, varied areas of flowers, a rockery and a cast-iron bridge from this first period have been followed by recreational facilities.

This park was influential not only in Britain, but also abroad. In 1850 it was visited by Frederick Law Olmsted, and was decisive in inspiring his design for New York's Central Park. *Open all year.* ♿. *Refreshments. Birkenhead, Merseyside, bounded by Park Road North, Park Drive and Park Road West.*

Blenheim Palace

One of the most important park and garden landscapes in Britain, of *c.*2500 acres, Blenheim was given by the nation as an expression of gratitude to the Duke of Marlborough following his victories over the French. The palace, designed by Sir John Vanbrugh and modified by Hawksmoor, was built between 1705 and 1726, and the layout of the vast park and its gardens has been continuously developed since the early 18th century.

The first layout was by Henry Wise, in rigid geometric style, with a formal "bastioned" parterre to the south-east of the palace, and a 2-mile avenue extending away from the north-west front to Ditchley Gate. This avenue passed over Vanbrugh's great bridge, which spanned the modest River Glyme. Vanbrugh also made the surviving 8-acre walled kitchen garden.

In 1764–74 Capability Brown was called in to "landscape" this formal scheme; his principal achievement (and his greatest single work in England) being the creation of the lake, realised by damming the Glyme with the Great Cascade, nearly a mile to the south. Brown swept away most of the formal elements, but in the early 20th century several important formal features were added for the 9th Duke of Marlborough by the Frenchman Achille Duchêne. He designed the Italian Garden to the east in 1908, and the Water Parterre, with fountains, to the west of the palace in 1925–30. In recent years extensive replanting and the development of trees – singly, in avenues or in woodland – has taken place. *Open mid-March–end October, daily. Telephone (0993) 811325.* ♿. *Refreshments. Blenheim Palace is in Oxfordshire and can be reached from the A34, at the south-west end of Woodstock.*

Boughton House

While the fabric of Boughton House began with a monastic building in the 15th century, the 150 acres of gardens and park took shape when the house itself was remodelled and enlarged between 1683 and 1695 for the 1st Duke of Montagu.

This remodelling, in continental style, was matched by a grand formal layout in the French manner, with parterres and a geometrical basin to the north. The great outline of this scheme survives as a broad, grassy sweep to the lake, while beyond to the horizon it is flanked by majestic beech and chestnut. Elm avenues have been replaced with lime. Further geometrical avenues and an extension of the water features were added from 1715 onwards and the water scheme of the lake, canal, cascade and Star Pond were restored in 1976.

Open late July–late August; late April–end July and end August–early October, daily except Friday. Telephone (0536) 51573 or 82248. ♿. *Refreshments. In Northamptonshire, 3 miles north of Kettering, on the A43.*

Bowood

The lake and surrounding landscape at Bowood in Wiltshire is the finest surviving example of the art of Capability Brown, who was called in by the 1st Earl of Shelburne in 1757.

The great house built in this period for the Earls of Shelburne was demolished in 1955–6, leaving a complex of buildings including the stable courts and chapel which have been adapted as the present residence. The mid-18th-century walled garden remains to the north, and in the early and mid-19th century a scheme of formal gardens was developed on the terraces to the south of the stable court (the present Bowood House) with statuary, topiary and formal bedding.

By damming the waters of two streams – the Whetham and the Washway – Brown created an apparently "natural" lake some 1½ miles long. Round it, the ground was skilfully contoured, and at the northern end Brown's dam was further developed in 1785–7 with a superb cascade and grotto. The pinetum, developed in the mid-19th century, has been extended to become an arboretum with over 200 species of trees and shrubs. The gardens, lakeside walks and arboretum cover some 100 acres.

A separate area, the Rhododendron Gardens, was developed from 1854 onwards around the mausoleum (by Robert Adam, 1761), three-quarters of a mile west of the house. The plantings now include over 150 varieties of rhododendron and azalea in a 60-acre woodland.

House, gardens and grounds open late March–mid-October. Rhododendron Walks, mid-May–mid-June. Telephone (0249) 812102. ♿. *Refreshments. Garden centre all year. On the A4, between Calne and Chippenham.*

Bramham Park

Within much larger park and woodland, the 66 acres of gardens at Bramham Park were first laid out between *c.*1670 and 1710 for Robert Benson, and possibly designed by Benson himself. Somewhat altered in the 1720s for George Lane Fox, the gardens are one of the most interesting survivals of a large formal layout.

On the main axis behind the house was a formal parterre – now a rose garden, with clipped yews – leading to the great T-shaped canal. Between the house and the parterre the Broad Walk extends beyond the gardens into parkland. It begins with the Ionic Temple, continues to Obelisk Pond, then the Great Cascade, followed in Black Fen Wood by the rotunda and another obelisk.

Aligned with the house, or the arms of the canal, or with each other, are more remarkable buildings or monuments: the Gothic temple, the Four Faces monument, the Open Temple, and the Gothic summerhouse (the latter, *c.*1845). Within the park there are outstanding beech avenues, and fine mature trees in woodland.

Open mid-July–end August, Sunday, Tuesday, Wednesday, Thursday. Also dates in April, May and August. Telephone (0937) 844265. ♿. *In West Yorkshire, 5 miles south of Wetherby, on the A1.*

Castle Ashby

There are more than 500 acres of parkland at Castle Ashby, and an enclosed deer park was here from around the 11th century. "Landscaping" however did not occur until 1761 onwards, when Capability Brown was called in.

A formal garden scheme, with avenues out into the park, had by then been established, and Brown's work involved both the removal and the "softening" of the avenues – by cutting them into sections and rounding them into "clumps" – and considerable planting. Much of his planting remains, especially chestnut and beech. Park Pond and Menagerie Pond were made by Brown.

Just as notable are the formal gardens laid out in 1865 by Matthew Digby Wyatt between the house and the park. They remain as an exceptional example of Victorian formal garden design.

Open daily, 10am–dusk. ♿. *Refreshments. 6 miles east of Northampton.*

Castle Howard

The landscape of Castle Howard is immense; some would say *heroic;* Horace Walpole called it *sublime.* The central 3000 acres are backed by a further 2000 acres of woodland to the north, while the approach drive from the south is nearly 4 miles long, passing gates and fortified walls and monuments at extended intervals. Beside the house, the gardens cover about 100 acres.

The park and garden layout was developed between *c.*1698 and 1738 for Charles Howard, 3rd Earl of Carlisle, his main architect being Sir

Castle Howard: the Atlas Fountain, with statues by John Thomas, was erected in 1853

John Vanbrugh, with further architectural or landscape contributions by Hawksmoor, London and Switzer.

South of Vanbrugh's house (1700–21) was originally a parterre, modified in the 19th century by the addition of the Atlas Fountain in the 1850s, and given lawns and yew hedges *c.*1890. Eastwards, the Broad Walk leads to Ray Wood, with the flanking terrace walk lined by statues and leading to Vanbrugh's Temple of the Four Winds. From this point, one of the supreme views of English garden landscape stretches out from the east round to the south-west, from the Mausoleum (it would "tempt one to be buried alive", wrote Walpole in 1772) to the New River Bridge and the South Lake, and to the Pyramid on the far horizon. North of the house, the Great Lake was added in 1795–9, and in the 19th century a splendid rhododendron collection was established in Ray Wood. In the huge walled kitchen garden, begun *c.*1703, there is now one of the largest collections of old roses in the country. *Open late March–end October. Telephone (065 384) 333.* ♿. *Refreshments. 15 miles north-east of York, and 3 miles off the A64.*

CHATSWORTH

Chatsworth is distinguished by its almost continuous process of evolution. More than in any other garden in the country, one may see a palimpsest of "garden history" displayed, from the 16th century to the present day.

The gardens – *c.*107 acres – are within 1100 acres of park and woodland, which rise up on all sides round the house and gardens. A park, to the east of the house, was enclosed by the early 16th century, and by 1570 Queen Mary's Bower – a raised garden platform in parkland – was built to the west. The turreted Stand on the brow of the land to the north-east was erected *c.*1581.

Between 1685 and *c.*1703, a vast geometrical layout comparable in scale, complexity and character to Versailles, had been created by George London. The Frenchman Grillet made the cascade, *c.*1696, and Thomas Archer designed the pavilion at its summit in 1703.

From *c.*1755 to 1764, Capability Brown transformed the parkland (and simplified much of the gardens), adding plantations round most of the horizon. The course of the River Derwent was "improved", and Paine's bridge added *c.*1763.

From 1826 Joseph Paxton worked here. His Great Stove (1836–40) was demolished 1920, and a maze has been created within its outline. His Emperor Fountain (1834–44) still soars up from the Canal Pond. Development of the gardens in the later 20th century has been extensive, imaginative, and in keeping with the evolving character of the whole.
Open end March–end October. Telephone (024 688) 2204. ♿. *Refreshments. Chatsworth is 1 mile east of Edensor, on the A623.*

CHELSEA PHYSIC GARDEN

The Chelsea Physic Garden was founded in 1673, with an area of 3½ acres. The founders were the Worshipful Company of Apothecaries, who wished to establish a centre for the collection, study and dissemination of medicinal plants. This activity has continued to the present day, and has been extended to cover general instruction in aspects of botany and horticulture.

Originally the site extended to the bank of the Thames. In 1874, when the Chelsea Embankment was completed, access to the river was cut off, and the Physic Garden was reduced to some 2½ acres.

The first layout of the Physic Garden was geometrical – small rectangular beds in which groups of plants could be grown and studied. Though the layout has been varied over the centuries, such *pulvilli* or "teaching beds" still form part of its scheme today.

Famous names associated with the Physic Garden include Sir Hans Sloane; Philip Miller, author of the *Gardener's Dictionary* and curator from 1722 to 1770; William Forsyth, Sir Joseph Banks and Robert Fortune. The rockery is partly composed of lava from Iceland, brought back by Banks in 1772, and is the first European rockery conceived as a special growing-place for rock plants. The garden contains an impressive variety of plants, shrubs and trees.
Open April–October, Sundays and Wednesdays. For further times telephone (01) 352 5646. ♿. *Located in Chelsea, with the Chelsea Embankment to the south.*

CHISWICK HOUSE

Chiswick House (or Villa) was built in the 1720s for Lord Burlington, who was himself the main designer, inspired by Palladio's *villa Rotonda* near Vicenza. The gardens – 65 acres – were laid out first by Charles Bridgeman, then by William Kent, between *c.*1723 and 1738, and include many classical statues. To an extent they attempted to echo – if not to recreate – the setting of an ancient Roman villa.

Bridgeman's work was still in the formal tradition, including a goose-foot pattern of paths lined by clipped hedges, with garden buildings at the end – a temple, a column and a bridge. Beside the Ionic Temple, with a circular pool in front, is the lake, running for 350 yards. Designed by Kent, it is the first "natural" lake in 18th-century gardening, and has at one end Kent's cascade, which is the first example of a deliberately "ruined" garden building to be built. In the mid-19th century, a formal garden was laid out to one side of Burlington's scheme, with the Camellia House (restored 1985–6).
Grounds open all year. For times when the House is open to the public, telephone (01) 995 0508. ♿. *Refreshments. In Burlington Lane, London, ⅓ mile from the Chiswick flyover.*

Chelsea Physic Garden: founded in 1673

CHRIST CHURCH

The college gardens of Christ Church in Oxford comprise of several separate areas totalling 2½ acres, within larger grounds, and with extensive walks in Christ Church Meadows to the south.

Christ Church was founded in 1546. The principal quadrangle, Tom Quad, dates from the 16th century, and since 1670 has had a central stone-lined basin with the Mercury Fountain, surrounded by lawn within the raised paving of the quadrangle. Peckwater Quad was built in the 18th century, and *Oxonia depicta* (1733) shows it laid out with a pattern of grass plots. These were in fact not executed until 1978.

The Dean's Garden is noted for its associations in the 1860s with Lewis Carroll (C. L. Dodgson), Alice Liddell (daughter of the Dean) and the chestnut tree in which the Cheshire Cat appeared and disappeared. The Master's Garden was made in 1926. In the Priory Garden is the oriental plane planted by Dr Pococke in 1636, on his return from Aleppo.

To the south and south-east of the college buildings are Christ Church Meadows, with tree-lined walks down to the River Cherwell and various college barges. The walks enclose the meadows, which are still used as grazing land.
Gardens open evenings daily and Sunday. Walks round Christ Church Meadows open all year. Telephone (0865) 276150. ♿. *Located in Oxford, St Aldates, with entrance on Christ Church Meadows.*

CIRENCESTER PARK

Cirencester Park – all 2500 acres of it – was developed from *c.*1714 onwards for the 1st Earl Bathurst, advised until 1744 by the poet Alexander Pope. It is one of the grandest examples of a landscaped park in England, and may count as one of the earliest "essays" in a more natural style, after the formal geometry of gardens inspired by Louis XIV's Versailles.

The Broad Avenue, aligned on Cirencester Church, and the Elm Avenue, aligned on Cirencester House, stretch out west over the countryside, joined and crossed by lesser avenues or rides. At intersections or focal points there are several garden monuments: the Hexagon, Pope's Seat, and Round Tower, the Square Tower and Queen Anne's Monument. Deep in the woodland to the west is Alfred's Hall, begun in 1721 and a strong contender for the earliest of 18th-century mock-Gothic garden buildings.
Main walks and rides open daily. Parking near Cicely Hill entrance and near several other entrances. Located in Gloucestershire, on the western side of Cirencester.

CLAREMONT

Claremont was one of the earliest "landscape gardens" to be created in this country. A formal layout by Vanbrugh, *c.*1714–26, included the tall, castellated belvedere overlooking the gardens, a broad walk down the hill slope to a bowling green and on to the Amphitheatre, whose grassy banks (laid out by Charles Bridgeman *c.*1724) have been restored in the 1980s. Below the Amphitheatre is the lake, originally round and "softened" by William Kent in the early 1730s, who added the island and its temple *c.*1738. A cascade by Kent was replaced by the present grotto, 1750–68.

In the late 1760s Capability Brown was brought in by the 1st Lord Clive, who demolished Vanbrugh's original mansion, replacing it in 1772 with the present house, designed by Brown and Henry Holland. Brown's landscaping included the extension of the grounds to embrace the hill which was previously beyond the line of the former Portsmouth road. Both Brown and Kent planted many belts and clumps of trees, notably conifers, which were enriched in 1816–31 for Princess Charlotte and Prince Leopold.
(a) Claremont Landscape Garden (National Trust) open all year, closed Christmas Day and New Year's Day. Telephone (0372) 53401. ♿. Refreshments. On the east side of the A307, ½ mile south-east of Esher. (b) Claremont House (The Claremont Fan Court Foundation Limited) open February–November, first complete weekend in each month. Telephone (0372) 67841. Claremont is in Surrey, ½ mile south east from Esher on the A244.

CLIVEDEN

The first Cliveden House (now some 170 acres of gardens and grounds with *c.*250 acres of woodland) was built on high ground close to the east bank of the Thames in the 1670s for the 2nd Duke of Buckinghamshire. The first house was burnt in 1795 and the second in 1849; the present house was built on the same site in 1850–1 for the 2nd Duke of Sutherland by Sir Charles Barry.

A strictly formal garden scheme was set out by 1690, with a brick terrace to the south of the (first) house, overlooking a formal parterre. By about 1735 the Octagon Temple by Leoni (now a chapel) had been built on the western edge of the parterre, with a view over the Thames. In the later 18th century the parterre was replaced by a plain lawn, but after Barry's new mansion had been built, the present layout of the Great Parterre was made in 1851–3 by John Fleming. The lower terrace and the Borghese balustrade, between the upper terrace and the parterre, were added in 1896, while the group of sculpture representing Pluto and Persephone was added after 1893, leaving the scheme of terraces and the Great Parterre very much in the form we see today.

The grounds round Cliveden House retain traces of an early formal layout by Bridgeman, *c.*1723, and are marked also by surviving buildings and sculpture. North of the house, and west of the approach avenue, a rose garden was laid out *c.*1850, redesigned by Geoffrey Jellicoe in 1959. The valley to the west and south-west of the house – Rhododendron Valley and Spring Drive – was developed with informal planting of trees and shrubs, while the main drive from Feathers Lodge was developed after 1893, including the Shell Fountain by T. W. Story (1897). The Water Garden north-east of Rhododendron Valley, with pond, island and pagoda, made from 1893 to 1900, was restored in 1974.
Open March–end December. Telephone (062 86) 5069. ♿. Refreshments available April–October. Located in Buckinghamshire, 2 miles north of Taplow on the B476.

DUNCOMBE PARK

Like Cirencester Park in Gloucestershire, Duncombe Park is one of the earliest grand "essays" in the transitional period between the formal and the landscape garden.

In 1713–14, Thomas Duncombe had his grounds laid out with lawns, avenues and walks through woodland, near the edge of the escarpment overlooking Ryedale. Two temples – the Ionic Rotunda, possibly by Vanbrugh, and the Tuscan Temple, possibly Sir Thomas Robinson – are set on "bastions" at the opposite ends of a grassy terrace overlooking Ryedale. The bastions, though clearly visible from the outer or lower side, serve the purpose of a ha-ha wall by allowing a fine view outwards – from the temples – without the impediment of a raised wall or fence.

Thomas Duncombe aimed to connect his gardens with the escarpment overlooking the ruins of Rievaulx Abbey, three miles to the west, but this aim was not realised until *c.*1758 when his grandson acquired the land.
Open May–August, Wednesday. Telephone (0439) 70213 or contact Tourist Information Centre, Helmsley Market Place. No parking. In North Yorkshire, 1 mile west of Helmsley.

DUNSTER CASTLE

A medieval deer park and woodland of 375 acres surround the wooded hill on which Dunster Castle stands. Much remodelled by Anthony Salvin in 1867, the Castle was begun in the 13th century, and the garden history of Dunster may well have begun soon after, though surviving details are mainly from the early 1700s.

In the 1720s, the castle keep was levelled to form a most pacific garden feature: the walled bowling green. The summerhouse dates from 1727, and in this period the western side of the castle mound was terraced for a small vineyard.

"Picturesque" features were later added – the 17th-century Castle Mill was remodelled around 1780, and a bridge and cascade were built nearby. In the mid-19th century, exotic plants were grown on the sheltered terraces below the castle. The conservatory is Salvin's, built in 1867.
Garden and park open April–October, Sunday–Thursday. Telephone (0643) 821314 for varying hours. ♿. In Dunster, Somerset, 3 miles south-east of Minehead, on the A396.

EAST LAMBROOK MANOR

A little over an acre in size, the garden round the 15th-century manor house was not begun until 1939. Created by Walter and Marjorie Fish (he died in 1947, she in 1969) and since maintained by devoted owners, it is a marvel of compressed exuberance – and order.

As in all great gardens, whether vast or minute, there is a *framework*, formed here from the walls of the garden, the paved paths and the small terraces which accommodate the changing levels of the ground. But this is no abstract garden; it is one alive with a multitude of plants, set together, opposed and combined with a surety of touch which transcends all possibility of "overcrowding". Most of the plants are, necessarily, small to middle-sized, with wonderful early spring delights, such as hellebores and bulbs, followed by iris and euphorbia.
Open daily except Sundays (other than Bank Holiday Sunday). Closed Christmas and New Year. Telephone (0460) 40328. Limited parking. Located in Somerset, 2 miles north of South Petherton, off the A303.

ENDSLEIGH

In 1810 Jeffry Wyatt (later Sir Jeffry Wyatville) built Endsleigh House for the 6th Duke of Bedford, in thickly wooded, steeply sloping grounds overlooking the River Tamar. The year before, Humphry Repton was called in to advise on the building of a "picturesque" cottage (the present Endsleigh House, now a hotel) and his building and landscape proposals, illustrated in his Red Book of 1814, were mostly carried out. It

Great Dixter: the five-acre garden was originally laid out by Lutyens

is one of the most unspoiled of his schemes to survive. The grounds and gardens round the house – some 75 acres including woodland planted as an arboretum later in the 19th century – have been restored, and the larger woodland of over 250 acres still extends beside the river valley.

Repton's proposals included architectural terraces, a geometrical bedding scheme and a central fountain. Half a mile to the south-east is the Swiss Cottage, with an Alpine garden, and westwards from the house is Pond Cottage, with the dairy, "embosomed in all the sublimity of umbrageous majesty". All three are by Wyatt.
Cottages within the grounds may be rented through the Landmark Trust. Telephone (062 882) 5925. Endsleigh is in Devon, 3 miles from Milton Abbot, off the A384.

Farnborough Hall

The terrace-landscape of Farnborough Hall, in Warwickshire, is a mid-18th-century creation by gifted amateurs – the owner Thomas Holbech and his friend Sanderson Miller.

From 1745 onwards, Holbech and Miller landscaped the 160-acre park, developing a sequence of four pools lying round the western and northern sides of the Hall, and the great winding terrace, which stretches southwards for nearly half a mile. Along or near the terrace are four monuments or garden buildings – the octagonal Deer Larder, the Ionic Temple, the Oval Temple and the Obelisk – all built in the mid-18th century. The point of the terrace – and the remarkable merit of the entire scheme – lies in the superb and subtly changing views, both of the pools within the grounds and, especially, of the countryside to west and north-west, over towards Edge Hill. These views are grievously threatened by the progress of the M40 motorway.
Grounds and Terrace walk open early April–end September, Wednesday and Saturday, plus May Day Bank Holiday, Sunday and Monday. Terrace walk only, Thursday, Friday, Sunday. Telephone the National Trust (0684) 850051. ♿ difficult. 6 miles north of Banbury, ½ mile west of the A423.

Godinton Park

The topiary-bastioned enclosure of the Hall and gardens at Godinton in Kent is approached through broad parkland, with a scattering of mature trees. The park has existed for centuries – to the north of the house lies the bare trunk of an oak which was recorded in *Domesday Book*.

The gardens – some 12 acres – were designed in 1902 by Sir Reginald Blomfield, at the time of his restoration of the house. To the north, east and south, the yew hedges were planted in 1902–6. The west is enclosed by the walls of the kitchen block and the 18th-century kitchen garden.

Within this enclosure, the gardens are divided into several areas, separation being aided by a slight fall in the ground. To the north, four Acers stand in the corners of the forecourt; to north-east, pyramidal yews and columnar cypress surround a statue of Pan, who gazes south along the lawn towards a female statue. Beyond, topiary hedges enclose a formal sunken pool garden, graced by lilies and overhung by weeping willow. Beside these, within the enclosure, are a rose garden and an avenue of cherry and sorbus, leading south to a raised balustrade, with views out southwards to the village church.

Beside the kitchen garden is the Italian Garden. The small loggia looks south over a formal pool, flanked by fine borders, and on to an open colonnade and statues, with glimpses beyond to the 5-acre woodland garden. In contrast to the formality of other areas, this is "wild", with many different mature trees and a "natural" underplanting of spring flowers.

This is Blomfield's supreme garden, and one of the most beautiful in the country.
Open Easter Weekend, then June–September, Sunday and Bank Holiday only. Telephone (0233) 37311. ♿. Off the A20, 1½ miles west of Ashford.

Goodwood House

Goodwood Park extends for roughly 1000 acres. It has several distinctive areas and features including the racecourse, laid out in 1802 along the top of the downs.

Goodwood House was begun in the 1720s, and its successive enlargements by Sir William

Hampton Court: centuries of formality

Chambers in the 1760s, and by Wyatt from 1787, were reflected in the surrounding landscape scheme. Between the house and the stable buildings (1757–60, by Chambers) is a fine, small formal garden.

In the mid-18th century, the 2nd Duke of Richmond and his Duchess were noted for their garden enthusiasm. The Duke was an ardent dendrophile, and by mid-18th century his collection here included thirty types of oak and over 400 trees and shrubs from the Americas. The Duchess and her daughters were responsible for the decoration of the Shell House (which is not normally open), the most perfectly preserved example of its kind. On top of the hill in front of the Shell House is Carne's Seat, *c.*1743, by Roger Morris – one of the most elegant of all garden pavilions.

Open May–early October, Sunday and Monday, and extra days in August. Telephone (0243) 774107. ♿. Refreshments. In West Sussex, 3½ miles north-east of Chichester.

Great Dixter

The house at Great Dixter is originally mid-15th-century, with the addition of a 16th-century wing brought from Benenden in Kent in 1910 and another in matching style added by Edwin Lutyens in the same year.

Lutyens was also the first designer of the 5-acre gardens, in 1911, with further features and many modifications by the owner, Nathaniel Lloyd, Mrs Lloyd and their son Christopher Lloyd. The gardens extend round the house in a related, interconnected sequence, divided by walls and, principally, by topiary hedges. They are further separated and distinguished one from another by changes in level and excitingly different layouts and planting schemes. While the topiary shows a sensitive versatility, the variety and inspiration of the planting is proof of continued and genial application. A flowery meadow to the front door is flanked by a sunken garden with low-growing plants and a formal pool, while a rose garden, enclosed by bastions of yew, leads to orchard trees, grass and daffodils, overlooked by Lutyens' terrace and steps. Then there is the Long Border – 70 yards of grouped and blended shrubs and herbaceous plants.

Contemporary as a creation with Hidcote Manor, Great Dixter is of equal importance as an early exemplar of a garden divided into "rooms".

Open daily April–mid-October, except Monday, but open Bank Holiday. For further dates telephone (079 74) 3160. Refreshments sold locally. In East Sussex, 8 miles north-west of Rye.

Greenwich Park

Greenwich Park originated as a medieval hunting park; it was enclosed with a wall in 1619–24. After the Restoration the park was given a formal layout of avenues up the sloping ground to the south. It has been suggested that the design was by one of the French gardeners Le Nôtre or Mollet. A plan exists by Le Nôtre for an *unexecuted* garden at Greenwich, and this is his only sure design for any English garden.

In 1675–6 Wren's Royal Observatory was built on the ridge south of the Queen's House. There are magnificent views north, down to the Queen's House and the Royal Naval College, over the Thames, and to the Island Gardens on the north bank, created there in the 1890s.

In the later 19th century, large and varied ornamental gardens were laid out in the southern part of the park, with a lake, tree collection and fine displays of bedding. Another feature is the excellent bandstand of 1891.

Open all year. Park good all year round, flowers April–July. ♿. Refreshments. Close to the south bank of the Thames at Greenwich.

Grimsthorpe Castle

The vast landscape surrounding Grimsthorpe Castle has included a park since medieval times. In the 1690s, formal gardens were laid out to the south of the castle by George London. The walled kitchen garden to the east and long approach avenues survived in outline all through the 18th century. Capability Brown was called in between 1771 and 1772. The upper part of the park is crossed by a stream and lakes, with a causeway – the Red Bridge (mid-18th century) – carrying the Four Mile Riding, the western approach, across.

In the 19th century, the area of London's parterre was redeveloped as a formal garden. The walled kitchen garden has been redesigned by Lady Ancaster with areas for herbs, vegetables and fruit trees, and fine herbaceous borders. There is also a knot garden.

Open late July–early September, daily except Monday and Friday. ♿. Refreshments. Located in Lincolnshire, 4 miles from Bourne and 9 miles from Colsterworth, on the A151.

Haddon Hall

Within wider, wooded parkland of medieval origin, the 6-acre gardens of Haddon Hall in Derbyshire may well go back to the beginnings of the Hall itself, which dates from the 12th century. It was enlarged in the early 17th century, and the main structure of terraces on which the gardens are set dates from this period.

These gardens are necessarily terraced, since the Hall is built on a steep bluff (with fine views over the River Wye). The highest terrace was, until 1650, a bowling green, then a winter garden, and is now a rose garden with lawns and clipped yews. From this level, steps lead to the Fountain Garden, with the pool enclosed by a lawn and rose beds. Below, the lowest terrace has more lawns and roses, herbaceous borders and a massive yew. A long flight of steps leads down to a pack-horse bridge over the river.

Open early April–end September, daily except Monday, and Sunday and Monday in July and August. Telephone (062 981) 2855. Refreshments sold. Situated 6 miles north-west of Matlock, on the A6.

Hagley Hall

The landscape at Hagley – some 450 acres – was being shaped by the 1st Lord Lyttelton in the late 1740s, several years before the present Hagley Hall was built for him in 1754–60 by Sanderson Miller. The terrain is wooded and sometimes steeply undulating, adorned at different points with garden buildings and monuments, most designed by talented amateurs.

The two most important buildings are the castle, by Sanderson Miller, 1747–8 (the first mock-Gothic *ruin* to be built in the 18th century) and the Temple of Theseus, designed by James "Athenian" Stuart, and built in 1759. This is the first building in Britain in the "primitive Doric" style. This temple, half a mile north of Hagley Hall, is cut off from the main area of the park by the Birmingham road, as is the Obelisk. Other features in the park or related woodland are the Ionic Rotunda, sited beside a chain of small pools, the Prince of Wales' Column, and the remains of Thomson's Seat, commemorating the poet James Thomson.

Open January–February, daily except Saturday. Also open Spring and August Bank Holidays. Telephone (0562) 882408. Refreshments available. In Hereford and Worcester, just off the A456 Birmingham–Kidderminster road.

Hampton Court

The park at Hampton Court – some 660 acres – was enclosed when the palace was built for Cardinal Wolsey (*c.*1515), and further developed for Henry VIII from 1530. Development of the parkland has been related at several points with that of Bushy Park, adjacent to the north.

East of the palace, the semi-circular framework of the Fountain Garden, with its vistas down the Long Water and radial avenues on each side, was developed between the 1660s and 1711. The Fountain Garden was at its most elaborate in the 1690s, consciously imitating the manner of Versailles, with an embroidery parterre designed by the Huguenot *émigré* Daniel Marot. Later much simplified, the scheme was given exuberant bedding displays in the mid-19th century, still maintained round the semi-circle, while huge cones of clipped yew survive from the late 17th century. There are some magnificent 20th-century herbaceous borders along the Broad Walk.

To the south of the palace the 16th-century Privy Garden is now dominated by a 19th-century shrubbery, while the adjacent 17th- or early 18th-century areas beside the Banqueting House (the Pond Gardens) have fine 20th-century planting in several styles. North of the palace, Henry VIII's enclosed garden areas now include the Maze (*c.*1695), the Wilderness, and Tiltyard, with separate rose gardens, plantings of ornamental trees and shrubs, lawns and borders.

Capability Brown was Master Gardener at Hampton Court from 1764, but did not change the gardens apart from planting the Great Vine west of the Pond Gardens.

Gardens open all year. Spring and summer flower displays in different areas. ♿. Refreshments. Beside Hampton Court Bridge, on the north side of the Thames.

Hardwick Hall

Hardwick Hall was built for 'Bess of Hardwick' in 1591–7, and the 7½ acres of the gardens were enclosed at this time. Their present layout and planting however generally date much later.

The forecourt garden now has a geometrical layout of lawns and beds, but in the early 19th century there was a parterre laid out here with Bess's monogram 'ES' (Elizabeth Shrewsbury), which appears in the strap-work cresting of the parapet, repeating the decorative motif used within the Hall.

The main garden, to the south, is quartered by two alleys of trees: an east–west hornbeam alley, crossed by a yew alley running north–south. Within these four areas, there is a lawn; an old orchard (mainly apples, with mulberries to one side); a modern orchard, with pears and crab-apples; and a modern herb garden, laid out in the 1970s – one of the largest, most complex and best-planned in the country.

Open early April–late October, daily (closed Good Friday). Telephone (0246) 850430. ♿. Refreshments sold. Located in Derbyshire, 2 miles south of the A617, 6½ miles north-west of Mansfield.

Harewood House

The undulating terrain at Harewood was landscaped in several periods, and by several designers, from the mid-18th to early 19th centuries. Though Capability Brown's name is most often referred to (he was consulted in 1758, and employed between 1772 and 1781), other practitioners include a Mr Woods and a Mr White in the 1760s, James Webb from 1782 to *c.*1819, and both Repton and London in the early 1800s.

The principal landscape feature is the lake, with a fine cascade. Upstream are lesser ponds, and woodland or plantations surround most of the valley. A Triumphal Arch stands on the north-eastern approach drive, and on the south-eastern approach are the Lofthouse Gates, the New Bridge and the Rough Bridge.

In 1841–8 Sir Charles Barry added the extensive terrace gardens beside the house. The planting scheme, simplified in the early 1900s, has been partially recreated in 1983.

Open April–end October, daily; February, March and November, Sundays only. Telephone (0532) 886225. ♿. Refreshments. Situated in West Yorkshire, 7 miles south of Harrogate, 8 miles north of Leeds, on the A61.

Hatfield House

The complex and beautiful gardens of Hatfield House date from 1609, when Mountain Jennings drew up plans for Robert Cecil, the first Earl of Salisbury. These were executed in the East Garden. The planting was influenced by John Tradescant, whose importance as an introducer of foreign plants and flowers to England cannot be overestimated.

The gardens, some 50 acres, within park and woodland of over 500 acres, are still related to the early 17th-century scheme, but were restored and developed in the 19th and 20th centuries. The present variety of features, in the East and West Gardens, is outstanding.

In the East Gardens – descending from Hatfield House – the upper garden was restored in the 1970s, with a formal bedding scheme between the topiary walks. Below, the lawn leads through fruit trees to the maze (1841), and to the "New Pond", backed by shrubs and woodland beyond.

In the West Gardens formal frameworks enclose a scented garden, herb garden, herbaceous borders and the sunken knot garden, begun in the early 1980s and now one of the most important examples of historical garden recreation.

The park and West Gardens are open late March–early October except Monday, but open Bank Holiday Monday; the East Gardens are open Monday only, except Bank Holiday Monday. Telephone (070 72) 62823 for exact details and other times. Refreshments. In Hatfield, Hertfordshire, opposite the station.

Hestercombe: one of the best surviving examples of formal design by Lutyens and Jekyll

HELMINGHAM HALL

The 4-acre walled garden at Helmingham in Suffolk is both beautiful and unique. It is moated, but separate from the main moat which surrounds Helmingham Hall. Its medieval deer park – around 400 acres – contains some of the oldest oaks in the country, many from the 14th century or before. The magnificent 350-yard oak walk from the lodges to the Hall was planted *c.*1700.

The moated enclosure for the walled garden was built by the 15th century, and the present walls are dated 1749. Within, the layout is divided by paths, and the planting of vegetables and soft fruit is backed by fine espaliered fruit trees and has exuberant herbaceous borders.

Outside the walled garden and within the moat are the Spring Border, the West Border, and an area of lawn with a topiary, statuary, quince and mulberry trees. Outside the moat are the Apple Walk, Meadow Garden and Shrubbery Walk. North-east of the Hall, outside the Hall moat, is a knot garden made in 1982.
Open May–late September, Sundays only. ♿. *Refreshments. 9 miles north of Ipswich, on the B1077.*

HESTERCOMBE

The formal garden layout beside the house at Hestercombe – some 4 acres – is one of the best surviving examples of the partnership of Edwin Lutyens and Gertrude Jekyll. The main feature is the Great Plat (or parterre) – a square sunken garden surrounded by roughstone terrace walks. Steps lead down to the diagonal grass cross-paths and the sundial at the centre.

The terraces to left and right each have a central water-channel, with several small round pools. The water flows from a circular pool set in an alcove in the wall above, which is covered with an overgrowth of wistaria. The far terrace to the south has a massive pergola, with climbing roses, vines, clematis and lavender underplanting. The upper terrace leads on the eastern side to the rotunda, and thence to the east water garden, the orangery and lawn, and the Dutch Garden. The latter – a raised terrace – has foliage bedding, with contrasting arrangements of yuccas and roses.
Open all year, Tuesday, Wednesday and Thursday, plus Sundays in July and August. Telephone (0823) 87222. Best for flowers June to early August. Partly ♿. *In Somerset, 4 miles north-east of Taunton.*

HEVER CASTLE

The 20th-century gardens at Hever were made for William Waldorf Astor (later Lord Astor) in the early 1900s. The gardens – some 30 acres – and the 35-acre lake were designed by Frank Pearson, and were completed by 1908.

Round the castle to the south and east are notable works in topiary – free-standing clipped yews to the south; a topiary chess garden and maze in Anne Boleyn's Garden (the space between the inner and outer moats) to the east. There is also a fine pergola, embraced by wistaria and roses and strengthened by laburnum and apples. The silver garden was added in 1970.

Two hundred yards to the east is the 5-acre Italian Garden, an enclosure of walls and hedges, with lesser compartments along the sides and ending to the east with the loggia overlooking the lake. Within the Italian Garden is a splendid outdoor collection of classical and Renaissance sculpture, given brilliant colour by flowering shrubs, roses and bedding. A hedged sunken garden, with a pool and herbaceous borders, is set in the centre.

Informal areas of shrubs and ornamental woodland extend southwards from the Castle, beside the Golden Stairs, and up to the raised length of Anne Boleyn's Walk – a grassy, tree-lined ride which forms the 500-yard southern boundary, and provides splendid views of the ornamental woodland to the west, the Castle, the Italian Garden and the lake to the east.
Open late March–early November, daily. Telephone (0732) 865224. ♿. *Refreshments. In Kent, 3 miles south-east of Edenbridge, off the B2026.*

HIDCOTE MANOR

One of the most influential of 20th-century gardens, the 11 acres of Hidcote Manor in Gloucestershire were laid out and developed between about 1908 and 1948 by Major Lawrence Johnston. In 1948 they were presented to the National Trust.

Johnston's plan involved a main T-shaped framework of walks lined by clipped hedges, with ways through at several points to the garden areas (or "rooms") which were to the left and right of the T's "stem". Each of these areas – and there are many of them – is to some extent enclosed and sheltered by hedges, and given its own particular character by means of an individual layout and planting. The areas closest to the top of the T (and those higher up) are formal and architectural, while those further down merge with an informal woodland area which Johnston called "Westonbirt".

There is a fine area of kitchen gardens and orchard above Johnston's ornamental gardens, and there are also distinctive views out over the countryside. The concept of the "garden room" was first elaborated here at Hidcote, and at Great Dixter in East Sussex, and was later extended to Sissinghurst in Kent.
Open April–end October, daily except Tuesday and Friday. Telephone (038 677) 333. Partly ♿. *Refreshments. 4 miles north-east of Chipping Campden.*

HIGHCLERE PARK

The parkland round Highclere Castle comes to some 1500 acres – a smaller deer park was here in the middle ages, beside a 14th-century bishop's palace and long stretches of the medieval park pale (or embankment) remain. The original building was replaced in the 18th century, and largely rebuilt by Charles Barry in 1839–42.

Capability Brown was called in by Henry Herbert, 1st Lord Carnarvon, in the 1770s to reshape earlier 18th-century landscaping. Today, Jackdaw's Castle stands opposite the house to complete one vast vista northwards, while Heaven's Gate, *c.*1739, completes another to the south. Milford Lake and Duns Mere were made or enlarged from earlier ponds in the 18th century. The early 18th-century walled garden has dividing hedges of yew round beds of roses.

At the start of the 19th century, ornamental shrubberies and woodland were planted with exotic trees, and Highclere was noted for its success in raising hybrids – two of which bear the Latin name for Highclere: *Ilex aquifolia altaclarense* and *Rhododendron altaclarense. Telephone (0635) 253210. In Hampshire, 4½ miles south of Newbury, west of the A34.*

HOLKHAM HALL

Holkham Hall has one of the supreme 18th-century landscapes. The estate comprises park, woodland and agricultural land of some 3000 acres, and the central landscape was developed mainly in the 1720–30s by William Kent, in 1762 by Capability Brown and in 1801–3 by John Webb. Extensive formal terraces and parterres were built in the mid- and late 19th century by Eden Nesfield and William Burn.

Holkham Hall was designed by Lord Burlington and Thomas Coke, later Lord Leicester (1697–1759), with advice from Kent. Kent's landscape scheme was a part-formal, part-natural layout, with the lake west of the Hall, and striking garden buildings – the obelisk, the Temple and Triumphal Arch.

In the 19th century the formal garden included the orangery by William Burn, south-east of the Hall, and a temple at the east end of the long terrace. In this period, Pleasure Ground Wood – essentially an arboretum – was developed on the eastern side of the Hall.
Telephone (0328) 710227. Refreshments available. In Norfolk, 14 miles from Hunstanton, at Holkham on the A149.

HOUGHTON HALL

Sir Robert Walpole's plans for the parkland at Houghton began as early as 1707 but the present Hall was not built until 1722–35. The stable courtyard (the "Square") was built to the south-

Knole: fallow deer grazing in the park, which dates from the 15th century

west in 1733–5, with the walled kitchen garden further south-west.

The plan for the park was implemented in the mid-1720s, with a vast layout of rides, avenues and woodland plantations round the Hall. The old village of Houghton was also removed, to be re-established as "New Houghton" ¾ mile further to the south. This event was one of the sources of Goldsmith's poem the "Deserted Village". The original layout, possibly by Charles Bridgeman, involved formal gardens beside the Hall, with avenues aligned both on the Hall and on features in the landscape, such as the Water Tower, built in 1730–1 and designed by Lord Pembroke.

Though the formal layout round the Hall has gone, the lines of the main avenues, or the vistas between areas of woodland, remain in open grassy parkland.

Open April–end September, Sunday, Thursday and Bank Holiday. Telephone (048 522) 569. ♿. *Refreshments. In Norfolk, 13 miles east of King's Lynn, 10 miles west of Fakenham.*

Hyde Park

In the 16th century, Hyde Park was a deer park, but from the 17th century onwards it has been open to the public. It was not given any "design" until it was landscaped by William Kent, who created the Long Water and the Serpentine in about 1730 by damming the waters of the River Westbourne.

The park – some 320 acres – is criss-crossed by walks and horse rides, including Rotten Row, running roughly along the south boundary from Hyde Park Corner to the (vehicular) West Carriage Drive. Many mature trees, including planes, chestnut and lime, are planted along these drives and paths, and beside the undulating sweeps of grass. The site of the gallows at Tyburn is at the north-eastern corner of the park, close to Nash's Marble Arch, which was re-sited here in 1851, and to the area of Speakers Corner.

Open all year. ♿. *Refreshments. East of Kensington Gardens, with Bayswater Road to the north, Park Lane to the east.*

Iford Manor

This terraced hillside garden of 2½ acres is the masterpiece of Harold Peto, who lived here from 1899 until his death in 1933.

The steeply sloping ground beside and to the rear of Iford Manor was probably first shaped into terraces in the early and mid-18th century, and some of the walks in Iford Wood, which rises up behind the house, may then have been laid out. Some of the mature trees – cedar, plane, chestnut, beech – may also have been planted in the 19th century, but the principal layout, and all the architectural adornment, was Peto's work.

Over many years the three main terraces were given courtyards, seats, colonnades, separate columns, balustrades and connecting flights of steps. A variety of garden buildings and features were also added, such as a pool with fountain; a well-head (Byzantine); a summerhouse (Spanish); a garden house (18th-century), and cloisters (medieval), with accompanying items of statuary, urns and other sculpture. Steps up into the woodland lead past a Japanese garden, now in restoration, to a column dedicated to "Edward the Peacemaker" (Edward VII).

Fine planting of trees and shrubs softens the strongly Italianate architectural character, as do sloping lawns and the gentle views out from the garden over the River Frome to the south-west. The medieval bridge over the river has an 18th-century statue of Britannia, placed there by Peto.

Open May–August, Wednesday and Sunday. For details and other times, telephone (022 16) 314 or 2840. Refreshments Sundays only. In Wiltshire, 7 miles south-east of Bath, on the A36.

Kedleston Hall

Kedleston Hall is famous as the home of the Curzons, notably of Lord Curzon, Viceroy of India from 1898 to 1904. But for architects it is above all a treasure-house (literally) of early work by Robert Adam, who remodelled the existing house from 1758–9 onwards, designed many of the garden buildings, and also played a major part in landscaping the park.

The park – some 500 acres – encloses a smaller area of gardens, *c.*20 acres, which had been included in a formal layout by Charles Bridgeman in 1722–6, but Adam's larger landscape swept this away. Most important is the long Serpentine Lake, with islands, which he created in front of the Hall in the 1770s, with a three-arched bridge (there is a cascade beneath) and a fishingroom-cum-boathouse-cum-bathhouse.

The gardens round the Hall also contain features by Adam, but several were moved from their original sites when Lord Curzon remodelled the gardens in the 1920s. The Circular Garden now contains Adam's (or George Richardson's) summerhouse, a carved lion (by Joseph Wilton) on an Adam plinth, and a vase commemorating

Levens Hall: Britain's outstanding topiary garden

the poet Drayton. Adam's orangery stands beside the lawn, and his aviary is located beside the swimming pool.
Open early April–late September, daily (closed Good Friday). Telephone (0332) 842191. ♿. Refreshments. Situated 3 miles north of Derby, from the A38.

KENSINGTON GARDENS

Kensington Gardens, part of the royal parks, began with a formal layout beside Kensington Palace in the late 17th century, when the Palace itself was remodelled by Christopher Wren. The orangery was built in 1704–5.

The park to the east was laid out by Stephen Switzer and Charles Bridgeman in the early 18th century, still in formal style. The main survivals from their period are the Round Pond and the avenue running eastwards beyond (which are aligned on the eastern front of the Palace) and the Broad Walk. Around 1730 William Kent "softened" this design, and he is credited with the creation of the Long Water and the Serpentine at the eastern end of the gardens.

In the 19th century two important formal features were added to the gardens – the Italian Garden, *c.*1860, at the northern end of the Long Water, with its strongly architectural character (pavilion, stairs, balustrades and sculpture), and the Albert Memorial, 1863–72, near the southern boundary. Early in the present century the enclosed sunken garden was created close to the east side of Kensington Palace, with profuse displays of massed flowers round a paved rectangular pool.

Kensington Gardens are now notable for their spacious grassy areas and tree-lined walks. Famous sculptures include Watts' *Statue of Physical Energy* (1907) and *Peter Pan* (1912) by Frampton. South of the Round Pond, the band-stand has been painted by a number of contemporary artists, including Kathleen Browne and Mary Rodd.
Open all year. Spring and summer flower displays in the sunken garden and along the Flower Walk. ♿. Refreshments. West of Hyde Park, between Bayswater Road and Kensington Road.

KNOLE

The deer park at Knole in Kent goes back to the 15th century, and was enlarged several times until the 19th century. There are still fallow and Japanese deer in the park, although part is a golf course, and the whole is crossed by long straight avenues, which were most probably planted in the 18th century.

The rectangular walled enclosure with the house and gardens was complete by the late 16th century, though the wrought-iron gates are a century later. The gardens were laid out formally by a Thomas Akres (or Acres) in 1710–11, and much of his plan survives in outline, providing the lines for walls, paths and divisions between the different areas.

The house stands in the north-west quarter of the rectangle. To the west, south-west and south are areas of lawn, divided by terraced slopes or pergola; a herb garden; an orchard; a lawn planted with rhododendron and azalea, and heroic growth of wistaria along the north-west wall. The Wilderness, in the far south-eastern section of the garden, has fine mature trees, with a unique group of limes. A boggy area is planted with flags and giant ferns.
Park open daily to pedestrians. Garden open May–September, first Wednesday in each month only. Telephone (0732) 450608. ♿. At the south end of Sevenoaks town, east of the A225.

LEONARDSLEE

Planned and planted in wooded terrain from 1889 onwards by Sir Edmund Loder, the 100 acres of Leonardslee Gardens are among the most noted in Britain for their rhododendrons, azaleas and camellias. *Rhododendron loderi* was bred here.

The gardens extend over both sides of a southwards-falling valley, in which a chain of hammer ponds provide a wonderful "natural" focus. The house – built in 1855 – stands near the top of the valley, with a terraced lawn flanked by magnolia, camellia and a fine tulip tree. The collection at Leonardslee includes conifers, maples, oaks, hardy palms and a splendid variety of rare species from Asia and North America, many of them now fully mature, well set out, and with superb views over the Wealden Forest.
Open mid-April–mid-June, daily; July–October, Saturday, Sunday only. Telephone (040 376) 212. Best in May and October. Refreshments. Located in West Sussex, 4½ miles south-east of Horsham, on the A281.

LEVENS HALL

The 10-acre garden beside Levens Hall was laid out in 1689 by Guillaume Beaumont. His formal scheme extends to the north, east and south, and has survived for three centuries with no reduction in area, albeit with distinctive growth in the topiary specimens.

This is Britain's outstanding topiary garden, rare even in Europe as a survivor from the 17th century. Since then the clipped trees have grown – defying the shears – into fantastic and unforgettable shapes, made more striking by thoughtful underplanting of box-edged borders and vivid annuals.

On the west side of the garden a terrace wall, *c.*1694, overlooks a deer park of some 200 acres and is a forerunner of the 18th-century ha-ha, examples of which can be seen at Rousham, Stowe, or West Wycombe.
Open Easter Sunday–mid-October, Sunday–Thursday. Telephone (053 95) 60321. ♿. Refreshments. In Cumbria, 5 miles south of Kendal – exit 36 from the M6.

Longleat

The vast landscape park at Longleat – some 690 acres – was shaped in the mid-18th century by Capability Brown. But long before he was called in by Lord Weymouth in 1757, the area round the 16th-century house had been given a formal, enclosed scheme of gardens, shown in a painting by Jan Sieberechts in the 1670s, and had been much extended – still in formal style – into parkland in the 1690s.

When Brown was called in, he replaced the 17th-century formal layout by lawns, with scattered clumps of trees, and made the course of the "Long Leat" into a chain of "natural" lakes. Humphry Repton was employed from 1803, and he enlarged two of the lakes, putting an "island" between them. The orangery (by Wyatville), the boathouse and the Palladian bridge date from the early 19th century.

By the mid-19th century formality returned, with a flower garden (between Longleat House and the orangery) celebrated for its extravagant bedding displays. This garden survives, having been redeveloped by Russell Page in the 1940s.

The Safari Park, maze and other attractions have been created in the last 25 years.

House, with gardens, open all year except Christmas Day. Telephone (098 53) 551. Safari Park, mid-March–end October. Telephone (098 53) 328. ♿. *Refreshments. In Wiltshire, 4 miles south of Frome, on the A362.*

Magdalen College

The various garden areas of Magdalen College, Oxford, date from widely different periods and include some 36 acres. The college was founded in 1458, and the main quadrangle, enclosing a simple lawn, dates from later in the 15th century.

To the north-east of the college, beside the River Cherwell, are the tree-lined Water Walks and Addison's Walk, dating from the 17th century, with splendid river views down to Magdalen Bridge and Magdalen Tower and up towards Parson's Pleasure. To the north of the college is the walled Deer Park. Deer were first recorded here in 1706–7 and are still a noteworthy element of a garden only a few yards from Oxford High Street.

Open all year. For hours of opening, consult Magdalen College, telephone (0865) 276000. ♿. *Located on the north side of the High Street beside Magdalen Bridge.*

Melbourne Hall

"To suit with Versailles" – this was the claim of George London and Henry Wise when they submitted plans for a terraced garden to Thomas Coke of Melbourne around 1698. His garden had already been given a small formal layout by 1630, but the new French-style plan was adopted, and laid out by 1703 or 1704.

The gardens – some 16 acres – have two main areas: first the symmetrical terraced parterre, descending from Melbourne Hall towards the geometrically-shaped pool (the Great Basin) and the iron "arbour" or summerhouse by Robert Bakewell (1706); second, to the left of the Great Basin, the woodland garden, also in Continental style, laid out *c.*1704, with outstanding lime walks intersecting at focal points.

There are superb early 18th-century lead statues in the gardens at Melbourne, mainly by Van Nost – *putti*, a Mercury, Perseus and Andromeda, and a great Four Seasons vase.

The parterre was grassed over in mid-19th century, but the garden is otherwise an intact survival of a plan in the style of Le Nôtre.

April–September, Wednesday, Saturday, Sunday and Bank Holiday Monday. Telephone (03316) 2502. ♿. *Refreshments sold. Located 8 miles south of Derby, on the A514.*

Mount Edgcumbe

Sited on the Rame peninsula, the present 860-acre park and gardens of Mount Edgcumbe were formed in the 18th and 19th centuries, but a deer park had existed south of Mount Edgcumbe since 1539, and a formal layout of gardens and avenues beside the house was made in the 17th century, of which the broad avenue leading to the house is the main feature to survive.

In the mid-18th century the gaunt ruin or folly was built on high open ground ⅓ mile south-east of the house. From this point alone, views east over the Hamoaze to Plymouth and south to the sea justify the existence of the landscape park. But they are repeated, with many a variation, from other vantage points in the grounds, some elevated, others close to the shore, and mostly adorned with 18th-century monuments – from Picklecombe Seat, from the Ionic Rotunda (Milton's Temple), or from the late 16th-century Blockhouse. From Thomson's Seat, with its back to the sea, one can hear the waves.

The gardens, occupying some 7½ acres north-east of the house, are enclosed and separated from each other – and protected from sea winds – by holm oak hedges. They are largely early 19th-century in origin, though the English House may have been begun in the 1730s, and the orangery was built by 1788. The varied floral planting schemes and separate formal bedding schemes laid out round the house in mid-19th century are now in the course of restoration.

Mount Edgcumbe has been a Country Park since 1971.

Open all year. Telephone (0752) 822236. ♿. *Refreshments. Mount Edgcumbe is located on Rame peninsula, 12 miles from Torpoint or from Trerulefoot (A38); or by Cremyll (pedestrian) ferry from Plymouth.*

Newstead Abbey

Newstead Abbey was founded in the 12th century, and acquired by Sir John Byron after the Dissolution. It remained with the family, and was the English home of the poet Byron.

Formal gardens extend round three sides of the Abbey, their outlines going back to monastic times, though the walls are mostly 18th-century. The Monks' Garden has trees and shrubs in geometrical beds. Beside it, on the lawn, is a monument to Byron's dog Boatswain. The Eagle Pond, surrounded by steep terraces, may well have been a monastic stewpond, while the adjacent Spanish Garden, close to the Abbey, has box-edged knot patterns, laid out early in the 20th century. Other 20th-century gardens are within the old walled kitchen gardens to the south-east: the Iris Garden and the Rose Garden.

Several ponds or lakes lie to the west and south of the Abbey. The Upper Lake was enlarged in the late 1740s, with the Fort and Cannon Port to the north and south. The Garden Lake, made in the mid-19th century, has a relatively recent garden beside it – 20th-century rock and heather gardens above, and a 19th-century Japanese garden with maples, stone lanterns and cranes below.

Open all year. Telephone (0623) 793557 or 792822. Partly ♿. *Refreshments available. Located in Nottinghamshire, 11 miles north of Nottingham, on the A60.*

Nuneham Courtenay

In the 1750s the 1st Earl Harcourt built himself a Palladian villa, overlooking a broad sweep of ground sloping down to the Thames with fine views beyond, including a glimpse of the distant spires of Oxford. To "improve" the landscape, the village nearby was removed in 1761 to its present site. In 1764 the medieval village church was replaced by a new church in classical style, designed by "Athenian" Stuart. Oliver Goldsmith's poem "The Deserted Village" was particularly inspired by this forced removal.

In 1771, influenced by the "Elysee" garden in Rousseau's *La Nouvelle Héloïse*, the poet William Mason designed an enclosed "secret garden" (Flora's Garden) roughly in the area of the old churchyard, in which his Temple of Flora, and parts of the orangery and grotto, survive.

Capability Brown landscaped the wider scene in 1779–82, and the landscape was given a remarkable "eye-catcher" in 1787 when the Carfax Conduit from Oxford was re-erected in open ground to the north-west of the house.

In 1832 the house was given a formal terrace and balustrade with a bedding scheme by W. S. Gilpin, who also began a pinetum (enlarged as an arboretum in the 20th century, and since 1962 an extension of the Oxford Botanic Garden).

Open 4 days a year. Telephone (086 738) 551. ♿. *Off the A423, 7 miles south of Oxford.*

Oxford Botanic Garden

The Oxford Botanic Garden was founded in 1621 by Henry Danvers, Earl of Danby. It is the oldest surviving botanic garden in Britain (the next being the Chelsea Physic Garden). Its initial walled area was 2½ acres, given a superb entrance gateway by Nicholas Stone in 1632–5. A further area of 3 acres outside the walls has a delicious frontage on the River Cherwell.

The first keeper was Jacob Bobart, appointed in 1642, and at first the formal, four-square division of the enclosure was intended to receive plants from the "four quarters" of the world, set out in rectangular beds for convenient study, usually related to their medicinal properties. The need for "teaching beds" in which, for example, groups of plants grown in evolutionary order may be studied, is still apparent in the geometrical plan.

The garden has many distinctive areas, those outside the walls including a water or bog garden, a remarkable range of greenhouses, gardens for roses, irises and alpine plants and a small pinetum. In 1962 the scope of the Botanic Garden was extended by the acquisition of the arboretum at Nuneham Courtenay.
Open all year. Closed Good Friday and Christmas Day. ♿. Opposite Magdalen College, beside Magdalen Bridge.

Painshill

In the late 1730s Charles Hamilton acquired some 200 acres of rough ground in Surrey, sloping down towards the River Mole. He created a fine garden, which included a large winding lake, a sequence of enchanting garden features – rockwork cascade, gothic temple, ruined abbey, grottoes, ruined mausoleum, Turkish tent, Temple of Bacchus, hermitage and belvedere – and an immense variety of rare trees and shrubs, particularly from North America.

By 1773 Hamilton had overspent and had to leave, and his gardens entered a long period of gentle decline. Happily, this process was reversed in the 1980s, when 158 acres of the original estate were acquired for restoration. The Painshill Park Trust has already succeeded in saving several of the buildings, and in recreating part of Hamilton's distinctive planting scheme. It is one of the most important garden restoration projects to have been undertaken in this country.
Visiting by appointment with the Painshill Park Trust. Telephone (0372) 62111. ♿. Off the A245, between Cobham and the junction with the A3.

Parham House

Parham House dates mainly from 1577, and was extensively restored in the early 20th century. The deer park at Parham – over 600 acres – has existed virtually as long as the house, and, though first landscaped in the late 1770s, remains much as it may have been in the 17th century, running close up to the house.

The 7-acre gardens – lawns, fine trees and shrubs, and a delightful small lake, overlooked by a walled terrace – have been remodelled in the later 20th century. There is a formal, circular garden feature comprising of box hedges clipped to form the numbers and points of the clock, with a sundial at the centre.

On the south front of the house, a small terrace with statuary and formal bedding has views over parkland and the main lake. St Peter's Church stands isolated in the park, since the medieval village there was demolished in 1778–9.

The 4-acre walled garden to the north of the house retains its original quadrant division, with broad walks separating each section. In the south-west quadrant there is an orchard.
Open Easter Sunday–October, Sunday, Wednesday, Thursday and Bank Holidays. Telephone (090 66) 2021. ♿. Refreshments. In West Sussex, 4 miles south-east of Pulborough, on the A283.

Regent's Park: seasonal bedding schemes, with avenues and walks by John Nash

Penshurst Place

The medieval deer park at Penshurst in Kent covers some 200 acres, lying mainly to the north and east of the rectangular area of Penshurst Place and its walled garden of 11 acres. In the park is a sizeable lake, with a 400-yard double poplar avenue (planted in 1965) between it and the walled garden enclosure. A lime avenue, first planted in the 1730s, stretches along the outer side of the north garden wall.

The gardens within the wall were first laid out in the 16th and 17th centuries, and their main outlines survive, shaped by two straight paths which effectively quarter the entire enclosure. The *plan* shown in Kip's view of 1719 has changed little, though the *planting* has been changed often.

The Italian Garden retains the 19th-century plan (itself derived from the 17th century) but with varied modern planting in the box-edged beds. Eastwards, on slightly falling ground, is a rose garden and a nut garden, beside a double border of foliage plants. Long herbaceous borders flank the main axis.

In recent years the main eastern areas of the gardens have been extensively developed from earlier orchard and vegetable gardens. They retain many lines of mature yet ordered apple trees. Beside the 17th-century pool, Diana's Bath, there is a paved silver garden, a grass theatre and a magnolia garden, all enclosed by clipped hedges. The north-eastern quarter is the latest to be developed. It has been designed by Lord de L'Isle, with a Union Jack pattern, and is overlooked to one side by a "mount" round which the rose, thistle, leek and shamrock are laid out in box.
Open April–late October, Tuesday–Sunday plus Bank Holiday Monday. Telephone (0892) 870307. ♿. Refreshments. Located in Penshurst village, on the B2176.

Petworth House

The medieval deer park of Petworth House – some 750 acres – was landscaped by Capability Brown in 1752–4, and has since then survived in a state of sublime simplicity.

The house, with medieval fabric, was remodelled in 1688–96, and then given formal gardens with a geometrical layout, probably designed by George London. All traces of these formal gardens have gone, swept away when Brown redesigned the "Wilderness" as the present Pleasure Grounds – with the Doric temple and the Ionic rotunda set among shrubs and meandering paths. The Pleasure Grounds were modified in the 1850s with the planting of exotic shrubs and trees, many of which, mature in the 1980s, were destroyed in the 1987 storm.

Brown's parkland, enclosed in a 14-mile boundary wall, includes the 13-acre Upper Pond, with superb views to and from Petworth House, the 7-acre Lower Pond, and spacious sweeps of grass enclosed by woodland and belts of trees. Many of the mature oak, beech, lime, sweet and horse chestnut trees were destroyed in the hurricane of October 1987.
Deer park open all year. Pleasure grounds April–end October. Telephone (0798) 42207. ♿. Refreshments. In Petworth, West Sussex, 5½ miles east of Midhurst.

Prior Park

Ralph Allen's grand house, designed by John Wood the Elder, was built between 1735 and 1748, and the relatively small landscape – 55 acres – round about was developed in two stages: first from 1734, by Allen with advice from the poet (and garden enthusiast) Alexander Pope, who died in 1743, and then, from 1762 to 1765, by Capability Brown.

In the first stage, the layout was in the rococo style, with belts of trees round the edges of the steeply descending valley below the house, curving paths in and out of the bordering groves, and delicate garden features such as a small pool and stone-lined rills, rustic summerhouse, and a shell-lined grotto.

In 1756 Allen had built the Palladian bridge, the most important of the three made in British landscape gardens (the first, at Wilton in 1737, the second at Stowe the year after). It was not effectively "landscaped" until Brown's work in 1762–5, when the entire valley vista was simplified to become a single scene, viewed from the house downwards or from below the bridge up towards the house with equal delight.
Open daily. Prior Park is situated in Avon on the eastern outskirts of Bath.

Regent's Park

At the end of the 18th century farmland extended over the area of some 470 acres which is now Regent's Park. The park (which was first intended to be named "Marylebone Park") was planned by John Nash in 1811, and laid out over the next twenty years. The public part opened in 1835.

Nash's design included formal avenues and walks, now given fine areas of seasonal bedding, and the great sinuous boating lake. Belts of trees along the boundaries enclose undulating lawns and a variety of features, both public and private. The original scheme envisaged private houses and their gardens to be part of the park (such as The Holme and St John's Lodge beside the Inner Circle). Other areas were also used for distinctive purposes – the Royal Zoological Society acquired a site in the northern quarter for its zoo in 1827 and the Royal Botanic Society acquired a site within the Inner Circle in 1835 (this area was redeveloped as Queen Mary's Gardens in 1932, with a now-renowned rose garden). In the present century a remarkable variety of sports facilities has been developed in the park, and its character has been further extended by the building of the Central London Mosque on the western boundary in 1974–82.
Open all year. Spring and summer flower displays in different areas. ♿. Refreshments available. Located north of Marylebone Road and Regent's Park tube station.

The Rievaulx Terrace

The 75 acres of woodland here serve a sublime and single purpose: they are a background to the curving, ¾ mile grassy terrace which overlooks the wide expanse of Ryedale, and in particular the great gaunt ruins of Rievaulx Abbey.

In the early 18th century, Thomas Duncombe, from Duncombe Park three miles to the east, had thought of cutting and levelling this terrace, but the aim was not realised until his grandson Thomas Duncombe acquired the land in about 1758. As at Duncombe Park itself, the terrace views are given noble buildings at each end – the Ionic temple or Banqueting House to the west, the Tuscan Doric rotunda to the east. They were built *c.*1758, and probably designed by Sir Thomas Robinson.
Open April–end October. Telephone (043 96) 340. ♿. The Rievaulx Terrace can be found in North Yorkshire, 2½ miles north-west of Helmsley, on the B1257.

Rousham

The landscape garden at Rousham – some 30 acres – was laid out *c.*1715–20 by Charles Bridgeman in a semi-formal style, then extensively remodelled by William Kent between 1733 and 1740 in a "natural" manner, given arcadian allusions by sculpture and classical buildings. The landscape combines numerous brilliantly separated internal scenes and remarkable views out over the Oxfordshire countryside. It is Kent's best surviving work.

There is a formal lawn – once a bowling green – in front of the house, with views out to rural scenes, and Kent's primitive "eye-catcher" arch on the hillslope a mile away. Venus' Vale, with a pool and rocky cascade, is enclosed by groves of trees, while the Cold Plunge – a formal pool – is fed by the Serpentine Rill. From Townesend's Temple a grassy walk leads to the medieval Heyford Bridge and the Statue of Apollo is at one end of the Long Walk, leading to Praeneste – an arcaded viewing-point facing the river.

The old kitchen gardens, with 17th-century walls, have 19th- and 20th-century planting – fine herbaceous borders, old fruit trees and a formal box-edged rose garden.
Open all year. Landscape garden excellent all year round. Telephone (0869) 47110. ♿. Rousham Park is 12 miles north of Oxford, off the A423.

The Royal Botanic Gardens, Kew: the crocuses

ROYAL BOTANIC GARDENS, KEW

The present botanic gardens at Kew – some 300 acres – began in 1759 with 10 acres inside much larger royal gardens begun thirty years before for Queen Caroline. The landscaping – first by Bridgeman, then by Capability Brown – was continued 1757–61 by Sir William Chambers, who added some bizarre garden buildings (including a mosque, a Chinese bridge and a menagerie) of which several classical temples, the Ruined Arch, the orangery and the great Pagoda survive.

The development of the botanic aspect of the gardens was emphasised from the 1770s by Sir Joseph Banks, receiving newly-discovered plants and trees from many countries. In 1841 the gardens were made a public research institute, and relandscaped by Nesfield. The Palm House was built in 1844–8, and the Temperate House in 1859–62. Since then there has been continuous development of the gardens, and research and teaching facilities.

Open all year except Christmas Day and New Year's Day. Excellent variety of features throughout. ♿. *Refreshments. On the south bank of the Thames, at Kew.*

ST JAMES'S PARK

St James's Park, a royal park, was a formal layout by Charles II, with straight tree-lined avenues beside The Mall and a long, straight canal between Horse Guards Parade and Buckingham House, now Buckingham Palace.

In 1828–9 this formal scheme was remodelled by John Nash (who had built Buckingham Palace in 1825, incorporating part of the earlier Buckingham House). Nash's park layout drastically reshaped the lake, giving it a sinuous shoreline and two islands, while the paths wind gently round the lake and through the undulating landscape. The open lawns are skilfully divided by clumps of trees, allowing many superb and varied views, with glimpses of Big Ben, Buckingham Palace or the buildings of Whitehall.

There are bedding displays beside the northern paths, fine mature trees and many water birds.

Open all year. Spring and summer bedding displays. ♿. *Refreshments. Located between The Mall, Horse Guards Parade and Birdcage Walk.*

ST PAUL'S WALDEN BURY

The early 18th-century layout of St Paul's Walden Bury in Hertfordshire is unique in the British Isles, with a wholly formal plan set in undulating and "natural" woodland surroundings.

When the house was built, around 1730, for Edward Gilbert, the garden framework was laid out at the same time. The lawn in front of the house leads to a diamond-shaped scheme of hedge-lined rides through woodland to either side, extending for nearly half a mile to the north. The rides follow the contours of the land, and so the views, leading to statuary or to garden buildings, are given fascinating variations. Within the "diamond" of paths is the *giardino segreto* of the Running Footman, with an 18th-century temple and central lawn.

In the present century, there has been notable development of the areas to east and west of the house, with a flower garden beside the rotunda, a rhododendron garden and a rose garden.

St Paul's Walden Bury is the birthplace of Her Majesty Queen Elizabeth the Queen Mother.

♿. *Refreshments. 5 miles south of Hitchin, on the B651.*

THE SAVILL GARDEN

Within the boundaries of Windsor Great Park, the Savill Garden's acres of landscaped wild and woodland gardens form a fascinating contrast with the undulating park and woodland beyond.

Created between 1932 and 1939 by Sir Eric Savill (who later made the Valley Gardens north of Virginia Water), the garden began as a woodland area with decidedly watery connections, and was first affectionately called the "Bog Garden". King George VI renamed it in 1951. Its area has been extended in the 20th century.

Two ponds give a landscape focus to the varied woodland glades, where mature trees (oak, beech, chestnut) give shelter to exotic underplanting – specimen trees and shrubs at one level, and much smaller plants at another. These areas are all "natural" in their layout, and include the rare and beautiful moss garden beneath beech trees near the Upper Pond.

Since 1947 a terraced alpine garden and a formal rose garden have been developed, with herbaceous borders enclosed by cypress hedges. In 1977, a 2 ½-acre Dry Garden was created.

Open all year. Closed Christmas Day. Refreshments. In Surrey, off the A30, on the road between Egham Wick and Bishops Gate.

SCOTNEY CASTLE

In the mid-1830s Edward Hussey employed Anthony Salvin to build him a new house and took advice from William Sawrey Gilpin about his gardens. As a result of their deliberations, Salvin's new mansion was sited 300 yards away, high up to the north-east of the medieval Scotney Castle. An angled terrace was built to overlook a rough quarry and the moated castle below. The castle itself was partially demolished to give it "picturesque" quality; the quarry was adapted as a rock garden and the 8 acres of gardens between the mansion and the castle were carefully planted with trees and shrubs chosen to vary and adorn the original woodland. Many were destroyed in the 1987 storm and replanting is in progress.

In the forecourt of the old Castle is a herb garden made by Lanning Roper. The gardens are surrounded by farmland and woodland.

Open April–mid-November, Wednesday–Sunday, plus Bank Holiday Monday. Closed Good Friday. Telephone (0892) 890651 for varying hours. ♿. *1 ½ miles south-east of Lamberhurst, on the A21.*

SEZINCOTE

Sezincote in Gloucestershire is one of the most important "oriental" buildings in this country, and the 10-acre gardens share this distinction. The house was built for Sir Charles Cockerell around 1805 and designed by his brother Samuel Pepys Cockerell, with advice from Thomas Daniell. The park and gardens were contemporary with the house. Humphry Repton was probably the designer of the 250-acre park, creating the lake eastwards from the house, and he may have collaborated with Thomas Daniell, who designed several garden features in Indian style.

In the formal garden south of the house is Daniell's octagonal fountain and steps, a sundial and a grotto in the bank beyond. In the woodland glades to the north he made the Indian Bridge, the shrine with the figure of Surya, and the three-headed serpent fountain in the Snake Pool.

In the mid-20th century these gardens were restored and further developed by Lord and Lady Kleinwort, in collaboration with G. S. Thomas.

Sheffield Park: Capability Brown landscape with outstanding trees and shrubs, and chain of lakes along a valley

The formal garden was given a firmer, symmetrical Indian design round the fountain with tapering yews flanking the axes, and an Indian pavilion to the south; the wood stream garden to the north has been given flowering shrubs and trees, planted informally.
Open all year (except December), Thursday, Friday, Bank Holiday Monday. Located 1½ miles south-west of Moreton-in-Marsh, on the A44.

Sheffield Park

The present house at Sheffield Park was built in the late 18th century for J. B. Holroyd, the 1st Earl of Sheffield. In 1776 he called in Capability Brown to landscape the sloping valley to the south-east, and Brown almost certainly created the two furthest of the present four lakes. Almost a century later, the 3rd Earl of Sheffield brought in James Pulham to make the two lakes nearer the house, with a waterfall, a bridge and a cascade down to one of Brown's lakes.

It was the 3rd Earl who gave this valley and chain of lakes its distinctive character – by planting a varied selection of exotic trees, mainly conifers, as well as Japanese maple. From 1904–34, a further variety of autumn-colouring trees and shrubs was added by A. G. Soames.

Subsequently, the estate – of *c.*183 acres – was divided, and in 1954 the National Trust bought the main, eastern area of 100 acres, and has since continued to develop the garden. The house – Sheffield Park – is in separate private ownership.
Open mid-March–early November, daily except Mondays, but open Bank Holiday Mondays and then closed on following Tuesday. Telephone (0825) 790655 for varying hours. ♿. *Situated in East Sussex, 5 miles north-west of Uckfield, on the east side of the A275.*

Shotover

The grand house at Shotover was begun around 1714 for James Tyrell, and has a distinctly Continental character. Gardens within a park and woodland of some 210 acres were laid out from *c.*1718 onwards, the scheme being more or less complete by the early 1730s.

It is still a largely formal layout, with its most striking feature, the great eastern vista, extending from the house for nearly half a mile – first a lawn, then a pool and then the rectangular canal, stretching out to the distant Gothic pavilion (probably built *c.*1721 by Townesend) which closes the view. This canal – the longest formal garden canal in England – echoes both the Long Water at Hampton Court and the far grander canals of Louis XIV's Versailles. Yet the pavilion or "temple" at the far end is remarkable for its innovation – it has pointed arches, and battlements along the top. It is one of the first garden buildings of the "Gothic Revival". Either way, from the house or from the pavilion, it is one of the finest formal garden vistas in the country.

West of the house are pools, with serpentine paths through shrubbery and woodland, and an eight-sided temple by William Kent.
Telephone (086 77) 4095. ♿. Refreshments. Near Wheatley, on the A40, 6 miles east of Oxford.

Shugborough

At Shugborough, the parkland and gardens of some 400 acres were laid out from 1743 onwards for Thomas Anson, with the advice and enthusiasm of his brother George Anson the circumnavigator, who had returned to England in 1744, and James "Athenian" Stuart. Between them, they were responsible for the primitive Doric temple, *c.*1758 (second only in this style to Stuart's Temple of Theseus at Hagley (1758)); the Arch of Hadrian; the Lanthorn of Demosthenes; the Tower of the Winds; the Chinese House (1747, by Brett, but with George Anson's advice), and the Ruins beside the river. The latter, *c.*1749 and attributed to Thomas Wright, was George Anson's project, and in his absence the workmen built it far too "completely". "Then comes Mr Anson with axes and chissels to demolish as much of it as taste and judgement claimed", restoring the edifice to a "ruin".

In the 19th century, a wild garden with trees and shrubs was established, as well as a formal layout before the river front of the house, which has been restored in recent years.
Open April–late December, daily. ♿. Refreshments. 6 miles east of Stafford on the A513.

Sissinghurst Castle

Laid out from 1930 onwards, and largely complete by 1939, the gardens fill the several distinct areas left in the framework of buildings, walls and moat belonging to the mainly mid-16th-century castle. The tower (from which one looks with delight) is visible in the upper centre of the scheme from most points in the gardens.

The property, then derelict, was acquired in 1930 by Vita Sackville-West, the wife of Harold Nicolson, and together they created the gardens – he being credited with the design, she with the choice and arrangement of plants.

Influenced by the "garden rooms" of Hidcote and Great Dixter – both conceived early in the 20th century – they made a complex scheme of gardens at Sissinghurst, linked by paths or doorways, but separated by walls or hedges so that each had a distinct and memorable character without conflict with its neighbours.

The gardens include the Tower Courtyard, 1931–2, with "purple" border; Rose Garden and Rondel, 1933–4; the White Garden, 1946; the orchard, leading to the moat, and with delicate views beyond; the Cottage Garden, 1931; the Lime Walk, 1932–3; the Nuttery, and the Herb Garden, 1938.
Open April–mid-October, Tuesday–Sunday. Telephone (0580) 712850 for varying hours. ♿. Refreshments. In Kent, off the A262, 1 mile east of Sissinghurst village.

Sledmere House

The landscaped park and plantations at Sledmere are a fine example of Capability Brown's work. He was called in by Sir Christopher Sykes in 1771, and his plans were implemented *c.*1790.

The park covers some 900 acres, and is enclosed on the horizon by Brown's belts or plantations – Avenue Wood, Castle Wood and Cherry Wood. From the house there are fine views to distant "eye-catchers", such as a classical portico, and the mock-Gothic Sledmere Castle, built *c.*1790.

The 18th-century walled kitchen garden now has a fine collection of roses.
Open end April–early October, daily except Monday and Friday. Also open all Sundays in April, Bank Holiday Mondays and Easter Weekend. Telephone (0377) 86208. ♿. Refreshments. In Humberside, 24 miles east of York on the main York–Bridlington road. 8 miles north-west of Driffield.

Stancombe Park

Round the 19th-century house there are expansive views out over the countryside and a succession of superb and varied garden areas developed since 1964: shrubbery and foliage plants beside the drive, and, to the south, a sequence of formal gardens with fine borders, rope-pergola and rambler roses, and pleached limes.

But to one side, along a winding path, there is the "secret garden", a magical ten acres created *c.*1850 by the Rev. David Edwards. Through the woods one reaches winding tunnels, leading suddenly to the hidden lake, enclosed by rose-pergola on two sides, clipped box-hedges on the third, the whole overhung and surrounded by splendid trees – mature copper beech, chestnut and oak – and brightened by flowering shrubs. To one side of the lake is a Doric temple; to the other, a grotto – part Gothic, part Egyptian.
♿. Refreshments available. In Gloucestershire, half-way between Dursley and Wotton-under-Edge, on the B4060.

Stansted Park

Stansted Park extends on a heroic scale round the house, with 650 acres of parkland and another 1200 acres of forest. This parkland – originally, in the 12th century, a deer park – was given a partly formal layout early in the 18th century, and from this period dates the great beech avenue stretching westwards from the house and through the forest. First planted in the 17th or 18th century, and the avenue is as long as any in the country.

The parkland and grounds were "landscaped" in the 18th century. Garden buildings include a Palladian temple and the Racton tower.

Much replanting of trees has taken place in recent years. There are walled gardens and a fine early 20th-century arboretum, with examples of cedar, pine and tulip tree now reaching maturity.
Open May–September, Sunday, Monday, Tuesday. Telephone (0705) 412265. Refreshments. Garden shop. In West Sussex, 4 miles from Rowlands Castle.

Stancombe Park: one of the most mysterious – and rewarding – gardens in the country

Stanway House

In the late 17th century the deer park at Stanway was given formal avenues, and a walled kitchen garden was laid out to the north-east of the house and a walled ornamental garden to the south.

Then, in the 1730s, a water scheme involving a pool (or reservoir), a cascade with six waterfalls, and a canal was developed on ground rising eastwards from the house, and in 1750 the Pyramid (a square, open-arched tower with pyramidal top) was built in front of the highest pool, overlooking the House 300 yards away.

Today, the walled kitchen garden remains, and the area of the walled ornamental garden has a lawn with shrubbery and trees. The Pyramid still overlooks the house, with vast views out westwards and with a spreading grassy slope in front of it (where the cascade once was) down to a broad terrace, still called "Canal" despite the water's being drained in the mid-19th century.
Open June–August, Tuesday and Thursday. Partly ♿. Refreshments in the village. Located 1 mile off the A46 Cheltenham–Broadway road, on the B4077.

Stonor Park

There has been a deer park of some 120 acres at Stonor since the 13th century, attached to the ancient manor house begun *c.*1190, remodelled and enlarged firstly around 1600 and then again by John Aitkins *c.*1785. It has been the house of the Stonor family for over eight centuries.

The deer park was enlarged around 1800 to make a landscape park of some 270 acres, incorporating woods, tree-lined rides, undulating parkland and gardens.

The walled garden, begun in the 17th century or possibly before, encloses both the kitchen gardens, and a fine scheme of 17th-century formal gardens behind the house.
Open frequently from May–September. Telephone (049 163) 587. ♿. Refreshments. In Oxfordshire, 5 miles north of Henley-on-Thames on the B480.

Stourhead

The landscape of Stourhead in Wiltshire was created between 1741 and 1785 by Henry Hoare; modified by his grandson Sir Richard Colt Hoare from the late 1780s until 1838; and has been preserved with little change until the present day. The gardens of 40 acres, with a large surrounding estate, was given to the National Trust in 1946.

Stourhead was built in the 1720s. From 1741, Henry Hoare developed the gardens in the steep-sided valley south of, and out of sight of, the house. Having as inspiration the literature and architecture of ancient Rome, the landscape of the Campagna, and the paintings of Claude Lorrain and Gaspard Poussin, he created one of the most beautiful landscape gardens in England.

The lake was created from a group of fishponds by putting a dam across the valley, and it was surrounded by several buildings with classical forms or connections – the Temple of Flora, the Pantheon, the Roman Bridge and the Temple of Apollo. To these was added the Bristol High Cross, re-erected in 1764 close to Stourton parish church, overlooking the northern tip of the lake.

All these survive, though several other lesser items have gone, Hoare also built architectural features in the wider landscape which survive – the obelisk, northwards from the house, and the convent and Alfred's Tower in and beyond the woodland to north-west.

His grandson added only one important building, the Rustic Cottage, but is significant for introducing ornamental trees and shrubs round the lake, which give the gardens the additional quality of an arboretum.
Open all year. Mid-May–mid-June for rhododendrons. Telephone (0747) 840348. ♿. Refreshments. Situated off the A303, 3 miles north-west of Mere.

Stowe

The present gardens at Stowe – some 400 acres, surrounded by further park, woodland and agricultural land – were developed from modest beginnings in the 1680s, round a mansion built for Sir Richard Temple. Throughout the 18th century the garden scheme grew, and changed, with the development of the house and changing tastes.

From the first formal layout near to the house, Charles Bridgeman extended avenues far into the countryside, given focal points by monuments and temples designed mainly by Vanbrugh, Gibbs and William Kent. In the 1730s Kent took over from Bridgeman. The main axis from the house – once a hedge-lined parterre leading to a formal eight-sided pool – was "softened", and to the east Kent created the "Elysian Fields", a small valley with a stream, which he adorned in the mid-1730s with two temples. Further to the east, the half-mile expanse of Hawkwell Field was developed with two classical temples, the Palladian bridge and a Gothic temple.

Other areas were developed at the same time, or after, including the Grecian Valley with the Temple of Concord and Victory (1742–*c.*1762). By the late 1770s the Stowe landscape was virtually complete. Though many of the lesser garden monuments have gone, over thirty survive. Since 1923 the house has been a school.

Stowe has associations with Capability Brown who was appointed its head gardener in 1741 and who was married at Stowe Church.
Open April and July–end August. Closed during term time. Telephone (0280) 813650. ♿. Refreshments. 4 miles north of Buckingham.

Studley Royal

John Aislabie had been Chancellor of the Exchequer at the time of the South Sea Bubble, and when the "crash" came in 1721 he was disgraced and retired to Studley Royal. By 1728, the straightened River Skell had been adorned with the adjacent Moon and Crescent Ponds, and, by 1732, the Fishing Lodges at one end and the Rustic Bridge and grotto at the other end of the canal had been built. Also added was the Banqueting House, the rotunda and part of the Octagon Tower. The Temple of Piety completed the area of canal and Moon Ponds.

This area – thought by many to be the purest examples of formal gardening in England – was not Aislabie's only garden or landscape concern. He wished also to include in his property the extensive ruins of Fountains Abbey, half a mile westwards along the valley, an interest in "medieval scenery" running parallel with Thomas Duncombe's admiration of the ruins of Rievaulx Abbey a few miles away. Aislabie died before he could achieve the completion of his scheme, but his son added the Fountains Abbey property to the Studley Royal estate in 1768, thereby bringing together in one landscape garden the prized qualities of the *beautiful* and *sublime*.

The wider landscape at Studley includes the avenue aligned on Ripon Minster, 3 miles to the north-east.
Open daily, except 24 and 25 December. Telephone (076 586) 333 for varying hours. ♿. Refreshments. Situated in North Yorkshire, 2 miles west of Ripon.

Syon Park

Syon Park, once well outside the capital, now remains as one of the great landscape parks (some 205 acres) within the area of Greater London.

Beginning as a monastic establishment, Syon was granted to the Duke of Somerset in 1547, and important garden activity began almost at once directed by Dr William Turner, who created a botanic garden in the grounds.

The park was landscaped by Capability Brown in the 1760s, when the lakes were created. Woodland and a botanic garden were established round the northern lake and enclosing Flora's Lawn.

The 3rd Duke of Northumberland had the Great Conservatory (to the north of the House) built between 1827 and 1830 by Charles Fowler, with a formal flower garden, pool and fountain in front. He was also responsible for extending the botanic collection. The gardens have been continuously cared for and developed since then.
Gardens open all year. Closed on Christmas Day, New Year's Day. Parkland is not open to the public. Telephone (01) 560 0881. ♿. Refreshments. Garden centre. On the north bank of the Thames, between Isleworth and Brentford.

Stourhead: a masterpiece of 18th-century romantic landscape by Henry Hoare, inspired by the paintings of Lorrain and Poussin

Tresco Abbey

This garden, begun in 1834, is the most convincingly "sub-tropical" of any in the British Isles, and the general plan of the garden – a series of broad, steeply rising terraces – gives additional coherence and distinction to the planting.

The gardens cover some 17 acres, with a further 45 acres of woodland. When Augustus Smith leased the Isles of Scilly in 1834, he began to build his house, Tresco Abbey, on the island of Tresco, and to develop his garden at the same time, including the planting of shelter belts – holm oak, Monterey pine and Monterey cypress. Beginning with the area of the 12th century Priory ruins, 50 yards south-west, he proceeded to the building of the main terraces, which were complete by 1855. There are rockery areas nearby, while to the west and in the lower regions of the garden there are open lawns, areas of orchard, and, on the southern boundary, the Valhalla, a 19th-century building containing figureheads from ships wrecked on the coast.

Throughout the gardens the planting has been continuously directed by the search for species, mainly sub-tropical, which will thrive in the benign conditions at Tresco. From time to time, lists of plants flowering on New Year's Day have been compiled and these compare well with the lists produced at La Mortola in Italy, a garden begun at Cecil Hanbury in the later 19th century with similar horticultural aims. Exuberant growth characterises many of the species, whether trees, shrubs or smaller plants. Collections of aeonium, and profuse growth of agave, aloe, yucca, mesembryanthemum, protea, tree ferns, bamboo and echium can be found there.

Open daily except Sunday. Refreshments available. Tresco can be reached by ferry from Hugh Town, St Mary's.

Virginia Water

Like most garden lakes, whether "natural" or "formal", Virginia Water is an *artificial* lake, formed by damming a valley and letting the water from local streams build up round the "natural" contours of the land. It was a two-stage affair, begun in the early 1750s with a dam, grotto and a "Chinese" yacht, the *Mandarin*. A storm and a flood breached the dam in 1768, and a far larger lake was then made, completed by 1782 with Thomas Sandby's magnificent cascade. The ruins on the south shore were not erected until 1826 – the columns came from Leptis Magna.

There are wonderful walks round the lake, and the modern Valley Gardens – rhododendrons and dwarf conifers – extend to the north-east.

Open all year. Parking near to the Wheatsheaf Hotel. Located in Surrey, north of the A329, by its junction with the A30.

Warwick Castle

At its largest, the landscaped park round Warwick Castle – partly beside the Castle to the north, but mainly south of the River Avon – extended to some 800 acres, and its oldest components must go back to the medieval origins of the Castle itself.

In 1749 Capability Brown began removing the small formal gardens which lay round the Castle, replacing them by lawns and scattered trees. Round the area of the Castle Park, south of the river, he added belts of trees and designed a long winding carriage ride within these boundary belts.

Formality returned to the grounds near the Castle in 1868–9, when Robert Marnock laid out the parterre garden in front of the late 18th-century Gothic conservatory, and designed the formal Rose Garden between the Castle and Castle Lodge. Both of Marnock's features survive, the Rose Garden being restored in 1985–6.

Open all year except Christmas Day. Telephone (0926) 495421. ♿. Refreshments. In the centre of Warwick.

Westonbirt Arboretum

In 1829 Robert Stayner Holford began the arboretum at Westonbirt as an extension to the park round Westonbirt House (now Westonbirt School), and the three early avenues in the arboretum are aligned on the house. The planting of chosen trees – particularly North American conifers – was followed by Sir George Lindsay Holford (1860–1926), who began a collection of maples and started another area with rhododendron. The arboretum is now over 300 acres, the variety of the trees is encyclopaedic, and their appearance unforgettable. It is Britain's best.
Open all year. Particularly good for autumn colour. Located in Gloucestershire on the A433, 5 miles north-east of the junction with the A6.

Westonbirt School

In the 1860s Westonbirt House was built by Lewis Vulliamy for Robert Stayner Holford.

Vulliamy laid out a grand series of terraces along the southern side of the house – some 200 yards across, and descending in three stages to a circular pool and fountain. Eastwards from the upper terrace is the Italian garden, with enclosing walls, buildings and pavilions on three sides, and with stone-edged beds in the centre. To the south, there are views out over a circular pool set in the wall. The terraces and the Italian garden are remarkable examples of highly formalised and architectural garden design, with its surviving formal bedding and mature trees – Lebanon cedar, deodar, copper beech.

Part of the wide parkland around the house has been planted with ornamental trees and shrubs to make a woodland garden with a lake.
Visiting by appointment. Telephone (066 688) 233. ♿. Gloucestershire, 3 miles south of Tetbury, on the B432.

West Wycombe

The landscape park at West Wycombe is the creation of an *amateur*, an eccentric and talented owner-designer – Sir Francis Dashwood.

West Wycombe House was begun around 1710, and much extended and remodelled between 1739 and 1780 for Sir Francis. Round this house – itself an exceptional building – he created the landscape, the development of which can be seen from paintings by Hannam, *c.*1751, and Daniell, 1781, in West Wycombe House.

In the late 1730s the lake was formed to the north-east of the house, and in the grounds were built the Temple of Venus, the Temple of the Winds and the Temple of Apollo. On Church Hill, half a mile northwards, the parish church was topped with a large gilded sphere, visible from the grounds, and in 1748–52 the chalk of the hill was tunnelled to form the labyrinthine caves. On the side of the hill, Dashwood built the gaunt hexagonal mausoleum in 1764–5.

From the 1770s Dashwood employed Nicholas Revett as architect. Revett remodelled the west portico, and built the Round Temple south-west of the house and the distinctive Music Temple on the main island in the lake. Other features were built or adapted in parkland to the east.

The house and grounds were given to the National Trust in 1943. Considerable replanting of over-mature trees, the restoration of garden features, along with the creation of new ones, took place in the 1980s.
Open (a) April–May, Monday–Thursday, Bank Holiday Sunday and Monday, (b) June–August, Sunday–Thursday. Telephone (0494) 24411. ♿. Refreshments available at West Wycombe Caves. Located at the west end of West Wycombe in Buckinghamshire, off the Oxford road (A40).

Wimpole Hall

Wimpole Hall's fabric goes back to *c.*1640, with many enlargements and alterations thereafter, particularly by Gibbs, Flitcroft and Soane. The gardens – some 20 acres – and the surrounding parkland of 350 acres have likewise been much developed, and their complex history is well-documented.

The park has existed since 1302, but the gardens were probably not laid out until the 1640s, then enlarged in the 1690s, and again in *c.*1720–31 by Charles Bridgeman. He extended long straight avenues from the house – in particular, the broad double elm avenue to the south. This magnificent feature was replanted with limes in the late 1970s.

Bridgeman's relatively formal layout was "softened" in the mid-18th century, and further so in 1767–73 by Capability Brown. To the north Brown opened up one of Bridgeman's avenues to form a broad vista with a ruined folly. Brown also created (or enlarged) two lakes, of which one survives, now adorned with a mid-19th-century Chinese bridge.

Immediately north of the house, a formal layout with parterre and clipped hedges was created in the mid-19th century. Railings and specimens of yew and box remain from this scheme, as do the shrubberies and numerous exotic trees, single or in groups, to the west and north-east, from the same period – mature Indian bean, manna ash, Chinese juniper, Bhutan pine.
Open April–end October, daily except Monday and Friday, but open Bank Holiday Monday. Closed Good Friday. Telephone (0223) 207257. Daffodils in April. ♿. Refreshments. 8 miles south-west of Cambridge, off the A603 at New Wimpole.

WILTON

Wilton House was extensively developed for the 4th Earl of Pembroke in the 1630s. The architect was Isaac de Caus, advised by Inigo Jones. De Caus was also responsible for a magnificent formal garden layout with parterre, fountains, sculpture and a grotto to the south of the house, which may be considered the first essay in England in imitation of the (then) new French formal style. The layout was crossed roughly midway along its length by the River Nadder, hidden at points by dense hedges.

By the early 18th century this scheme had been simplified, and in the 1730s it was abandoned completely when the Palladian bridge was built across the Nadder. The river was dammed to form a lake, and the surrounding terrain was "landscaped" to resemble an idealised countryside. This is the first of three such bridges built in English 18th-century gardens, the others being at Stowe (1738) and Prior Park (1756).

In the 1820s an Italian garden was added to the west of Wilton House, with a formal layout, statuary, central fountain and several garden buildings – orangery, loggia and the Holbein Porch (this area is not open to the public).

East of Wilton House are lawns and ornamental woodland. The forecourt garden to Wilton House, with a central fountain surrounded by pleached limes, was redesigned in 1971 by David Vicary.

The walled kitchen garden to the north-east of Wilton House is now a garden centre.

Open end-March–mid-October. Telephone (0722) 743744. ♿. Refreshments. Garden centre. In Wiltshire, on the A30, 2½ miles west of Salisbury, in the town of Wilton.

WINDSOR GREAT PARK

The vast area of Windsor Great Park – now around 5600 acres – has been a royal park for centuries and encloses a variety of areas with different uses – forest, woodland, farms, heathland, gardens and ponds, and several royal or private residences. The boundaries extend (approximately) between the Home Park of Windsor Castle to the north and Virginia Water to the south.

The parkland was first enclosed by 1086 and extended to the present area by about 1365. Lines of great avenues, some replanted, remain from the 17th century – the Long Walk and Queen Anne's Ride. Virginia Water to the south was created in the mid-18th century for the Duke of Cumberland, and the Savill Garden in the 1930s. Several farms have been developed within the park, by George III and Prince Albert.

Public access is possible all year at many points, though some parts are entirely private. It is located in Berkshire between Windsor, Sunninghill and Virginia Water. (See also entries for Virginia Water *and* Savill Garden.*)*

WOBURN ABBEY

Since the foundation of Woburn Abbey in 1145, the grounds – some 3000 acres of undulating park and woodland, with a chain of small lakes – have been "landscaped" (in the 18th and early 19th centuries), while the 41 acres of gardens round the house have been imaginatively developed since the early 17th century. A part of the house itself is the grotto, by Isaac de Caus, one of the earliest surviving grottoes in this country (*c.*1630).

In the 1790s Henry Holland built the Chinese Dairy, with a covered way leading to the north stables, curving round the shore of a small lake. Decisive landscaping came with Humphry Repton, who was called in by the 6th Duke of Bedford in 1804. His Red Book (1805) led to landscaping work lasting until 1810, and to many garden buildings, including the aviary (1808). In 1833, the eight-sided Chinese Pavilion by Wyatville was built within a maze on an island in a small lake to the south-east of the house. In this period there was comparable enthusiasm at Woburn for the collection and cultivation of rare grasses, heathers and willows and catalogues of the Woburn collections were published in 1816, 1822, 1829 and 1833.

In the 1930s the ornamental gardens were redeveloped by Percy Cane, while the amenities of the gardens and grounds of Woburn Abbey have been considerably extended since the 1950s.

Open January–March at weekends and end March–end October daily. Telephone (0525) 290666. ♿. Refreshments available. Located in Woburn, off the A4012, 8½ miles north of Dunstable.

WREST PARK

The gardens at Wrest, some 125 acres, were founded in the late 1680s in a strictly formal layout aligned on the now demolished original house, with two fountains, two mazes, and a long rectangular canal stretching away from the house. At the end of the canal, Thomas Archer's magnificent Banqueting House was built in 1709–11. By the 1730s lawns and tree-lined walks had replaced the mazes. East of the canal, the Bowling Green House by Batty Langley was built *c.*1735.

Between 1758 and 1771 Capability Brown created the tree-lined, gently curving "river" which now winds round three sides of the formal garden scheme, hidden from the central layout by groves of trees. There is a monument to him in woodland east of the canal. To the north-west, screened by trees, are the hermitage, Cold Bath House and small cascade, founded in the 1770s.

In the 19th century, the building of a new house 250 yards further away from the site gave room for new, formal gardens, with a terrace, sculpture and parterres to the north of the canal; a conservatory and an area of massed bedding west of the house; and an orangery to the south-west. The surviving complex of the old formal canal, with its terrace and parterres, enclosed by Brown's serpentine "river", is one of the most subtle and interesting of English landscape gardens.

Wrest Park is now the National Institute of Agricultural Engineering. The grounds are in the care of English Heritage.

Open April–September at weekends and Bank Holidays. Telephone (0525) 60718. ♿. Refreshments. Wrest Park can be found in Bedfordshire, ¾ mile east of Silsoe, off the A6.

Westonbirt Arboretum: contains 300 acres of trees and shrubs. This is the acer glade

INDEX

J

L

BIBLIOGRAPHY

Allen, M., *Fisons Guide to British Gardens*, 1970
Anthony, J., *The Gardens of Britain*, vol. 6, 1979
Batey, M., *Alice's Adventures in Oxford*, 1980
Batey, M., *Oxford Gardens*, 1982
Bisgrove, R., *The Gardens of Britain*, vol. 3, 1978
Blunt, Wilfrid, *The Art of Botanical Illustration*, 1950
Bowden Smith, R., *The Water House, Houghton Hall*, 1987
Brookes, J., *The Garden Book*, 1984
Brown, J., *Gardens of a Golden Afternoon*, 1982
Brown, J., *Vita's Other World*, 1985
Cantor, Leonard (ed.), *The English Medieval Landscape*, 1982
Carter, G., *Humphry Repton*, 1982
Church, Thomas, *Gardens are for People*, 1983
Coats, Alice, *The Quest for Plants*, 1969
Coombes, A. J., *Bowood's Trees and Shrubs*, 1983
Cooper, P. M., *The Story of Claremont*, 1975
Crowe, S., *Garden Design*, 1981
Davies, H., *A Walk Round London's Parks*, 1983
Davies, J., *The Victorian Kitchen Garden*, 1987
Fish, M., *We Made a Garden*, 1983
Fisher, J., *The Origins of Garden Plants*, 1982
Fleming, L., and Gore, A., *The English Garden*, 1979
Gray, R., and Frankl, E., *Cambridge Gardens*, 1984
Green, D., *Gardener to Queen Ann*, 1956
Green, D., *The Gardens and Parks at Hampton Court*, 1974
Greenoak, Francesca (ed.), *The Journals of Gilbert White*, vol. 1, 1986
Harris, L., *Robert Adam and Kedleston*, 1987
Harwood, T. E., *Windsor Old and New*, 1929
Hellyer, A., *The Shell Guide to Gardens*, 1977
Hepper, F. N., *Royal Botanic Gardens, Kew*, 1982
Hill, T. (R. Mabey, ed.), *The Gardener's Labyrinth*, 1987
Hussey, C., *English Gardens and Landscapes*, 1975 (revised edn)
James, N. D. G., *The Trees of Bicton*, 1969
Johnson, Hugh, *The International Encyclopedia of Trees*, 1984
Johnson, Hugh, *The Principles of Gardening*, 1984
Jones, B., *Follies and Grottoes*, 1974
Kellman, M. C., *Plant Geography*, 1975
Kelly, J., *The Gardens of Abbotsbury*, 1985
Kitz, N., *Painshill Park*, 1984
Lemmon, Kenneth, *The Gardens of Britain*, vol. 5, 1978
Lemmon, Kenneth, *The Golden Age of Plant Hunters*, 1968
Lloyd, C., *The Mixed Border*, 1985
Lloyd, C., *The Well-Tempered Garden*, 1985
Maclean, Teresa, *Medieval English Gardens*, 1981
Morton, Earl of, *Chelsea Physic Garden*, 1985
Muir, Richard, *The Countryside Encyclopedia*, 1988
Neidpath, J., *Stanway House*, 1984
Newton, N. T., *Design on the Land*, 1981
Paterson, A., *The Gardens of Britain*, vol. 2, 1978
Plumtre, G., *Collins Book of British Gardens*, 1985
Prest, J., *The Garden of Eden*, 1981
Rackham, Oliver, *The History of the Countryside*, 1986
Raphael, S., *An Oxfordshire Garden*, 1982
Roach, F. A., *Cultivated Fruits of Britain*, 1986
Rohde, E. S., *Oxford College Gardens*, 1932
Rohde, E. S., *The Old English Gardening Books*, 1974
Sackville-West, V., *The Illustrated Garden Book*, 1986
Sales, J., *West Country Gardens*, 1980
Scott-James, Anne, *The Cottage Garden*, 1977
Sidwell, R., *West Midland Gardens*, 1981
Stroud, D., *Capability Brown*, 1975
Stuart, David, and Sutherland, James, *Plants from the Past*, 1987
Synge, P. M., *The Gardens of Britain*, vol. 1, 1977
Taylor, C. C., *The Archaeology of Gardens*, 1983
Taylor, G., *Old London Gardens*, 1977
Taylor, J., *Conservatories and Garden Rooms*
Thacker, Christopher, *The History of Gardens*, 1985
Thacker, Christopher, *Three Paths to Paradise*, 1988
Thomas, G. S., *Gardens of the National Trust*, 1979
Thompson, F., *The History of Chatsworth*, 1949
Toogood, Alan, *The Conservatory for Plants and People*, 1985
Turner, T., *English Garden Design: History and Styles Since 1650*, 1986
Wade Martins, S., *Holkham Park*, 1983
Wilkinson, G., *A History of Britain's Trees*, 1981
Williamson, T., and Bellamy, L., *Property and Landscape*, 1987
Willis, P., *Charles Bridgeman*, 1977
Woodbridge, K., *Landscape and Antiquity*, 1971
Wright, T., *The Gardens of Britain*, vol. 4, 1978